W9-AON-577

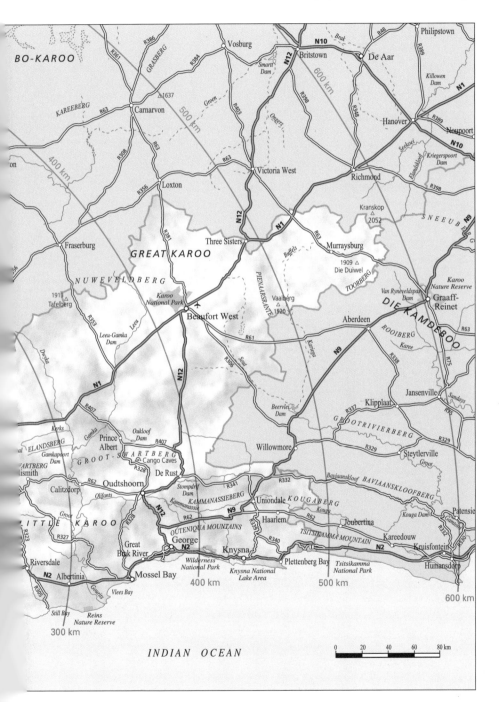

BO-KAROO

KAREEBERG

R386

GRASBERG

R361

R384

Vosburg

Smartt Dam

N10

Bruk

N12

Britstown

De Aar

R48

Philipstown

R389

N1

Killowen Dam

R63

Carnarvon

△1637

Groen

R403

Orange

R398

R48

Hanover

R389

Neupoort

N10

R308

R63

R356

Loxton

R63

Victoria West

Richmond

Seekoei

Elandskloof

Kriegerspoort Dam

R398

Kranskop △ 2052

SNEEUBERG

N9

Fraserburg

GREAT KAROO

NUWEVELDBERG

R381

Three Sisters

N12

N1

R63

Buffels

Murraysburg

1909 △ Die Duiwel

TOORBERG

Karoo Nature Reserve

Van Ryneveldspas Dam

DIE KAMDEBOO

Graaff-Reinet

1913 △ Tafelberg

Karoo National Park

Leeu

Beaufort West

PIENAARSRANTE

Vaalberg △ 1520

Aberdeen

ROOIBERG

Karee

R63

R353

Leeu-Gamka Dam

R306

Soul

R61

Karega

N9

R338

R75

Dwyka

N1

R356

N12

Beervlei Dam

Jansenville

Sundays

R75

R407

Kerks

Oukloof Dam

R407

Willowmore

R337

Klipplaat

GROOTRIVIERBERG

R329

Steytlerville

R329

ELANDSBERG

Gamka

Gamkapoort Dam

Prince Albert

GROOT-SWARTBERG

Cango Caves

R328

De Rust

R62

Stompdrif Dam

R341

R332

Baviaanskloof

BAVIAANSKLOOFBERG

Groot

WARTBERG

ismith

Calitzdorp

Oudtshoorn

Olifants

Kammanassie

KAMMANASSIEBERG

N9

Uniondale

KOUGABERG

Kouga

Kouga Dam

Patensie

Cumba

LITTLE KAROO

R328

N12

R62

OUTENIQUA MOUNTAINS

Haarlem

R62

Joubertina

Kareedouw

R323

R327

Groot

Great Brak River

George

N2

Knysna

R339

R340

TSITSIKAMMA MOUNTAIN

N2

Kruisfontein

R352

R330

Riversdale

N2

Albertinia

Mossel Bay

Gourits

Wilderness National Park

Knysna National Lake Area

Plettenberg Bay

Tsitsikamma National Park

Humansdorp

Still Bay

Reins Nature Reserve

Vleis Bay

300 km

400 km

400 km

500 km

500 km

600 km

600 km

INDIAN OCEAN

0   20   40   60   80 km

The
Essential Guide
to South African Wines

The Essential Guide to South African Wines

Publisher: Cheviot Publishing cc
Editor: Harry Stephan Ph.D.
Designer: Rob House
Photographer: Jaap Scholten
Illustrator: Daniel Botha
Proofreader: Rhonda Crouse
Cartographer: John Hall
Reproduced by Unifoto (Pty) Ltd, Cape Town
Printed and bound in Singapore by Star Standard Industries PTE

First published in 2006 by Cheviot Publishing cc

The Essential Guide to South African Wines © 2006
Cheviot Publishing cc

Cheviot Publishing cc
P.O. Box 5, Green Point 8051, South Africa
www.cheviot-publishing.com
Reg. No. 2005/010348/23

ISBN 0 - 620 - 35500 - X

Acknowledgements

Firstly, our heartfelt thanks to the subject experts who acted as contributors to this publication, for their invaluable contribution in sharing their knowledge, experience and passion for South African wine.

- Dawid Saayman for his invaluable effort as chief contributor in setting out the Pockets as well as on the subject of South African *terroir*;
- Prof. Eben Archer for information on viticulture in South Africa;
- Loftie Ellis and Louis Nel for information on oenological aspects and local wine styles;
- Charl Theron for an historical overview of the South African wine industry;
- Eben Sadie for his contribution on a vision for the future of the South African wine industry;
- Dr Andy Roediger for information on wine tasting and wine styles;
- Cathy van Zyl (MW) for her contribution on collecting South African wine;
- Tanja Beutler and Clive Torr (CWM) for information on the Garagiste Movement of South Africa.

A great thank you goes to our editor, Dr Harry Stephan, and to the Unifoto team for all their enthusiasm and support in the production of this publication.

Thank you to Andrew Jefford and Michael Fridjhon for honouring us with forewords to this book. We are privileged to have their support.

We would like to thank the following people for their roles in creating this publication:

Jaap Scholten, whose dedication to this project was limitless, in every aspect from the inception of this idea to its fulfilment;

Christa von La Chevallerie for her tremendous enthusiasm and invaluable PR in collecting relevant data;

The staff of *Stellenbosch Management Services* for secretarial support;

eNetworks for providing computer hardware and technical support;

The *South African Wine and Brandy Company* and *The South African Brandy Foundation* for their support;

All the participating wineries taking sponsored profiles to represent the local industry. Thank you for your support and the opportunity to photograph your properties.

Thank you to our families and friends for their love and support that carried us through this project.

We acknowledge our Creator who afforded us this opportunity to live a dream and have others to share our delight.

Thank you all.
Elmari Swart & Izak Smit

Contents

6

Foreword

Wine is the song of the earth. Virgin scrub may give us a visual reading of a hillside, with its muscles of rock, its horizons of light, its tracks of wind. Other crops – wheat, cotton – may allow us to gauge a soil's generosity and calibrate human ingenuity. Only wine grapes, sensitively shepherded through fermentation, reflect their place of origin with nuanced exactitude, offering a sensual grid reference for the human nose and mouth to savour. Since no two places on the face of the earth are the same, every vineyard's song is different.

Pursuing those differences is the point of all fine winegrowing. For commodity wine, by contrast, the reflection of difference is at best a sideshow and, at worst, an irrelevant inconsistency to be blended or corrected away. We could call the former wines of place, and the latter wines of effect. Any competitive wine-growing economy needs both; there are drinkers thirsty for nothing but wines of effect, just as there are drinkers who search for the sensorial truths of landscape which only wines of place can reveal. For a wine nation to have a future, though, it needs wines of place. Wines of effect can usually be produced more cheaply elsewhere – where the weather is more regular, where mechanisation is further advanced, where wages are lower. Wines of place, by definition, are inimitable.

Among southern hemisphere nations, South Africa is notable for having set itself the challenge of producing great wines of place earlier than most. The means it chose to do this, though, were instinctive – via the cultivation of historic estates whose boundaries had often been established for centuries, originally with general farming aptitude in mind. Sometimes, serendipity means that these are indeed ideal sites in which to produce the fresh, lively and vivacious fine wines of South Africa; on other occasions, better sites beckon, a little higher up the hill, a little closer to the sea, a little further into the mountain range. Understanding is what we need now.

Elmari Swart and Izak Smit's book marks the first step on that road. Its exploration of *terroir* Pockets (the term is peculiarly appropriate to the rumpled Cape landscape) helps us grasp the parameters of each wine-growing location, while the winery profiles provide details not only of each estate's soils and slopes, but paint the vital human portrait for us too. Together they provide a framework for comprehension which the coming years, decades and centuries will deepen.

The understanding of *terroir* is a journey, not a destination. In the short term, the climate changes; in the long term, the earth moves. Drinking wines of place brings us closer to our land and our planet, and listening to the song of the earth in this way is a precious moment in the adventure of life.

Andrew Jefford

Foreword

While *terroir* has become something of a catch phrase among people who talk and write about wine, it is so poorly defined that one of France's leading wine writers, Michel Bettane has said "..."

It is possible to understand much of what is meant by a concept without being able to offer a rigorous definition. This does not mean that discussion of the subject will be free of controversy – on the contrary, lack of accuracy in definition is a recipe for a war. It does mean that a working model can be constructed and refined over time. Rutherford's concept of the atom has long been superseded, but the usefulness of his model is beyond dispute.

It has long been recognized that, in the world of wine, there is a correlation between place and product. The more limited the focus on site, the more accurately the sense of place is expressed. This is hardly surprising: wine – produced in a natural way – is a by-product of an agricultural environment. Whatever influences the performance of the vine has the potential to affect the taste, feel and evolution of what is produced from its grapes.

It is clear that precision of place yields – in principle – a more precisely unique wine. However, allowing that what is unique is not necessarily good, the identification of site and its rigorous transformation into a wine of origin is not necessarily a recipe for a quality product. Riesling, grown at Wadi Halfa in the Sahara, will certainly yield an unusual expression of the grape, but it is probable that it will find few aficionados.

South Africa has some of the oldest soils on earth, and a wine-producing region that is among the oldest of the so-called New World. Soil age is not a guarantee of quality, just as an established viticultural tradition does not promise commercial success. Wine production in Africa antedates even the most primitive winemaking in Europe by some 2, 000 years, but no one seriously argues that Egyptian wine offers a serious alternative to great Burgundy.

Given the quality and antiquity of South Africa's soils, the infinite climatic nuances in the viticulturally favourable southern regions of the land mass, the long-established winemaking tradition and the technical expertise of (particularly the new generation) winemakers, a *terroir* analysis of our major vineyard areas is long overdue. Site specificity without the ability to capture what is unique about place in a bottle of good wine is largely irrelevant, from a consumer perspective.

The extraordinary transformation of South African wine in the past decade has made a book of this kind a necessity rather than a luxury. South Africa has some of the world's greatest wine sites. It is time we identified them with the greatest precision, understood them in all their nuances, and sang their praises to fellow wine enthusiasts – wherever they may be living on the planet.

Michael Fridjhon

Authors' Note

Fine wine reveals two secrets to its students – a place of origin and an artisan's craft. Meeting the winemaker and visiting the site where the grapes are grown adds a new dimension to enjoying wine. We invite you to the Winelands of South Africa.

The concept of this book took shape in 2001, arising from the need to pay tribute to South African *terroir* together with human influences – fostering quality grapes to create great South African wines. This guide offers detailed information about wine production areas and wine styles by introducing a Wine Pocket System.

The task we set ourselves was to highlight:
- *Terroir* units as Wine Pockets in South Africa;
- The concept of *terroir*-specific wines;
- Influences distinguishing a Pocket's uniqueness;
- Natural factors impacting on wine quality;
- Vinification and wine styles;
- Flagship wines and their *terroir* foundations;
- Single vineyard identities and contributions;
- The uniqueness of South African wines.

The grape variety used to produce a wine is probably the most important factor in the taste of any wine, although this set of flavours is influenced by the location of vines and natural elements. Add to this the variations in soils and sub-soils, as well as the management to moderate influences and the result is a complex synergy of factors. The visible evidence of variable physical conditions clearly implies that each vineyard has a unique *terroir*, influencing the resultant wine. A richer wine experience can be created by exploring area differences as well as interpreting the process employed by viticulturists and winemakers.

No work of this kind can ever be complete. Future editions will elaborate on and refine the application of the *terroir* concept in South Africa, and place more detailed emphasis on the influence of winemaking and style differentiation.

We trust that this Guide, will make a meaningful contribution in highlighting the unique local viticultural diversity and various styles of world-class South African wines. Work on this volume was a great excuse to write about splendid landscapes and winemaking in this spectacular country – South Africa, "alive with possibility."

Elmari Swart & Izak Smit

Parameters of Consideration

The Essential Guide to South African Wines is a visual representation of the South African Winelands. The purpose of this book is to provide the wine enthusiast with knowledge about *terroir* and specialised day-tours, in a portable format.

The current demarcation system allows for area and region specificity. However, as the various levels of demarcation are somewhat daunting, the wine-producing regions of South Africa have been divided into 24 *terroir*-based Wine Pockets. Strict adjudication principles have been followed to distinguish *terroir* aspects and find synergies between areas of wine grape cultivation and varieties.

A Wine Pocket is a small demarcated area of wine grape production, where a level of homogeneity is found – not only in soils but also in the the shape of the landscape, climatic influences and cultivation of wine grapes. Such a set of conditions contributes to a recognisable wine style and distinctive characteristics, which differentiate the wine from its immediate surroundings. For this reason branded commodity wines have not been included, despite some very good examples.

The principles followed in this Guide include:
• Identification of Region and Pocket sites;
• *Terroir* (climate, soil, landscape and other aspects) and its influence;
• Cultivated varieties and age of the vines;
• Unique viticultural and vinification techniques;
• Complexity and consistency of flagship wines over vintages;
• Developing areas of viticultural interest.

This *Guide* is not intended to be another jargon-filled wine rating catalogue. We view all wine as individual and unique creations.

A representative number of wineries were identified in each Pocket, described in Chapter 2. All selected wineries were given the opportunity to sponsor a dedicated profile detailing their uniqueness and highlighting their flagship wines.

Wine Pockets present the wine traveller with a holistic experience, including food and accommodation, packed into day-drives. Relevant, vital local knowledge ensures the reader's enjoyment. Wine travellers do not have to be experts – this book is for the enthusiast, whether a connoisseur or novice. While the former may be intrigued by *terroir*, vinification specifics and particular wine styles, the latter may just wish to savour, compare and enjoy drinking some of the stunning wines on offer. The first Wine Pocket is a mere 15 minutes away from Cape Town International Airport, making it easy to integrate wine tourism into your visit to the Western Cape.

The unique Wine Pockets System will enhance your wine enjoyment as you discover and explore featured wine cellars and vineyards within a region's spectacular mountains and valleys.

11

Elmari Swart & Izak Smit

How to use this Guide

Whether you are a wine connoisseur using crystal drinking instruments or simply enjoying a glass of wine on occasion, this book will provide you with detailed information and vital local knowledge on South African wines.

The introductory chapter places South African wine in an historical and cultural context, and highlights a vision for the future. It summarises new developments such as Black Economic Empowerment (BEE), flying and garage winemakers as well as a local initiative to protect the indigenous fynbos heritage. The *terroir* concept is explained and a useful guide to key varieties is included. The bulk of the book is divided into 24 winemaking units, using the Wine Pocket system. This system provides insight into the major winegrowing areas, focusing on individual *terroir* Pockets, top producers and their flagship wines. Detailed maps and suggested day-driving routes include wine and local interests. All maps are orientated with North to the top of the page. Specially commissioned photographs illustrate key viticultural areas, while text boxes highlight significant facts.

Chapter 3 on wine tasting gives insights on serving and enjoying wine and recognising wine faults. The main wine styles are defined and illustrated per varietal for easy reference within the local market. Chapter 4 touches on ownership of property for wine production and suggests a list of South African wines for collection. Global Positioning System (GPS) waypoints are provided for use in your own GPS unit to locate places of interest. The last chapter provides vital local knowledge on everything from visiting South Africa and the Winelands in particular; to guidelines on

transport and storage of wine, and an essential wine dictionary. As you explore the world of South African wines, this book will prove a useful guide both at home and on your travels through the vineyards and wineries of South Africa. Enjoy wine responsibly, do not drink and drive!

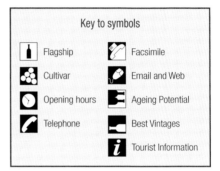

Key to symbols

Flagship
Cultivar
Opening hours
Telephone

Facsimile
Email and Web
Ageing Potential
Best Vintages
Tourist Information

Abbreviations for grape varieties

Cabernet Franc – Cab F
Cabernet Sauvignon – Cab S
Chardonnay – Chard
Chenin Blanc – Chenin Bl
Gewürztraminer – Gewurz
Malbec – Malb
Mourvèdre – Mouv
Nebbiolo – Neb
Petit Verdot – PV
Pinot Noir – PN
Riesling – Riesl
Sauvignon Blanc – Sauv Bl
Semillon – Sem
Shiraz – Shz
Tinta Barocca – Tinta B
Tinta Roriz (Tempranillo) – Tinta R (Temp)
Touriga Naçional – Touriga N
Viognier – Viog
Zinfandel – Zin

TERROIR
THE WINE-GROWING AREAS

Wine Pocket name

Colour photographs
A wealth of information is presented in full-colour photographs, providing a visual feast.

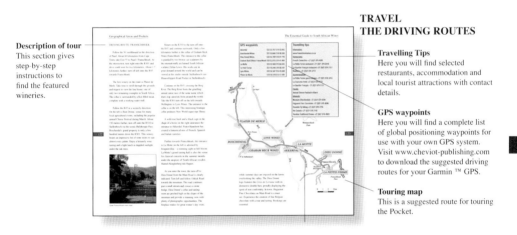

Franschhoek Pocket

Description of the Pocket
A detailed description gives an overview of climate, topography and other factors relating to the *terroir* of a Pocket.

Wine styles and top producers
The significant grape varieties cultivated are highlighted along with individual wine styles, the top producers and their flagship wines.

Key facts box
Here you will find information on the soil, climate and main grape varieties.

TRAVEL
THE DRIVING ROUTES

Description of tour
This section gives step-by-step instructions to find the featured wineries.

Travelling Tips
Here you will find selected restaurants, accommodation and local tourist attractions with contact details.

GPS waypoints
Here you will find a complete list of global positioning waypoints for use with your own GPS system. Visit www.cheviot-publishing.com to download the suggested driving routes for your Garmin ™ GPS.

Touring map
This is a suggested route for touring the Pocket.

13

TASTING
THE INDIVIDUAL WINERIES

Name of winery
This is the name of the winery or producer.

Flagship wine
Recognise the flagship wine with this full-colour pack shot.

Grape cultivation
This section focuses on the grape cultivation in the light of the specific *terroir*.

Winemaking
This section explains winemaking techniques and their importance to the wine style, focusing on the winery's flagship wine.

Information box
This box provides further information on the winery.

14

Chapter 1

15

A Recent Overview of the South African Wine Industry

Liquid assets – the wines maturing in these barrels at Vergelegen will fetch high prices

A Recent Overview of the South African Wine Industry

Recent plantings – vineyards at the top of Stellenbosch Kloof

The breathtakingly beautiful Cape Winelands are spread over a relatively small area, but the biodiversity of its winegrowing sites ensures that the area can produce an extensive range of wines to excite wine lovers the world over.

SHAPING THE INDUSTRY

Ironically, South Africa is often labelled as a "New World" wine-producing country; however, winemaking is anything but "new" at the tip of Africa. Vines were originally planted in the Cape of Good Hope in 1655 after the first wine cultivars were imported by the Dutch VOC. Although the Dutch were responsible for the birth of the local wine industry, their limited wine knowledge proved a definite constraint. Most of these early wines were made from unripe grapes and, together with the lack in hygiene and cellar technology, wines were over-sulphured. The revoking of the Edict of Nantes in 1688 by France's King Louis XIV resulted in Protestant Huguenots fleeing to the Cape. These immigrants were granted land in the secluded Franschhoek Valley, and their wine knowledge greatly improved local grape cultivation. The Vin de Constance, a dessert wine from the Constantia Pocket, became world famous and fuelled European demand for South African wines.

The local industry suffered many setbacks despite quality improvements and a newly found market. The dreaded root disease, *Phylloxera*, killed many vines during the 1880s. Overproduction followed in the early 20th century, when emphasis was placed on mass production. A ruling co-operative cellar, the Koöperatiewe Wijnbouwers Vereniging (KWV), was formed as a consequence with full government backing in order to control sales and stabilise pricing. A quota system (1957) limited vine plantings in new areas and the KWV quarantine system strictly dictated which new plant material could be imported.

These regulations limited producers' options and, as payments from the KWV were based on quantity, farmers failed to take into account quality aspects of their grapes and wines. The final blow came in the form of international trade sanctions during the 1980s as widespread protest against the apartheid regime became a reality.

THE TURNING POINT: NELSON MANDELA

Restrictions on international trade during the late 1900s forced producers to turn to the local market. This rather unsophisticated local market, when compared to international markets, did nothing but limit the winemaker's scope for creativity. It was only after Nelson Mandela's release from political imprisonment and the subsequent democratic elections in 1994, that serious international focus fell on the South African wine industry. Mandela's support for South African wines formed a necessary political stepping stone for the true emergence of Cape wine. Mandela toasted his 1993 Nobel Peace Prize with Cape wine.

CHANGES AND TRENDS

Following the political rebirth, international markets opened up and exports grew significantly, accounting for up to 45 per cent of local production. Inexperience and over-excitement resulted in some poor quality wines being exported, which did little to build the South African quality brand. Nor were there any true iconic wines to compete with the best international offerings. The South African wines were focused on price competitiveness. Once consisting of only a few producers and co-operative cellars, the wine industry has grown from just on 200 producers to nearly 500 producers during the past few years. Of these producers, 84 per cent are privately owned, which indicates a definite

trend towards greater hands-on involvement, increased quality and a definitive development in style. South Africa now competes at the highest level, both at international wine shows and for the wallets of wine enthusiasts.

THE OLD WORLD AND THE NEW WORLD

Mainly a geographical distinction between Europe (Old World) and the Americas, Australia and South Africa (New World), this distinction takes on a broader meaning in wine language. It differentiates between two philosophies of winemaking. Old World winemaking is defined by tradition; wine is made in the same place, in the same way and style as in the past. Nature is the key factor. Climate variations are expected, and wine is viewed primarily as an expression of *terroir* rather than individual varieties. Characterised by elegance, complexity and tightness, Old World wines tend to have lower alcohol levels (Alc. 11–12% by Vol.). Fruit flavours relating to each variety are less pronounced, and Old World wines have a greater maturation potential that can even run into decades.

New World wines, on the other hand, are defined by progress. New technology, innovative cultivation and exploration of uncharted areas are the order of the day. Wines are created to be consistent in quality, and the role of the vintage has somewhat diminished. The wines are defined by varietal characteristics and the expression of a wine's fruit characteristics. *Terroir* as a concept is only now being explored. New World wines are more powerful, with higher alcohol levels (as much as Alc. 16% by Vol.) and tend to have a more pronounced upfront fruitiness. Made for earlier consumption, these wines do have maturation potential, but not as much as the Old World wines.

South African wines are often described as lying somewhere between these two worlds, with the structure and restraint of the Old World and the fruit intensity of the New. Set to become a fully competitive world player, South Africa is one of the few New World wine countries which may have the ability to exhibit the fine qualities, elegance, balance and restraint comparable to truly great Old World wines. As the many new *terroir*-focused vineyards mature and winemakers gain an understanding of its interpretation, the sense of place in their wines will certainly deepen.

CHANGING GRAPE VARIETIES AND WINE STYLES

South Africa does not adhere to the strict regulations that govern most Old World wine areas, especially with regard to permissible varieties for certain blends, for example the Bordeaux blend. Since abolishing the quota system in 1992, the search for cooler, quality vineyards has taken entrepreneurs to the tip of Africa and to slopes on higher elevations at the snowline. In recent years, the planted area of five classic varieties (Cabernet Sauvignon, Shiraz, Merlot, Chardonnay and Sauvignon Blanc) has increased three-fold to 36 per cent of total plantings, largely at the expense

Pinot Noir – increasing its popularity

of Chenin Blanc. A local cultivar, Pinotage (a cross between Hermitage or Cinsaut and Pinot Noir), has recently also become a popular drinking varietal. Discussions on a classified "Cape blend", similar to a Bordeaux blend, but including Pinotage, are currently topical. Exchanges between local and foreign winemakers have influenced styles and varietal selections. French, Portuguese, Spanish and Italian grape varieties are now also being planted and they have attracted serious attention from blenders. This diversification of styles has presented a diverse spectrum from sparkling to fortified and from big, powerful, alcoholic wines to more elegant and delicate wines.

DEVELOPMENT AND TECHNOLOGY

New vinification techniques have also transformed winemaking: cold fermentation and use of specialised yeasts have led to a broader diversification of Sauvignon Blanc styles, while micro-oxygenation and finishing in small oak barrels has improved complexity and refined red wines in particular. In recent years more cellars are using modern technology, but most winemakers are still confident in traditional methods. For example, grapes are still fermented in large, open, wooden vats. Wine is also made without adding cultured yeasts (natural fermentation) and some wines are bottled without fining or filtration. Architecture within the winery has also developed, with the Cape now boasting some of the most impressive production facilities in the world.

BUSINESS AND FOREIGN INVESTMENT

The multi-million rand wine industry – a great tourism magnet in the Western Cape –

18

Modern technology – stainless tanks at Bein Wines

native countries. Wine consumption in South Africa is much lower than in most other wine-producing nations – just eight litres per capita per annum. In France and Italy consumers imbibe approximately 50 litres per capita per annum. Thus there is great scope for home-market growth as non-traditional consumers develop an interest in wine with rising living standards.

EMPOWERMENT INITIATIVES AND THE INDUSTRY STRATEGIC PLAN

Real success within the South African wine industry is crystallising as open minds and racial equality have come to the fore. The new democracy has brought about a re-structuring of traditional ownership patterns. Significant black-empowered ownership is developing, further instilling a culture of wine among a wider black population in South Africa. While the Black Association of the Wine and Spirit Industry (BAWSI) is working towards this objective, the South African wine industry drafted a Wine BEE (Black Economic Empowerment) charter in 2003. Under this charter, economic equity, enterprise procurement, skills and social development, as well as funding mechanisms have been put in place. A scorecard was developed to rate companies on their efforts to empower black and female workers.

is one of South Africa's most dynamic and exciting business sectors. In 2000, Stellenbosch Farmers Winery and Distillers Corporation merged to create Distell Group Limited, South Africa's largest producer and marketer of wines, spirits and ready to drinks (RTDs). The group is listed on the Johannesburg Stock Exchange, employs over 4,000 people and has an annual turnover in excess of US$800 million. South African Brewers (SAB) acquired Millers Brewing Company (the second largest brewery by volume in the USA) during 2002 and thus became the second largest brewer (by volume) in the world. With interests in Europe, Africa and the Americas, these companies resemble Fosters in Australia or Mondavi in the United States.

Since the 1990s, many international wine enthusiasts have also become involved in the South African wine industry. Some have set up joint ventures such as the husband-and-wife team of Zelma Long and Phil Freese as well as the French viticulturalist, Michel Rolland. Others have bought wineries, like Anne Cointreau-Huchon, a member of the Cointreau family, who now owns Morgenhof. The Swiss Buhrer family has revitalised Saxenburg. These investors infuse the industry with new ideas and increase exports through their ties to their

Individuals are also making a difference: wine farmers such as Charles Back of Fairview, Beyers Truter of Beyerskloof and Paul Cluver in Elgin have assisted farm workers to buy their own houses and set up their own winemaking operations. The private sector offers scholarships to young aspirant black winemakers to study viticulture and oenology at the leading University of Stellenbosch Oenology Department.

19

A second industry document, "South African Wine Industry Strategy Plan", is now accepted as the strategic framework for cooperation and action with specified goals on global competitiveness and profitability, equitable access, sustainable production and responsible consumption of alcoholic products. The plan aligns the visions and goals of the wine industry to grass root action plans managed by several supporting bodies.

BIODIVERSITY

The Cape Floral Kingdom is internationally recognised as a global biodiversity hotspot and World Heritage Site, one of the richest and most threatened reservoirs of animal and plant life on earth. A new partnership between the wine industry and the conservation sector aims to minimise the loss of threatened natural habitat and contribute to sustainable wine production through the adoption of biodiversity guidelines. By promoting cultivation practices that enhance biodiversity in vineyards and increasing the area set aside in contractual protected areas, the initiative will create a unique selling point for Brand South Africa. The world's first biodiversity wine route has recently been established. It includes Elgin, Bot River and Walker Bay.

FLYING, GARAGISTE AND OTHER WINEMAKERS

Flying winemakers made a significant contribution in shifting the international wine industry's focus from "wine is made in the vineyard", to an internally consistent and mutually supportive system integrating viticulture, cellar technology and grape processing. These trained winemakers (mostly Australian) travel the world and make wine for established as well as up-and-coming cellars in various countries, gathering and exchanging a wealth of knowledge and international winemaking experience.

Another type of winemaker is emerging from the industry – the **Garagiste** or garage winemaker. These are small-scale producers, who buy grapes from growers and vinify them themselves. Garagiste wines are hand-made in very limited volumes and illustrate the individuals' passion and dedication to wine as an art form, while most of them keep day jobs. The wine is usually of outstanding quality where only the best grapes and wood barrels are used.

In South Africa, as in most other wine-producing areas, **wine merchants** buy

Blue Cranes – South Africa's national bird among indigenous fynbos

buy grapes or wines from selected areas to blend and bottle wines under their own labels. Some merchants are involved in the actual winemaking process, while others buy the finished wine, which they mature, blend and bottle. Some outsource their winemaking operations to particular cellars, where they have the wine made according to their prescriptions, dictating viticulture and vinification practices. In many instances these wines still represent *terroir* characteristics and styles. Examples are Stellenbosch Bottling, Douglas Green Bellingham (DGB) and Jean Daneel.

There are over 60 **co-operative wineries** in South Africa, focusing on specific grape varieties, blends of varieties, dessert and distilled wines. Most co-operatives source wines from the vineyards in their immediate proximity. Various co-operatives have adopted a company structure, aligning themselves with current trends. A number have amalgamated and Distell, Rooiberg Cellars and Darling Cellars are good examples.

VISION FOR THE FUTURE

South Africa is still refining its identity and drawing closer to a system where individual regions may better suit specific grape varieties within an area than the marketing department. In new, cool areas like Elgin, Pinot Noir plantings are expanding. Sauvignon Blanc is becoming the grape of choice along the West Coast. In the Stellenbosch area, the Helderberg and Bottelary Pockets are redefining Cabernet Franc and Pinotage production respectively. Many new plantings of Shiraz in Paarl and the Swartland show great promise, and the true potential of old vine Chenin Blanc as a classic wine is gaining recognition. Winemakers are taking a more hands-off approach, allowing wines to express their specific vineyard origins.

Pride of South Africa – vines and proteas

Single varietal wines remain a consumer favourite, although specific blends are slowly gaining popularity. Recognising the importance of *terroir*, cultivation and winemaking, a blend in Constantia might consist of Sauvignon Blanc / Sémillon / Viognier, whereas the Swartland may blend Syrah, Mouvèrdre and Grenache. The Helderberg producers might find their rhythm with a Cabernet Franc / Merlot / Cabernet Sauvignon / Petit Verdot blend and Robertson might be producing single varietal Chardonnay. Areas showing great potential are Wellington and Tulbagh. Further a field, Napier and the southern coastal areas look promising with well-known producers developing virgin land. Stylish packaging, innovative and contemporary label design, together with new non-cork closures reflect South Africa's coming of age in the global wine village.

One of the great South African *terroir* wines is Kanonkop's Paul Sauer. The winery, in Stellenbosch-Simonsberg, has been producing its highly acclaimed flagship wine for over two decades. This is one of the most successful examples in terms of quality and consistency over time. Many new, young producers are following these footsteps to vinous greatness.

21

South Africa: A unique *terroir*

The South African winelands provide a constant interplay between ancient soils, valley slopes, soaring mountains and coastal breezes, resulting in an extraordinary biodiversity which is reflected in the indigenous flora of the area. With more than 9, 600 plant species, of which 70 per cent is endemic, the Western Cape is recognised as the smallest yet richest of the world's six great floral kingdoms. The conditions which support this remarkable biodiversity also support a large spectrum of grape varietals and wine styles.

Most of the Cape's wine-growing regions are influenced by either the Atlantic or Indian Ocean, which meet at the southernmost tip of Africa. The beneficial maritime influences (regular fog and cooling sea breezes), the moderate Mediterranean climate, the distinctive and varied topography and diverse soils all combine to afford ideal conditions to create wines of unique character and complexity. Coupled to this is a 300-year-old winemaking tradition and history that blends Old World restrained elegance with New World accessible fruit-driven styles. The result is wines that eloquently express the unique *terroir* of the Cape. No wonder this extraordinary wealth of natural assets and tradition instils South African wines with a unique sense of place. Today, more than 100, 000 hectares are planted to wine grape varieties, annually producing 620 million litres of wine.

DEVELOPMENT OF TERROIR IN A SOUTH AFRICAN CONTEXT

Terroir refers to the natural features of a body of land, which interact to create a unique set of conditions. These in turn confer specific characteristics on vineyards and wines. Although literally meaning "soil", *terroir* actually includes much more than simply that. The word refers to a combination of topography, climate, geology and soil variations. Identification of viticultural *terroir* now receives worldwide attention, and is backed by an increasing demand by the consumer for knowledge and understanding of the origin of each wine.

Falling in a warmer wine-growing zone, South Africa produces wines of pronounced diversity and vineyard site topography. The meso-climatic conditions are considered an

Calcareous soils as found in the Walker Bay Pocket

Natural *Terroir* Unit

A natural *terroir* unit (NTU) is a unit of the earth's surface characterised by relatively homogenous patterns of topography, climate, geology and soil. It has a scientific agriculture potential which is reflected in the characteristics of its products, resulting finally in the concept of *terroir*.

Zonation

Demarcating an area into units on a certain basis (for example *terroir* or climate).

Plutons

A dome like intrusion of igneous magma into the earth's crust, which occurred at great depths and consequently cooled slowly. These plutons have been exposed by erosion resulting in dome-like mountains such as the Paarl and Paardeberg Mountains and Darling Hills; or flat-topped erosion covered by sandstone deposits like Table Mountain and Simonsberg Mountain.

enormous asset, which makes zonation of high importance to the industry. As a result, South Africa has become a world leader in *terroir* research, using a multi-disciplinary programme to identify what constitutes *terroir* and its effect on grape quality as well as wine style. This information has significantly impacted site selection for individual varietals as well as viticultural practices including canopy management and trellising. It is now unlocking the potential of new wine-growing areas.

Geology – Although viticulture in South Africa is relatively young, the geology is not, resulting in some of the most ancient viticultural soils in the world. Geology forms the basis of *terroir*, as it dictates the chemical composition and shape of the land, how it changes over time and how soils are formed.

Massive pressures and upheavals over millions of years resulted in majestic mountain ranges with soaring peaks, steep slopes and deep valleys, creating a remarkable variety of meso-climates and soil types. This geological inheritance goes way back in time: The late Precambrian shale and schists deposited some 800 – 570 million years ago in a marine basin, presently occur at 20 – 200 metre altitudes. This deposit was folded and lifted due to tectonic movement of the Pan African event, which ended 550 million years ago and eroded into rolling hills.

Subsequently, intrusions of granite plutons occurred (600 million years ago), before the separation of Gondwanaland into the present-day Africa, Americas, India, Australia and Antarctica. A period of erosion and covering followed; intensive folding and lifting created the distinctive folded sandstone mountain ranges and valleys of the Cape.

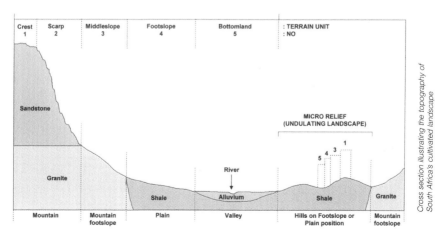

Cross section illustrating the topography of South Africa's cultivated landscape

Following the landscape – meticulous vine rows at Graham Beck Wines, Franchhoek

Topography – Topography describes the land surface features, its physical shape and has a strong interaction with soil and climate. Altitude, aspect (direction in which the slope faces) and inclination of a slope are three very important factors influencing viticulture. As the southern hemisphere seasons are directly opposite to those of the northern hemisphere, known influences will be exactly the opposite as well.

Climate – Viticulture originated at latitudes of 27°– 34° South, in areas with a Mediterranean climate. The Western Cape is cooler than its geographical position suggests, with vine-growing areas along the coastal zone seldom stretching more than 50 kilometres from the ocean. The coastal zone has warm summers and wet, cold winters, with frost rarely a problem. Rain falls mainly between May and August, and diminishes in a northerly and north-easterly direction, the latter the result of prominent mountain ranges. Temperature is a vitally important factor, influencing every aspect of the vine's functioning. The average summer daytime temperature follows an inverse pattern to the rainfall, increasing in a northerly direction and with distance from the ocean.

Soils – Soils are highly varied and often several different types occur within a single vineyard. Soil texture and structure depends on the clay content, which binds particles together and determines how water is retained or drained away. Excess water will cause vines to drown, whereas too little water (in sandy soils) will cause the vines to die of thirst. Too much clay causes the soil to compact when it experiences pressure – vine roots only develop in non-compacted soil areas. In very sandy soils, roots may develop only where they find water (e.g. drip irrigation) and not make use of the entire soil volume available. An evenly spread root system, both horizontally and vertically, is required for optimum plant health, giving it the best possible environment to survive and thrive. The organic and mineral content of soil feeds the vine; however, rich soils can cause excessive growth and mediocre fruit. Low fertility soils with a good structure and drainage are thus preferred.

> Gravelly or rocky soils are potentially good vineyard soil as gravel acts like natural mulch, shading the vine roots from the sun. The gravel and clay combination acts like a sponge, storing water during the rainy season and redistributing it back to the roots in the dry season. This ensures a constant feeding for the vines, giving them a more balanced water source, as opposed to simple irrigation.

Principle soils of South Africa

Sandstone		Lightly coloured, sandy with low nutrient and adequate water-retention properties. Contains calcium and quartz.
Granite		Red or yellow coloured, acidic and found on mountain foothill slopes and ranges of hills; good physical and water-retention properties. Quartz-rich, hard and acidic, easy-draining, low-fertile soil. Some of the best soils for viticulture.
Shale		Brown in colour, strongly structured, with good nutrient reserves and water retention.
Gravel		Free draining (benefit in wet conditions), low fertility, pebbly soil, retains heat of the sun and extends ripening beyond sunlight hours. Also retains moisture to cool soils.
Alluvial		Found on river banks and in flat land previously linked to a river. Potentially very fertile, yet sandy and silty. Not suitable for vigorous growers such as Shiraz.
Clay		Acidic. Retains water and is cool – benefit in warm conditions. In high quantities, prone to compaction and poor root development.
Limestone		Alkaline, easy-draining, calcium rich. Best suited to white cultivars (Chardonnay).
Loam		Equal parts of clay, silt and sand; potentially too fertile for grape cultivation.
Sand		Low fertility. Drains very well, prone to dryness, no storing of nutrients. Advantage of deterring *Phylloxera* beetle.

Maritime Climate

Close proximity to a large body of water such as an ocean defines a maritime climate. Key climatic factors associated with a maritime climate and their impact on vineyards is illustrated below.

In the Western Cape viticulture regions, the summer warmth is moderated by the constant interaction between the rugged mountain peaks and multi-directional valley slopes, as well as the proximity of two great oceans – the Atlantic and Indian. Cooling moisture-laden breezes blow in from the sea during the afternoon and seasonal fog is prevalent.

The Cape Doctor

As the Mistral in France, the legendary and sometimes ferocious south-easterly wind blows across the south-western Cape during the spring and summer months. Living up to its name, the Cape Doctor inhibits the development of diseases in the vineyards by drying grapes and dispersing air pollution, dust and pollen. It has a moderating effect on temperature, lowering it by several degrees, but rarely brings moisture to vineyards.

Aspect Vines on northern and western slopes experience warmer conditions due to higher interception of sunlight and as a result, grapes ripen more easily than those grown on flat land. Cabernet Sauvignon, Cabernet Franc and Pinotage, which require more heat, ripen later in the season. Cooler southern and eastern slopes (the latter warming faster and cooling earlier) host the more delicate varieties such as Sauvignon Blanc and Pinot Noir.

Flat terrain often experiences difficult drainage and ridges are made on shallow soils to increase soil volume.

Hill / Mountain Hills can offer protective rain shadows. They also provide shelter against damaging winds and reduce sun exposure. Small valleys in the folds of mountains provide sheltered land, but with the added benefit of run-off water.

Canopy The vine leaves not only ripen the grapes but also act as protection against harsh sunlight.

Sun Long hours of sunlight are adequate to ripen grapes fully.

Rain A maritime climate is subject to higher annual rainfall.

Wind Wind is an important factor as it influences the water requirements of the vines and reduces humidity and subsequent fungal diseases. Very strong winds may damage vines.

Levels of Climate

Macro – climate of a region, what is generally referred to as "climate".

Meso – differs from macro due to altitude, slope inclination, aspect or distance from the sea or large bodies of water, usually describes the climate of a vineyard.

Micro – climate immediately within and surrounding a plant canopy, can differ within location and time; a few centimetres and minutes can make a difference.

Ocean Close proximity of a large body of water moderates climate by providing cool air during the day and reducing the cold of night. The air movement it generates, assists in reducing disease by drying the surface of the grape bunches and leaves.

Altitude Maritime sites are often located at low altitudes.

Vineyard Humidity may cause fungal diseases. Vertical shoot positioning on a trellis system promotes circulation of air and minimises rot.

Row direction is used to maximise air flow between the rows and influences sun exposure.

Trellis system The height of vines is managed on a trellis system. Bringing the cordon arms closer to soil increases radiant heat and hastens ripening. It is also used to spread and open the canopy to sun exposure and protects shoots against prevailing winds.

Micro-climatic control is of great importance. In areas with relatively high humidity, leaf removal increases air movement to dry grapes; in sheltered areas sun exposure is increased to ensure proper ripening.

Continental Climate

A continental climate lacks the presence of large bodies of water which makes it drier and often sunnier. Continental areas experience wider temperature variations than Maritime areas; both from day to night and between seasons. These variations can be beneficial as cooler nights slow grape ripening and the long growing season yields riper fruit; however, frost can be a problem.

The aspect or orientation of a slope influences its *terroir*. In the southern hemisphere, north-facing slopes receive more sun and are warmer than south-facing slopes. The reverse is true for the northern hemisphere.

Shoot positioning Thicker canopy protects grapes from sunburn.

Soil A good soil structure is more important that its chemical composition, as the structure influences the water, air and nutrient content.

Steep slopes Slopes provide excellent drainage. In certain areas excessive sun exposure and heat restrict vine cultivation to cooler southern aspects. Slopes promote air circulation as warm air rises and cold air descends along the hillside. This air movement helps to reduce frost.

Altitude Vines are cultivated from a mere 50 metres above sea level to an altitude of 600 metres in the mountains. Increased altitude reduces average daytime temperatures and creates cooler conditions.

Rivers Bodies of water play a less important role in continental climates.

Grape varieties

The cultivar, or grape variety, is the heart of a wine and determines the basis of flavours.

Although in South Africa, there are no regulations on the selection of varieties, where they may be planted or what production yield per hectare of vines may be achieved (as is the case in France), the accepted standard for quality grape production is between five and 10 tons per hectare. A requirement for high quality grapes is a balance between its vegetal growth (trunk, shoots and leaves) above ground and the root system of a vine. This balance will naturally be influenced by soil types, climate, topography and sun exposure. Reducing yields does not always increase quality.

The noble varieties of France have been very popular in South Africa. Cabernet Sauvignon, Merlot, Chardonnay, Sauvignon Blanc and Chenin Blanc are firm favourites with many producers. Shiraz, under the guidance of mainly Australian winemakers, is rapidly increasing its popularity among South African wine drinkers and producers.

Fierce competition between producers has resulted in new varieties gaining in popularity. Viognier, Malbec, Grenache and Mourvèdre are increasingly used in high quality blends based on French styles and are also vinified to single variety wines.

South Africa's sunny climate seldom fails to ripen grapes fully. As sugar levels increase during ripening, the natural acid decreases. Simultaneously other chemical components (flavour, aromas and colour) are formed. Historically grapes were harvested on required sugar levels alone. Today, however, most producers harvest at a point referred to as "optimum ripeness". Difficult to define in terms of values, this is a combination of sugar, acid, tannin, colour and other chemical levels. These parameters (within a specified range) give an indication of grapes reaching optimal ripeness and are used to determine the moment of harvest. Although chemical changes continue inside the grape, its chemical makeup at the moment of harvest will determine the ultimate quality of a resultant wine, therefore the decision when to harvest is critical.

As wines easily attain sufficient alcohol levels (generally above Alc. 12.5% by Vol.)

The grape

The skin is the source of colour, tannins and flavour compounds, giving the wine its distinctive character. The stalks contain bitter tannins and are rarely used in winemaking.

The bloom or wax coat on the outside of the skin contains natural yeasts, which are used for spontaneous or natural fermentation. The wax also protects the grape from disease and pests.

The pips contain bitter tannins and will generally be removed during the winemaking process. The pulp is the heart of the grape and makes up the bulk of the volume. It comprises of water, sugar, acids and flavour compounds.

in the sunny ripening conditions, South African law does not allow sugar additions in winemaking. Addition of acid (naturally occurring in grapes: tartaric, malic) however is allowed to balance high sugar levels. Too little acid makes wine taste bland and lifeless; excessive acid stings the palate and makes wine undrinkable. Acid gives a wine structure and balance and remains one of the most important chemical components. Many aromas and flavours need a certain acid level to bring them to the fore.

Leading Varieties

Chenin Blanc — Earlier regarded as relatively ordinary. Historically grown with high yields and poor fruit concentration. **Wine:** Examples with high acid, pleasant citrus nose and wood are popular. **Area:** In most vine-growing areas

Chardonnay — Flourishes in poor, rocky soils, expressing typical butter, spicy and even nut flavours. In warm areas, rich and full bodied with softer acid. In cool conditions shows high, crisp acidity and strong mineral and flinty characters on limestone (Chablis style) (see Robertson). **Wine:** Many overoaked. Best maturation potential among whites, 3 – 4 years. **Area:** Stellenbosch Kloof, Robertson, Franschhoek

Sauvignon Blanc — Prefers cooler growing conditions with a refreshing acidity. **Wine:** Typically two styles: very tropical with citrus, guava and pineapple, or more green with grass cuttings, asparagus and tinned peas. **Area:** Durbanville, Constantia, Elgin, Cape Point

Sémillon — Often a blending partner, does well in cool areas. **Wine:** Peachy and citrus aromas and dense if aged well. **Area:** Franschhoek

Riesling — **Wine:** Few examples in German style, not popular in youth but dense and oily if matured (8 years +). **Area:** Constantia

Pinotage — A unique style, Cape Blend, incorporates Pinotage with various red blending partners. **Wine:** Red fruits: cherry, raspberry, strawberry and ripe plums. Some hints of violets. **Area:** Bottelary, Koelenhof, Robertson, Wellington, Tulbagh

Cabernet Sauvignon — Most abundant red. Ripens late, enjoys sites with long sun hours. High ratio of skin to juice, very good maturation potential due to high tannin content. Cool coastal Pockets see medium bodied, fruit-driven styles, turning more tannic and dark in warmer areas. **Area:** Stellenbosch-Simonsberg, Helshoogte, Paarl

Cabernet Franc — Grassy cousin of Cabernet Sauvignon, does very well as a blending partner. Is becoming popular as a single variety wine. **Area:** Helderberg

Pinot Noir — Requires meticulous handling. Prefers cool conditions, no direct sun and is sensitive to wind damage. **Wine:** Less intense with less tannin, but tends to elegantly restrained wines. Typical raspberry and strawberry flavours. **Area:** Walker Bay, Elgin

Merlot — Less tannin and more fruit driven, toffee and plummy characters. Good as single variety wine with softer mouthfeel and early drinkability, or used to soften blends. **Area:** Polkadraai, Annandale

Malbec — Spicy red grape, not as tannic as Cabernet Sauvignon. Good blending partner for red blend.

Mourvèdre — Favourite blending partner of Shiraz. Typical blackberry flavour.

Shiraz — Dark-skinned grape, making very powerful wines. **Wine:** Smoky, leathery and spicy with some red berries, can be very peppery. Does well with some American oak, giving vanilla, toasty aromas. **Area:** Simondium-Klapmuts, Agter-Paarl, Swartland

Viognier — Gloriously perfumed grape. Newly planted, used as blending partner for Shiraz (Rhône style) or with whites, very few single cultivar examples. **Area:** Swartland, Stellenbosch

Port — Fortified red wines, typically from warm areas. Uses mainly Portuguese cultivars, Tinta Barocca, Tinta Roriz and Touriga Naçional. **Area:** Klein Karoo

Timeline

January	February	March April	May	June

Viticulture

Veraison

The berries increase in size and start to change colour as the first signs of ripening. Vineyard maintenance: Once fruit is successful, growers may remove underdeveloped bunches (green harvesting) to create an optimum yield.

Preparation for harvest

Harvesting equipment is prepared, although some white varieties may be picked earlier to obtain a more herbaceous flavour. Grapes are analysed chemically and with taste tests for ripeness and flavour development.

Harvest

Harvest is the busiest time of the year. Vineyards are dotted with the colours of pickers, as they harvest grapes as rapidly and gently as possible. Machine harvesting is not very common in South Africa.

Leaf fall

Leaves fall naturally from the vine after grapes have ripened. This marks the end of the reproductive cycle. Vineyard maintenance: After harvest, vines are given time to rest. Trellis systems are mended, dead wood is cut from vines and unproductive plants are removed. Soils are ploughed to break up any compaction.

Resting

After leaf fall, the vines go into a period of dormancy where they can survive extreme cold. Without sufficiently cold conditions, the next growing season will be poor. Vineyards in shallow soils are ridged to provide sufficient soil volume for roots.

Hazards, diseases and pests

A number of potential dangers face the vines during the course of the year. Hazardous weather conditions such as spring frost damage young growth, a hail storm can rapidly destroy a vineyard and very humid conditions may cause fungal infections. *Phylloxera*, the insect that nearly destroyed the European wine industry in the 19th century, attacks vine roots, but today most vines are grafted on resistant American rootstocks. Various insects can damage the vine and birds, deer and small rodents feed on the ripe grapes.

Winemaking

Prepare cellar for grapes, machinery, barrels and chemicals.

Harvest of first white grapes

Harvest

Grapes are delivered to the cellar for fermentation

Fermented red (and some white) wine is placed in barrel for maturation. Bottling of previous vintage.

White wines are stirred on lees in barrel. Malolactic fermentation is started. Wines are racked from lees.

Sorting, crushing and destemming

On arrival, grapes are sorted, removing MOG (material other than grapes) as well as rotten, underdeveloped and damaged grapes. Grapes are transported via a receiving hopper which feeds into a destemmer / crusher where stems are removed and berries are crushed between rollers to render sugar-rich juice. White grapes and Rosé grapes are pressed to remove skins, and pips and juice is cleared for fermentation.

Fermentation

Yeast may be added to convert sugar to alcohol and carbon dioxide, alternatively natural fermentation is done without yeast addition. Fermentation generates a large amount of heat and the temperature is carefully controlled to prevent loss of flavour. Red wine completes warm fermentation (25 – 30°C) in four to seven days, but is kept in vats for maceration. Juice and skins are mixed by punching down the skins into the juice, drawing juice from the bottom of the vessel and pumping it over skins floating on top. White wines are fermented cold (16 – 20°C) and may take three weeks. If grapes lack acidity, acid may be added.

Pressing

Once sufficient alcohol, tannins and colour is extracted, the liquid (free-run) is run into a different container. The remaining solid matter is pressed to produce a dark liquid (press wine). Press and free-run juice may be blended to achieve a full, rich wine.

Lees stirring – White wine may be stirred on its yeast lees to increase development of flavours.

July	August	September	October	November	December

Pruning and vine shaping

Vines are pruned to position correctly and shape the plant as well as ensure good future yields. Although pruning can be done by machine, most growers use skilled workers.

Budbreak

Vineyards start to bud and the first green growth is visible. Soil is ploughed to aerate it.

Planting new vines

Young vines are removed from the nurseries and planted. Vines are planted wider apart on steep slopes as well as in areas where mechanical harvesting is done. Row direction allows strong winds to flow through the rows and reduce damage to vines.

Flowering

Small green flowers bloom and over the next two weeks pollination and fertilisation occur. Vines are sprayed, where necessary, against insects and fungal diseases. Vineyards in warm, dry areas are less prone to disease.

Fruit set

The fertilised flowers now develop into berries; the others fail to grow and fall off. Vine training: Following flowering, shoots are placed in the wires (trellised vines) and tied together (bush vines).

Excessive canopy shade causes a decrease in bud fertility, sugar concentration, colour density, flavour and tartaric acid while it increases potassium concentration, pH and malic acid.

Fining, filtration and bottling of white wines from this vintage.

33

Malolactic fermentation

A second fermentation done by bacteria, which may be added or done naturally. Mainly for red wine and certain dense whites (Chardonnay). Malic acid is converted to lactic acid, reducing the acidity of the wine and increasing a soft mouthfeel. This is done in barrel or tank.

Fining and filtering

Fining removes tiny proteins using a carrier such as bentonite or egg white to bind with the suspended particles and cause them to sink to the bottom of the vessel. Filtration removes solids from a liquid. These clarification techniques assist in producing a clear wine, which is stable in the bottle.

Maturation

Maturation mainly applies to barrel aging. Reserved for high quality red and white wines, this may take a few weeks to over two years. The porous wood allows slow oxidation, softening tannins and increasing the flavour complexity. As wine matures, it produces sediment, which may result in undesirable flavours. Using racking, the wine is drained or pumped away into a clean vessel to continue aging. Certain white wines may mature in stainless steel tanks before bottling.

Blending and bottling

In most cases, a number of barrels or tanks are blended to create a singular wine, then allowed to settle in a tank. Mobile bottling plants assist smaller producers to bottle their wine, while larger producers use automated bottling equipment. The aim is to transfer the wine safely to the bottle and preserve its character using a slow, careful fill protected from oxygen.

Chapter 2

Geographical Areas and Pockets

Breathtaking Banhoek Valley with Simonsberg Mountain (1,319 m)

Geographical Areas and Pockets

Healthy chill – afternoon mists from the Atlantic Ocean cool the vineyards

Most vineyards are found in the south-western areas of South Africa, hosting a wide range of *terroir* units that suit a large range of wine styles. Wine-producing areas are not restricted by regulations that specify the planting of varieties in specific areas, therefore varieties that were not previously known to be suited to certain areas were planted by pioneering winemakers with great success.

Although the first wine was made in 1659, a recent renaissance in winemaking practices has lifted South African wines to new heights. A flood of innovation started in the late 1960s with the arrival of German winemakers, and surged again after 1992 when South Africa became more exposed to the international wine arena. The concept of *terroir* has slowly taken root in this relatively young wine country and, together with a better understanding of viticultural practices, has boosted wine quality to a point where South Africa now offers wine that equals and often exceeds international standards.

Cape Town, capital of the Western Cape Province, is South Africa's second largest city, with a population of approximately 3.5 million. It is the southern-most metropolis on the African continent, and enjoys a pleasant Mediterranean climate. The Western Cape's major wine-growing areas stretch from the heart of Namaqualand, north of the majestic Cederberg Mountains, to the Klein Karoo, well east of Cape Town. However, most of the 24 wine-growing Pockets are within easy reach of Cape Town, ranging from a 20 minute drive (Constantia) to a two-hour journey (Robertson).

Wine culture is well developed in the Western Cape, as the region has been producing wine for more than three and a half centuries. Jan van Riebeek, who arrived in Table Bay on 6 April 1652 to establish a refreshment station for the Dutch East India Company, saw his first vintage pressed in 1659.

Topography:	Mountains dominate, vineyards planted on slopes and valley floors
Soil:	Varies dramatically, mostly acidic and clay based
Climate:	Mediterranean – long, hot summers and wet, cold winters
Temperature:	February average 24°C
Rainfall:	Annual average range from 730 mm (Stellenbosch) to over 1,000 mm (Constantia)
Wind:	South-east in summer, also known as the Cape Doctor
Varieties:	Cabernet Sauvignon, Cabernet Franc, Merlot, Shiraz, Pinotage, Sauvignon Blanc, Chenin Blanc, Chardonnay, Sémillon, Viognier, Muscat, Riesling

Most of the Western Cape's wine-growing areas enjoy a Mediterranean climate, with winter rainfall and warm, dry summers. Both climate and soil variations ensure that a wide range of wine styles and types are produced. High quality red and white wines are made, along with an increasing number of sparkling wines. The fortified wines – including sherry, port and muscadel – are renowned for both good quality and affordable prices.

Gracious estates with distinctive Cape Dutch architecture, surrounded by verdant vineyards and a backdrop of mauve mountains, are as quintessentially Cape as Table Mountain. There are, however, several equally impressive cellars that are as modern as any in the world, some sunk into hillsides, others state-of-the-art steel and glass structures that soar skyward.

Temperature and rainfall conversion table (metric / imperial)

Metric	Imperial
Rainfall	
200 mm	7.9 in
400 mm	15.8 in
600 mm	23.6 in
800 mm	31.5 in
1,000 mm	39.4 in
Temperature	
10°C	50°F
15°C	59°F
20°C	68°F
25°C	77°F
30°C	86°F
35°C	95°F

Sky light – the impressive state-of-the-art cellar at Vergelegen

Cape Point Pocket

Coastal proximity – view over Cape Point Vineyards

Cape Point is the exception to vine plantings and cultivation in the Cape Winelands and represents the new face of South African wine. This Pocket is situated behind the south-western slopes of the Constantia amphitheatre of mountains. Vineyards are a maximum of three kilometres from the cold Atlantic Ocean, dominated by the artic Benguela current. The climate is Mediterranean, but the Pocket experiences strong maritime and mountain-shelter influences. The annual rainfall exceeds 1, 000 mm (40").

Apart from the south-western and west slopes facing the cold sea, the topography of the area resembles that of the neighbouring Constantia basin. Although the average summer daytime temperature is about the same as that of Constantia (20.6°C or 68°F), the Cape Point area is markedly cooler due to the proximity of sea breezes and synoptic winds, often combined with mountainous cloud cover.

The low daytime temperatures, mountain clouds and sea mists, which often cover the vineyards, produce near-perfect growing conditions for heat-sensitive grapes, such as Sauvignon Blanc and Sémillon. Sunlight hours during the growing season are also sufficient to ripen varieties such as Cabernet Sauvignon.

The Pocket's granite outcrops are highly weathered and stripped of their reddish-brown soil mantle, presenting more white-coloured soils. The hills and outcrops are extensively used as a source of kaolin, a good indication of the alkalinity of the soil. Due to varying soil fertility, marked differences in vine vigour occur between vineyards, and cultivation practices vary accordingly.

Viticulture is focused on utilizing the cool sea breezes to create slow, even ripening of grapes and continuous air movement to control humidity and combat fungal diseases. Vine row direction is orientated so that summer winds flow down the rows, while canopies are opened by removal of leaves and side shoots to allow sufficient sunlight penetration. The Pocket is still relatively young and although it is suited to both red and white noble varieties, not all of them are planted here. The Cape Point Pocket is currently recognised for its Sauvignon Blanc and Chardonnay production, with Sémillon beginning to show good potential.

Cape Point Vineyards excels in this category with the wines showing herbaceous flavours mixed with tropical fruit and a zippy finish. Recently, limited quantities of Pinot Noir, Cabernet Sauvignon and Shiraz vines have been added.

Soil:	sandstone on bleached granite
Climate:	cool, windy, high rainfall
White varieties:	Sauvignon Blanc, Sémillon, Chardonnay
Red varieties:	Pinot Noir, Cabernet Sauvignon, Shiraz
Wine styles:	red, white

Cape Point Vineyards *Cape Point Pocket*

The vines of Cape Point Vineyards are laid out near Cape Point, the southernmost tip of the Cape Peninsula. These vineyards are a mere 1,5 kilometres from the Atlantic Ocean. Thirty-one hectares of low-yielding vineyards are cultivated on decomposed granite and gravel soils, naturally limiting vigour and allowing for smaller grape berry production. This relates to greater fruit concentration and more intense wines. The white varieties are planted on soils with a higher percentage of clay. This favours Sauvignon Blanc wines, giving a mineral to steely character. The other wines also follow the mineral structure typical of the *terroir*. Three distinct styles demonstrate the complex potential of Sauvignon Blanc: • Stonehaven – an elegant, citrusy wine from grapes gown at a low attitude. • Sauvignon Blanc – a complex wine grown on granite and clay-rich elevated slopes. Blended with a portion of Sémillon and barrel-fermented Sauvignon Blanc and aged on the lees. • Isliedh Sauvignon Blanc – (pronounced ai-lay) a barrel-fermented wine grown on clay-rich soils, aged in wood for 10 months.

Sauvignon Blanc, Sémillon | Sauv Bl, Sém, Chard, Shz, Cab S
No tasting/sales at cellar, please contact cellar for stockists.
+27 (0)21 785 7660, +27 (0)21 785 7662 info@cape-point.com, www.capepointvineyards.co.za | Sauv Bl 5 y
Sauv 00, 01, 04. Sém 03, 05 | Southern-most vineyards in South Africa

Guarding the entrance

Making a statement

Proximity to the Atlantic Ocean

Biodiversity personified

Constantia Pocket

Beautiful history – Buitenverwachting's reception building

Historic Constantia is the site of Simon van der Stel's (one of the first governors of the Cape of Good Hope) 17th century wine farm and the source of the world-famous 19th century Constantia sweet dessert wines. Due to urbanisation, this small vine growing Pocket is squeezed in between the residential area of Constantia and Table Mountain, a World Heritage Site.

The Constantia Pocket nestles in a shallow mountain amphitheatre formed by the south jutting "tail" of Table Mountain (1, 000 m) extending into the Vlakkenberg (570 m), Constantiaberg (900 m) and Kalkbaaiberg mountain ranges. Constantia is considered a cool cultivation area, as the mean February temperature at harvest time is only 20.6°C. Facing south-east and opening directly onto False Bay (10 km), this area receives the full benefit of its cool and moisture-laden breezes. While the breezes moderate the daytime temperature, cloud cover and overnight condensation increase the relative humidity which often leads to the development of *Botrytis*. Strict viticultural management is required to avoid fungal infection or proper management for the production of sweet wines. An important feature of the Constantia Pocket is early morning sun which dries the vineyards from dew, aiding the prevention of vine diseases. An additional advantage is the afternoon mountain shadow which relieves the heat of day. Annual rainfall is relatively high (1, 050 mm) making irrigation unnecessary.

The mountain ramparts are remnants of a solidified sandy alluvial plain, called Table Mountain Sandstone. This formation rests non-conformably on a granite intrusion that was eroded flat before the deposition of the sandstone material. On the red granite base foothills, at altitudes of 100 to 300 metres, deeply weathered reddish-brown, acidic soils have developed with excellent water-retention and drainage properties.

This acidity is easily neutralised with the first soil preparation before planting and occasional lime additions. The high-lying vineyards cling to south-eastern and north-eastern aspects which are moderately cool, with some warm solar radiation from the North ensuring ripening. Vineyards located lower down on the foothills enjoy slightly longer sunlight hours. This allows red varieties such as Cabernet Sauvignon to ripen fully. However, these reds reflect definite cool climate characteristics with moderate (for South Africa) alcohol levels of 13 to 14 per cent.

Due to large topographical variations, long-term viticultural practices vary over short distances between farms and even between vineyards. Vine rows planted on the contours of steep slopes are wider, sometimes even forming terraces, while the vines on flat terrain have narrow rows. In many cases, these extremes are located very close or even right next to each other.

To combat the high humidity, row direction allows the prevailing summer south-easterly to flow through the rows and canopies are more open to facilitate air-flow and control fungal disease. With a few exceptions, all vines are cordon trained and shoots are vertically positioned in trellises to provide protection from the strong prevailing winds.

Although considered a cool climate, the Pocket's *terroir* is suited to both red and white varieties due to specific locational advantages such as sunlight exposure and slightly extended ripening conditions.

Heat-sensitive Sauvignon Blanc and Chardonnay excel in this particular cool climate, showing distinct varietal fruit and impressive concentration, while a naturally high acidity gives the wines longevity.

Steenberg Vineyard's Sauvignon Blanc shows complex herbaceous mixed with tropical fruit flavours. Constantia Uitsig is doing particularly well with a wooded Sémillon. Klein Constantia's Vin de Constance, historical favourite of Napoleon, is still an exceptional sweet wine, made from Riesling. White blended wines are also very popular with the Constantia producers.

Merlot and Cabernet Sauvignon-based blends are also popular. Groot Constantia and Buitenverwachting focus on these styles and their wines show great finesse. Small parcels of other red varieties show great potential. Red wines show fine berry fruit and tight tannins, reflecting the cool climate structure and elegance. Recently, the Constantia Pocket wineries decided to use a unique crested bottle for their flagship wines, promoting the collective range of their wines in premium glassware.

Soil:	red-brown sandstone on granite
Climate:	cool, windy, high rainfall, sunlight
White varieties:	Sauvignon Blanc, Chardonnay, Riesling, Sémillon
Red varieties:	Cabernet Sauvignon, Merlot, Shiraz
Wine styles:	red, white, sparkling

Vineyard perfection – Constantia Uitsig vineyards

DRIVING ROUTE: CONSTANTIA

Leave Cape Town on the N2 freeway, driving south-east to explore the oldest wine-producing area in South Africa – Constantia. The M3 freeway links to the N2; a few hundred metres further the N2 turns east towards Cape Town International Airport, while the M3 continues in the same direction – stay on the M3. The M3 winds its way through residential areas and changes name several times before regaining freeway status and descending a long, steep slope. Pass a four-leaf-clover intersection at the bottom of the hill and take the first turn-off left (Exit 15) to Kendal Road. Turn left and cross over the M3, towards the Constantia Mountain. At the next traffic light, turn right into Spaanschemat River Road (M42) and follow the road to a T-junction. Turn left into Constantia Main Road (M41), pass one set of traffic lights and take the second turn left where signs indicate Groot Constantia. Follow the road to the property, up a slight hill.

Groot Constantia has preserved many reminders of the luxurious lifestyle from the time of Simon van der Stel, including beautiful pediment gables and lush gardens with a historical bath. An orientation centre houses an exhibition of several artefacts and photographs depicting the history of the estate. Visit the manor house (Van der Stel's home, built more than 300 years ago) and original wine cellar, which now houses a display of drinking vessels and winemaking equipment.

Return along the same route to Spaanschemat River Road and follow the road in the opposite direction. Pass a famous local landmark, Peddlers on the Bend restaurant, up a slight hill and turn right into Klein Constantia Road. A few metres further, turn left at the sign to Buitenverwachting. An oak-lined driveway leads to paddocks and around the buildings to the tasting room and restaurant. Buitenverwachting was listed as one of the world's 50 top producers by *Wine Spectator* in 2004. The restaurant has been rated locally in the top 10 dining establishments for more than a decade.

Leaving Buitenverwachting, turn left into Klein Constantia Road and continue for a kilometre to Klein Constantia, home of Vin de Constance, a noble wine modelled on the famous South African sweet wine of the 18th and 19th centuries. Turn right and follow a gravel road to the tasting room, where a collection of old Vin de Constance bottles and a magnificent batik depicting four seasons in the vineyards are on display.

Return to Spaanschemat River Road and turn right. A few kilometres further, turn right to visit Constantia Uitsig. Sharing cellar space at Steenberg winery, Constantia Uitsig offers tasting facilities at its wine and gift shop. Adjacent Spaanschemat River Café boasts its own elegant cookbook. The world-class hotel and two fine-dining restaurants provide luxurious country charm.

Continue along the Spaanschemat River Road, which becomes Steenberg Road as it nears the mountain. The road turns on itself as it ascends a mountain slope. Turn right at the entrance to Steenberg. Follow the paved road up to the cellar and tasting room, which has a brilliant view over the area. Recently incorporated in the Kangra group of Graham Beck, Steenberg includes a championship golf course and a five star boutique hotel celebrating 17th century elegance and traditions. Catharina's restaurant, situated in the original winery (circa 1682), has been tastefully redecorated and now includes a cigar lounge.

GPS waypoints

Buitenverwachting	S34 02.470 E18 24.962
Constantia Uitsig	S34 02.857 E18 25.513
Groot Constantia	S34 01.425 E18 25.806
Klein Constantia	S34 02.283 E18 25.133
Steenberg	S34 04.504 E18 25.779

Travelling tips

Information:

www.constantiawineroute.co.za

Restaurants:

Simon & Jonkershuis (Groot Constantia) +27 (0)21 794 5128

Buitenverwachting restaurant +27 (0)21 794 3522

Catharina's restaurant (Steenberg) +27 (0)21 713 2222

Constantia Uitsig restaurant +27 (0)21 794 4480

La Colombe (Constantia Uitsig) +27 (0)21 794 2390

Spaanschemat River Café (Uitsig) +27 (0)21 794 1810

Accommodation:

Constantia Uitsig Country Hotel +27 (0)21 794 6500

Steenberg Hotel +27 (0)21 713 2211

Events:

Teddy bear festival (Buitenverwachting) 1 May

Leaving Steenberg, turn right at the gate and follow the M42 turning east, past the Barnyard Farm Stall. At the second traffic light it links up with the M3, returning to the city.

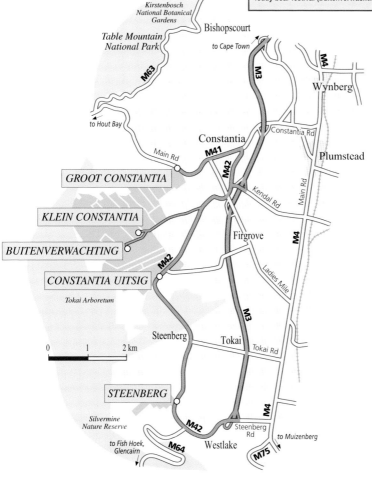

Groot Constantia *Constantia Pocket*

Simon van der Stel established Groot Constantia in the late 1600s. Today the granite soils and steep slopes of the Constantia Mountain provide the setting for its 100 hectares of vines. White varietals are planted on high, east-facing slopes and reds on the lower slopes which enjoy more sunlight exposure for development of colour and fruit flavours. With its close proximity to the Atlantic Ocean and its high altitude (240 m), the vineyards are relatively cool, ensuring slow, even ripening. Red wines are fermented at high temperatures (30°C), increasing colour development. The Bordeaux blend (Cabernet Sauvignon / Merlot / Cabernet Franc / Malbec) matures in 100 per cent new oak for 18 months, resulting in a powerful wine with fine tannin structure. Chardonnay is barrel fermented to add complexity and richness to the wine. Due to the cool conditions, wines have great density, elegant dry tannins and a long finish.

Governors Range – Reserve (Bdx blend: Cab S / Merlot / Malb) Cab S, Merlot, Shz, Chard, Cab S, Pinotage Daily 9 – 6 (Dec – Apr); 9 – 5 (May – Nov). Closed Easter Fri, Dec 25, Jan 1. +27 (0)21 794 5128 Fax +27 (0)21 794 1999 cellar@grootconstantia.co.za, www.grootconstantia.co.za red 5 – 12 y, white 2 – 3 y 04, 05 Tours on hour every hour, restaurant, BYO picnics, gift shop, conference venue, walks, museum

Klein Constantia *Constantia Pocket*

Klein Constantia has been lovingly restored to its former glory and is now home to Vin de Constance, South Africa's iconic sweet wine that has thrilled wine lovers for many years. The south-facing slopes of Constantia Mountain are ideal for heat-sensitive Sauvignon Blanc grapes which benefit from the cooling effects of high altitude as well as the nearby Atlantic Ocean. Red varieties are grown on fertile decomposed granite soils at lower levels. To constrain vigour, vines are planted to high densities with canopies carefully managed. Suckering opens the canopy to airflow, reducing humidity and fungal diseases. Vines are trellised to maximise the leaf surface exposed to sunlight for photosynthesis and to allow filtered sunlight to ripen the grapes. Vin de Constance is made with Muscat de Fontignan grapes, which are harvested at very high sugar levels, resulting in a naturally sweet dessert wine without *Botrytis*. Grapes are pressed and the cleared juice is cold fermented to achieve the rich, silky structure. Klein Constantia's white wines are aromatic and typically show minerality and lively acid.

Vin de Constance (sweet) Muscat F, Cab S / F, Shz, PN, Chard, Sauv Bl, R Riesl, Sém Mon – Fri 8 – 5 Sat 9 – 1 Closed publ hols +27 (0)21 794 5188 +27 (0)21 794 2464 info@kleinconstantia.com, www.kleinconstantia.com Vin de Constance 10 y, Red 8 y, Riesling 10 y Sauv 95, 96, 04, 05; Riesl 95; Reds 01 historic artefacts, magnificent wall hanging in tasting room

Quiet escape – luxurious Steenberg hotel

Aspect personified – mountain vines at Klein Constantia

Constantia Uitsig *Constantia Pocket*

Vineyards have flourished at Constantia Uitsig since the 17th century, but only in 1993 did the maiden vintage first carry the Uitsig name. Vines are cultivated on mountain slopes in sand and loam soils, at an altitude of 200 metres above sea level. Being in close proximity to False Bay, the vineyards enjoy cool ripening conditions. Grapes are harvested at night (2:30 – 10:00) to preserve the delicate flavours of particularly Sauvignon Blanc and Sémillon grapes. White varieties receive skin contact to increase fruit extraction and they are fermented cool to restrain alcohol production. Sémillon is barrel fermented (14°C) and wood matured for 12 months resulting in oily, lanolin characters with freshness and a lingering finish. The Chardonnay shows strong minerality and flintiness, typical of cold climate winemaking. Red varieties are warm fermented and oak matured to give lush, ripe fruit and soft silky tannins. Components are blended after wood maturation and the wine is bottle matured for another 18 months before release.

[i] Constantia Red (Cab S / F / Merlot), Constantia White (Sém/ Sauv Bl) 🍇 Cab S, Merlot, Sém, Sauv Bl, Chard 🕐 Mon – Fri 9 – 5, Sat Sun 10 – 4. Closed Easter Fri, Dec 25, 26, Jan 1 📞 +27 (0)21 794 1810 📠 +27 (0)21 794 1812 📧 thewineshop@uitsig.co.za, www.uitsig.co.za 🍷 white 3 y, red 6 – 7 y ⬛ white 01, 03 [i] 3 restaurants (top 10 of SA), luxury hotel, wine /gift shop, conference facilities, cookbook

Steenberg *Constantia Pocket*

Steenberg is the youngest (maiden vintage 1996) of the Constantia wineries. Sixty-two hectares of vines are spread along the eastern slopes of the Steenberg Mountain. The lower slopes (60 – 180 m) are exposed to early morning sun, which dries the grapes and prevents fungal diseases. Afternoon mountain shadows shelter vineyards from the strong prevailing winds, creating cool ripening conditions along with the beneficial ocean breezes. Low vigour, decomposed granite soils result in naturally low yields. The Sauvignon Blanc is made through a reductive process with 90 days lees contact. This aromatic wine shows typical cool-climate herbaceous and mineral flavours. The unconventional Catharina blend reflects Steenberg's signature Nebbiolo, with minty, berry flavours. The red wines express lower alcohol content due to cooler ripening conditions. The aromatic barrel-fermented Sémillon benefits from wood maturation. A small component of the Chardonnay for the 1682 Brut MCC is barrel fermented, enriching its mineral and biscuit flavours.

[i] Sauv Bl Reserve (single vineyard wine); Catharina blend (Cab S/F/Merlot/Shz/Neb) 🍇 Sauv Bl, Sem, Chard, Merlot, PN, Cab S, Cab F, Shiraz, Nebbiolo 🕐 Mon – Fri 9 – 4:30 Sat & Publ hols 9:30 – 1:30. Closed Easter Sun/Mon, Dec 25, 26, Jan 1 📞 +27 (0)21 713 2211 📠 +27 (0)21 713 2201 🌐 www.steenberg-vineyards.co.za 🍷 white 4 y, reds 8 y+ ⬛ Sauv 03, 04 Catharina 01, 02 [i] restaurant, hotel, cellar tours

Buitenverwachting *Constantia Pocket*

Buitenverwachting, first established in 1796, is a grand winery with an impressive façade. One hundred and twenty hectares of vines are cultivated on the slopes of the Constantia Mountain, where the early afternoon shade and prevailing ocean breezes cool the vineyards. The planting density is relatively high on the steep slopes due to fertile granite soils with good water retention. White varieties are planted on the coolest south and east-facing sites with reds on warmer north-east-facing slopes. Extended skin contact on Sauvignon Blanc concentrates its delicate flavours to an intensely aromatic wine, showing typical cool-climate minerality and naturally high acidity. These factors allow the wine to mature successfully and lees maturation softens the sharp acidity. Red grapes are cold soaked before and after fermentation, promoting colour and flavour extraction. Red wines, oak matured in 100 per cent new French barrels, are cellared for four years before release to soften and integrate the wood into a powerful yet majestically elegant and balanced finish.

[i] Christine (Bdx blend: Merlot / Cab S / F) 🍇 Sauv Bl, Cab S / F, Merlot, Malbec 🕐 Mon – Fri 9 – 5, Sat 9 – 1. Closed publ hols 📞 +27 (0)21 794 5190 📠 +27 (0)21 794 1351 📧 info@buitenverwachting.com, www.buitenverwachting.com 🍷 Sauv Bl 3 y; Bdx Blend 8 y ⬛ red 00, white 02 [i] older vintages available, tours by appt., restaurant (rated in top 10 in SA), picnics, Teddy bear fair 1 May

Durbanville Pocket

Rolling hills – the vineyards of Durbanville enjoy varying sun exposure

The Durbanville Pocket is made up of an open-ended tunnel between prominent, stand-alone north-south running hills known as Tygerberg (Eng. Tiger Mountain) and Kanonkop (Eng. Canon Head). The hilltops are elevated about 400 metres above sea level; however, the vineyards are concentrated mainly on lower east-facing slopes at altitudes of 100 to 350 metres, which enjoy long sunlight hours, assisting in the ripening of the grapes.

Although its macro-climate is comparable to that of Stellenbosch, this Pocket has a markedly cooler meso-climate than the Stellenbosch area. The reason for this is unobstructed exposure to two oceans, the Atlantic (10 km) and False Bay (28 km), as well as the general high altitude of the vineyards (up to 350 m). Even though the mean February temperature is 22.4°C, the duration of this high temperature during the day is relatively short due to the dramatic cooling effect of prevailing summer breezes,

taking effect from midday. This cooling effect may cause a decrease of as much as 5°C in vineyards exposed to the breezes compared to those sheltered between the hills. The relatively cool meso-climate permits the cultivation of all the noble varieties, but site selection is of great importance due to large variations in slope direction. In this way, cooler and warmer sites are created with the potential to ripen both heat-sensitive white varieties as well as hardy red varieties.

The annual rainfall is a mere 400 – 500 mm (15.7 – 19.7 in) and due to the isolated nature of this range of hills, there are limited water catchment areas and restricted water storage potential. Due to the lack of irrigation water, special emphasis is placed on rootstock choice, selecting drought-resistant rootstocks. Most vineyards are cultivated dry-land with supplementary irrigation given in extremely hot conditions to prevent permanent damage to vines. Subsequently deep root development (to access underground water) is a major feature of vineyards in this area.

Geologically, Durbanville differs from all other high-lying coastal-zone vineyard areas as the parent soil material found here is phyllite and greywacke formations (see box below). The dominant soils derived from these formations are highly weathered, reddish-brown and well drained with good water and nutrient retention properties. However, unlike typical Western Cape weathered soils, these are not acidic. Vineyards are cultivated without irrigation in an attempt to reduce excessive growth vigour on the fertile soils. With only a few exceptions, vines are spur pruned with emphasis on spacing of the shoots to ensure an open canopy.

The maritime moderating influences are reflected in the pronounced cool-climate characteristics of all the varieties, but in particular the sought-after Sauvignon Blanc grapes and wines. These wines show expressive fruity, cool nettle and green fig flavours. Other white wines are very food-friendly with a rich melon and citrus character, with a Chardonnay offering from Diemersdal and aromatic Sémillon from Nitida. Reds (Merlot and Cabernet Sauvignon in particular) are finely textured and accessible. Durbanville

Hills and Hillcrest are good examples. Altydgedacht's ripe Pinotage illustrates the heat collection to ripen this late variety in wind-sheltered sites.

The Philadelphia area just north of Durbanville is drier and viticulture practices are aimed at water conservation as well as increased water efficiency. The ocean influence is still very prominent and textured reds as well as ripe, juicy whites are produced by Capaia and Havana Hills. Soil preparation before planting and soil surface maintenance are of extreme importance to allow water into the soil and reduce run-off waste. Yields are low due to the cultivation conditions and preference is given to red varieties.

Phyllite – rocks which do not respond evenly to pressure and often have a distinctly wavy appearance

Greywacke – sandstone generally characterised by hardness, dark colour and angular grains of quartz and small rock fragments

---

Soil:	shale, red granite, schist
Climate:	warm with ocean influence, sheltered sites, moderate rainfall
White varieties:	Sauvignon Blanc, Chardonnay, Chenin Blanc
Red varieties:	Cabernet Sauvignon, Merlot, Shiraz, Pinotage
Wine styles:	red, white

47

Heart of gold – vineyards share Durbanville with wheat fields

DRIVING ROUTE: DURBANVILLE

The Durbanville Pocket starts some distance (30 km) to the east of Cape Town. The N1 northbound takes you out of the city, curving eastward towards Paarl.

Take Exit 23 to Willie van Schoor Road (R302 to Bellville/Durbanville). At the traffic light, turn left and drive along Willie van Schoor Road until it joins Durban Road, just past the Tyger Valley shopping centre. Turn left down Old Oak Road (M31) and right at the next traffic light onto Tygerbergvallei Road, driving in a northerly direction. As you leave the residential area, you pass through an archway of oak trees – a spectacular sight in late autumn when the leaves turn.

The first winery visit is Altydgedacht on the left. This beautiful traditional winery is a combination of old and modern, with a tranquil charm. A pond at the entrance to the tasting room hosts local bird life, many of which nest in the surrounding thickets.

Continuing northwards from Altydgedacht, you reach the T-junction of the R302 and the M13 (running in an east-west direction). After seeing this intersection with its traffic lights effectively in the middle of Altydgedacht's grounds, owner Oliver Parker commented that if God would kindly perform one more miracle, it would be good if Altydgedacht could be removed from this urban jungle far out to the North …

Turn right at the traffic light and drive in an easterly direction. At the next set of traffic lights, turn left (North) on St John's Road (M48), past the local polo club and race course on the right. At the first traffic circle (roundabout), take the first exit and continue driving north on Vissershok Road to visit

Meerendal. This historic property has been handsomely restored to its former glory by a group of wine enthusiasts. It now hosts not only the upgraded winery, but also a tasting facility, restaurant, functions venue, deli and children's play area.

Return to the traffic circle; take the first exit to the east on Vissershok Road. At the following traffic circle take the first exit, heading north on Koeberg Road (M58). This road runs more or less parallel to Vissershok Road. The next winery to visit is Diemersdal, the most northerly of the Durbanville wineries. The impressive white-washed entrance adorned by red irises bids visitors welcome.

Return along the same road to the T-junction close to Altydgedacht and continue westwards on the M13, towards the Atlantic Ocean. The road passes over the hill and descends to the entrance of Hillcrest. From the veranda of the Hillcrest's restaurant, you have a clear view of the Atlantic Ocean. Indulge in olives and olive oils from Hillcrest's own olive groves.

Durbanville Hills, the biggest producer (by volume) in this Pocket, has played a leading role in promoting Durbanville wines and tourism in this area. Its restaurant has spectacular views over the bay, and the tasting room serves wines, olives and olive oil.

Continue on the M13. At the T-junction with the M14, turn right to visit De Grendel. Once a diary farm, De Grendel now boasts some of the highest elevated Pinot Noir grapes after the Elgin Pocket. De Grendel's hillside vineyards are visible from Cape Town. The M14 leads back to the N1 freeway.

Poplars restaurant specialises in matching this Pocket's wine with exquisite cuisine.

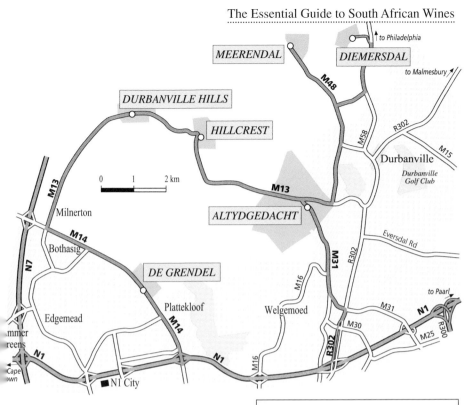

Travelling tips

Information:

www.durbanvillewine.co.za

Restaurants:

Poplars restaurant & venue +27 (0)21 975 5802

Meerendal restaurant & venue +27 (0)21 975 1655

Hillcrest restaurant +27 (0)21 976 1110

Durbanville Hills restaurant +27 (0)21 558 1300

Accommodation:

Poplars +27 (0)21 975 5802

Interests:

The Rose Garden +27 (0)21 948 1744

Tygerberg Nature Reserve +27 (0)21 913 5695

GPS waypoints

Altydgedacht	S33 50.691 E18 37.536
De Grendel	S33 52.002 E18 34.287
Diemersdal	S33 48.055 E18 38.399
Durbanville Hills	S33 49.232 E18 34.045
Hillcrest	S33 49.629 E18 35.422
Meerendal	S33 48.169 E18 37.173

Altydgedacht *Durbanville Pocket*

The Parker family has farmed Altydgedacht since 1852 – an astounding six generations with an unbroken 300-year winemaking tradition. Altydgedacht was one of the early wheat, wine and stock farms established in the late 1600s to supply ships sailing to the East. One hundred and sixty hectares of vines are cultivated on heavy clay and gravel soils on the gently sloping hills. Late summer mist and close proximity to the Atlantic Ocean contribute to cooler ripening conditions and cultivars are sited according to their heat preference. Intensive canopy management, including leaf removal and a vertical extended canopy, increase sunlight exposure, promoting flavour and colour development. The cool ripening conditions allow the grapes to hang longer than the norm, leading to more fruit-driven wine. The flagship Pinotage is from a single vineyard, made in a New World style with upfront fruit and ripe, juicy tannins. Altydgedacht also produces interesting Sauvignon Blanc, Barbera and a dry Alsace-style Gewürztraminer.

49

ℹ️ Pinotage, Gewürz 🍴 Pin, Barb, Sauv Bl, Gewürz
🕐 Mon ~ Fri 9 – 5, Sat 9 – 3. Closed Easter, Dec 25, 26, Jan 1
📞 +27 (0)21 976 1295 📠 +27 (0)21 976 4318
✉️ altydgedacht@mweb.co.za,
www.altydgedacht.co.za 🍷 8+ y 🍾 99, 01, 02
ℹ️ hands-on winery, rustic atmosphere, traditional buildings

De Grendel *Durbanville Pocket*

The Graaff family acquired the De Grendel (Dutch for "lock" or "latch") property in 1896, but only in 2000 were vineyards planted on the south-west-facing foothills of the Tygerberg Hills. Over 100 hectares of vines are cultivated on the marginal shale soils. The close proximity of the Atlantic Ocean, early morning mist and the south-easterly winds provide significantly cooler conditions. This in turn creates extended, even ripening of the delicate Sauvignon Blanc grapes. Under these conditions, sugar development slows down and grapes achieve phenolic and fruit ripeness without excessive potential alcohol due to high sugar levels.

A dense clay layer lying 1.5 metres below the ground reduces effective soil depth, restricting vertical root development and thereby naturally reduces growth vigour. The shallow soil necessitates a very low planting density of only 2, 200 vines per hectare to allow each plant sufficient soil volume. Subsequent lateral root development compensates for the loss in soil depth to ensure each vine has sufficient water and nutrient supply. These restrictive factors contribute to vines naturally producing smaller berries with a higher skin to juice ratio, improving the concentration of colour and flavour in the gapes.

White grapes are gently pressed and free-run juice is fermented cold to preserve the freshness and fruit flavours. The Sauvignon Blanc's complex fruit-dominated palate is lifted by four months lees maturation, resulting in an aromatic wine with khaki bush and grass, while the naturally high acidity provides freshness.

Making use of the aspect

ℹ️ Sauvignon Blanc 🍇 Sauv Bl, Merlot, Shiraz 🕐 Daily by appt 9 – 5. Closed Good Fri, Dec 25, Jan 1
📞 +27 (0)21 558 6280 📠 +27 (0)21 558 7083 ✉️ info@degrendel.co.za 🍷 red 5 y (expected)
🍾 04 (maiden vintage) ℹ️ farm produce, conservation area

Hillcrest Estate *Durbanville Pocket*

Hillcrest, located on the highest point of the Durbanville Valley, produced its maiden vintage in 2002. Twenty-five hectares were established on highly weathered, fertile granite soils with good water retention. Its altitude and close proximity to the Atlantic Ocean creates cool ripening conditions. Chardonnay and Sauvignon Blanc are cultivated on higher elevations (280 – 380 m) to maximise the cooling effect, while Cabernet Sauvignon and Merlot experience slightly warmer conditions on lower-lying sites. Strict canopy management controls vigour in order to achieve even ripening of the grapes. The single vineyard Sauvignon Blanc Reserve is vinified reductively and fermented at 12°C to preserve its delicate aromas. It is also given lees contact for three months to soften the racy acid structure and add mid-palate weight. The white wines show the typical citrus flavours characteristic of the area. Red wines receive a moderate 50 per cent new French oak, which imparts gentle wood aromas to support the dense fruit and spicy character.

ℹ️ Merlot, Sauvignon Blanc 🍇 Sauv Bl, Chard, Merlot, Cab S
🕐 Mon – Sun 9 – 6. Closed Easter Fri – Mon, Dec 25, Jan 1.
📞 +27 (0)21 976 1110 📠 +27 (0)21 976 8802
✉️ info@hillcrestfarm.co.za 🍷 whites 3 y, reds 5 y
🍾 04, 05 ℹ️ restaurant for breakfast, lunch, tours by appt, olive products, great views from lawns

---

Diemersdal *Durbanville Pocket*

Diemersdal's beautifully preserved Cape Dutch architecture, built in the early 1800s, reflects the meticulous care taken by six generations of the Louw family winemakers. A special feature is the cultivation of northern, southern and eastern slopes of the gentle hills. The fertile clay soils have good water retention, which makes dry-land cultivation possible. These favourable conditions increase growth vigour in the vine, allowing a higher grape yield of eight tons to be harvested per hectare without loss of quality. With the cooling effect from the nearby Atlantic Ocean and early evening mist, Diemersdal's vines are trellised closer to the soil surface to maximise radiant heat for full ripeness. Mature vines concentrate flavours in the red wines, with the high alcohol balanced by more complex fruit and wood flavours. The white wines enjoy lees contact adding a fuller mouthfeel to the pronounced acidity, typical of cooler ripening conditions. The reserve Chardonnay is 100 per cent barrel fermented.

ℹ️ Private Collection (Cab S / Shz / Pinotage / Merlot) 🍇 Shz, Cab S, Pino, Sauv Bl 🕐 Mon – Fri 9 – 4, Sat 9 – 3. Closed Easter, Dec 25, Jan 1 📞 +27 (0)21 976 3361 📠 +27 (0)21 976 1810
✉️ wines@diemersdal.co.za 🍷 8 y 🍾 NA ℹ️ traditional architecture, BYO picnics, walks

Durbanville Hills *Durbanville Pocket*

Durbanville Hills takes its name from the rolling hills of Durbanville. Collaboration between wine and spirit giant Distell, the local farmers and the Farm Workers Trust saw the maiden vintage crushed in 1999.

The shallow valley opens to the Atlantic Ocean (10 km) and, being shaded from the early sunlight, enjoys cool morning temperatures and late afternoon warmth. The frequent mists and prevailing south-easterly winds assist in cooling the vineyards. Over 700 hectares of vines are cultivated on the weathered shale soils, with good water retention allowing for dry-land cultivation (no irrigation). White grapes, on the south-facing slopes are protected from the heat of the day, while reds enjoy the sun exposure for ripe tannin development on north-facing slopes.

A medium canopy density prevents sunburn on the heat-sensitive Sauvignon Blanc by allowing filtered rather than direct sunlight onto the grapes. The red varieties specifically are managed to control canopy growth for smaller berry production and concentrated flavours. Some reds, requiring increased heat during ripening, are trellised very low to the ground to expose the grapes to radiant heat from the soil surface.

Reductive winemaking, employing dry ice (frozen CO_2), protects the white wines from oxidation. The red wines, however, are purposefully exposed to oxygen during regular pump overs, reducing excessive heat during fermentation and stabilising the colour and tannins. The Merlot shows chocolate and mint characters, while the ripe fruit-styled Sauvignon Blanc has subtle floral aromas with a slightly higher alcohol content when compared to the green pepper and grassy Sauvignon Blancs from the Constantia Pocket. Both these top wines are from single vineyards.

Modern cellar architecture

[i] Merlot, Sauvignon Blanc [symbol] Sauv Bl, Merlot, Cabernet Sauv [symbol] Mon – Fri 9 – 4:30, Sat, publ hols 9:30 – 2:30, Sun 11 – 3. Closed Easter, Dec 25, Jan 1 [symbol] +27 (0)21 558 1300 [symbol] +27 (0)21 559 8169 [symbol] info@durbanvillehills.co.za, www.durbanvillehills.co.za [symbol] white 5 y, red 10 y [symbol] white 99, 01, 05; red 01, 03, 05 [i] Vista of area and Atlantic Ocean, restaurant, gift shop, olive products, conference venue

Meerendal *Durbanville Pocket*

Meerendal was first granted to Jan Meerland in 1702 and by 1712 his widow established 60, 000 vines on the farm. The 1969 vintage carried the Meerendal name on the label for the first time. Today, 140 hectares of vines are cultivated on surrounding hills with various aspects providing interesting meso-climatic nuances.

A standard planting density is used on the poor shale soils, while the high clay content ensures very good water retention and facilitates dry-land viticulture even with the relatively low annual rainfall. Located only 10 kilometres from the Atlantic Ocean, vineyards benefit from cool ocean breezes creating slow, even ripening conditions. It is, however, the age of the vines that provides the greatest influence on the elegant style and concentration of flavours. The oldest Sauvignon Blanc, planted in 1980, makes up some of the youngest vines on this estate. The Pinotage was planted in 1955 and Shiraz in 1976. The Pinotage is still cultivated as bush vines, which means that the variety produces a deep red colour and robust flavours.

Sauvignon Blanc, in a typical greener, cooler-climate style, shows pronounced mineral and lime characteristics. Grapes are all hand harvested. Strict reductive techniques protect the young wine from oxidation and extended lees maturation (4 months) yields a deeply rich and aromatic white wine. Red wines are matured for 12 to 15 months in new and second-fill barrels. Silky tannins support the bitter chocolate and concentrated plum fruit of the Merlot while the Shiraz is typified by juicy tannins and black pepper flavour.

Paragliding over the vineyards

[i] Sauvignon Blanc, Shiraz [symbol] Sauv Bl, Merlot, Pinotage, Shz, Cab S [symbol] Mon – Sun 8 – 5. Closed Easter Fri, Dec 25 [symbol] +27 (0)21 975 1655 [symbol] +27 (0)21 975 1657 [symbol] info@meerendal.co.za, www.meerendal.co.za [symbol] Sauv 4 y, Blend 7 y [symbol] 84, 94, 98, 00, 03, 05 [i] wine and food destination, restaurant, bistro, deli, functions venue, children's facilities

Stellenbosch Area

Oldest town – charming Stellenbosch

Stellenbosch could well be regarded as the wine capital of South Africa. Hosting more private cellars than any other Cape Wine Area, Stellenbosch is also home to the country's largest wine and spirit producer, Distell and the centre of viticultural and oenological research and training.

Located on 34° latitude, the town is about 40 kilometres from Cape Town and 10 kilometres from the coast, with an elevation of approximately 300 metres above sea level. Founded in 1679 by Simon van der Stel, Stellenbosch is the second oldest town in South Africa (after Cape Town) and has become a premier tourist destination. Its colourful history is reflected in the neo-Dutch, Georgian and modern Victorian architecture, encompassing simple lines, fine detail and elegant proportions. The fertile valley was diversely cultivated to supply fresh produce to the visiting ships for their long voyages to the East.

Stellenbosch is also the oldest wine route in South Africa, drawing wine lovers and tourists from around the world. More than 100 wineries are open to the public, all within easy reach of the town centre. Almost all classic varietals are represented here except, to a lesser degree, some sweeter wines, where areas like the Orange River, the West Coast, the Klein Karoo as well as Worcester and Robertson, are better known.

Following closely behind Worcester and Paarl in terms of area under vine, the Stellenbosch area includes various meso-climates, aspects, elevations and soil types. It also has the advantage of frontage onto False Bay. The Cape Doctor (prevailing south-easterly) works its magic here, keeping vines cool and helping to control diseases by reducing relative humidity in the vine canopy. These factors allow wine production across the stylistic range, accounting for approximately 6.5 per cent of South Africa's total wine production.

Although many vines stretch up the mountain slopes, the lower, undulating hills are a carpet of vineyards. Even though land here is among the most expensive in the Cape Winelands, it does not deter winemakers from innovation and cutting-edge experimentation. The holy grail of *terroir* is chased by all. Specific attributes characterising the wines, the reds especially, are already discernible in places.

Although many of the farms have been handed down through generations, recent foreign investors are boosting local development. Many wineries offer tours and wine tasting to visitors, and settings range from the old-world charm of historic estates to large high-tech wineries, small family-owned boutique cellars and garagiste producers. With rolling hills and towering mountains as a backdrop and the ever-changing colour of the vineyards, the landscapes are constantly transformed. Harvesting is from late January to early April, when the smell of ripe grapes laces the air, creating an atmosphere of excitement. A drive around Stellenbosch and its Wine Pockets offers some of the best views of South Africa's stunning Winelands as well as festive gastronomical trips.

THE TOWN

The best way to explore the town is on foot as the narrow streets offer little parking space. Wandering around, you will find meticulously restored buildings. The giant oak trees lining the streets gave Stellenbosch the affectionate name of "Eikestad" – town of oaks. The historic architecture, parks and gardens contribute to its tranquil beauty. Stellenbosch has a small-town aura with a rich lifestyle in which music and the arts thrive. The Information Bureau supplies maps, contact details and opening times of most

attractions. Many attractions are centred on Dorp, Andringa and Ryneveld Streets with various arts and crafts stalls, coffee shops and fine restaurants.

Dining out in Stellenbosch is a special experience, whether alfresco under the oaks or the stars, or indoors in cosy, yet luxurious surroundings. From traditional Cape fare and European cuisine to the more exotic, there is something to tantalise the taste buds of the most discerning diner. Restaurants and eateries range from elegant Cape Dutch manors and country cottages to sidewalk cafés.

LOCAL INTERESTS

The mountains and hills surrounding the town offer unequalled opportunities for hiking, cycling, mountaineering and other adventure activities. For the wildlife enthusiast, there are several opportunities for encounters with animals, with parks, sanctuaries and reserves. Many wineries offer lunch, picnic baskets or dinner. Staying in one of the many Wine Pockets is an experience in its own right – see individual Pockets and Winery Profiles for more details. Township experiences in the areas of Kayamandi, Jamestown and Cloetesville are arranged at the tourist information centre.

EDUCATIONAL INSTITUTIONS

The University of Stellenbosch was founded in 1918 as a premier educational institution. A century-long tradition of quality education and research has ensured the university a place among the finest academic institutions. The Oenology and Viticulture Department, alongside the Institute for Wine Biotechnology, is the home of world-class wine research and cutting-edge technological development. Other institutions include the

Cape Institute for Agricultural Training at Elsenburg, educating students in various wine-related fields including microbiology and chemistry, as well as the Cape Wine Academy, a general wine education body which presents courses on the local and international wine industries and wine evaluation.

Soils:	Granitic foothills, exposed granite outcrops, shale
Climate:	Warm with ocean influence, sheltered sites, moderate rainfall
White varieties:	Chenin Blanc, Sauvignon Blanc, Chardonnay, Sémillon
Red varieties:	Cabernet Sauvignon, Merlot, Shiraz, Pinotage, Cabernet Franc
Wine styles:	red, white, sparkling, dessert, fortified

Travelling tips

Information:
www.wineroute.co.za

Events:
The Stellenbosch wine festival takes place annually in August, featuring local restaurants, delicatessens, wine and food personalities and Stellenbosch wines, in an extravagant three-day feast.

Natural environment:
The best panoramic view of the Stellenbosch mountains is seen from the lower end of Merriman Street (near the station). To the south is first the Helderberg and then Stellenbosch Mountain (1, 175 m) with the narrow Jonkershoek valley. To the north of this valley are the clearly discernible Pieke (twin peaks 1, 494 m). The mighty Simonsberg (1, 390 m) is connected to Botmanskop and the Jonkershoek Mountains at the saddle of Helshoogte, leading to Franschhoek.

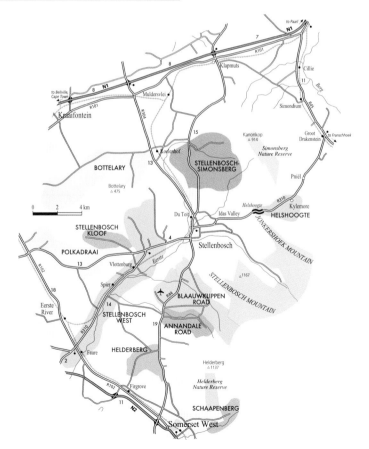

Bush vines at the foot of the Simonsberg Mountain

STELLENBOSCH TERROIR

The Stellenbosch landscape is generally characterised by remnant rugged sandstone overlaying granite plutons (forming the softer sloped foothills), exposed granite outcrops (giving rise to ranges of fairly high hills up to 400 m) as well as occasional shale. The close proximity of the ocean (about 25 km), with the cooling effect of summer sea breezes, ensures a macro-climate that is appreciably cooler than normally associated with latitudes of 33°55' – 34°10'. The average summer daytime temperature is around 20°C. The pronounced topographic and altitude variation further modifies the macro-climate, resulting in very different meso or topo-climates for different Pockets in the area, all benefiting to some degree from sea breeze effects.

The most dominant soils of the Stellenbosch area are derived from granite and are usually situated on the higher hills and mountain foothills. As a result of climatic conditions during their historical formation (rapid weathering, high leaching conditions)

and age (c. 50 Ma), these soils are a relic of the geological past and unique in the sense that they are acidic, acidity increasing with depth. These granite soils are yellowish to reddish-brown, with medium to high clay content. The good physical properties of the soil, as well as water drainage and holding capacity, makes dry-land (without irrigation) viticulture possible.

Pockets predominantly characterised by these granite soils are Stellenbosch Kloof, Devon Valley, Klapmuts-Simondium and those located on the Simonsberg Mountain (Helshoogte, Stellenbosch-Simonsberg, etc.). More strongly structured and duplex soils derived from granite and shale are features of Pockets like Polkadraai, Stellenbosch West, Annandale, Blaauwklippen Road and Bottelary. The Pockets of Jonkershoek, Helderberg and Schaapenberg have, in addition to granitic soils, a fair amount of well-weathered yellow or reddish-brown soils and some residual soils derived from shale, with remnants of the parent rock material often still very evident.

55

Stellenbosch Pockets

POLKADRAAI POCKET

Polkadraai is situated directly to the west of Stellenbosch and borders the suburb of Kuils River. The Pocket lies close to False Bay (12 – 15 km) and benefits greatly from cooling summer sea breezes, which create a considerably cooler meso-climate than the general macro-climate would indicate.

Follow the narrow roads trough the vineyards

The Pocket's *terroir* is characterised by hilly topography and subsequently varying elevations, providing sites on elevations of 60 to 400 metres. Slopes face predominantly south and south-west, favourably exposing vineyards to the cooling effect of the ocean. Some well-protected north-facing slopes are slightly warmer and are planted with red varieties.

Besides the differences in elevation, the layered soils vary from granite-based on the higher elevated positions (150 – 400 m), to shallow, sandy soils in lower-lying areas. Lime additions are required to neutralise the acidity of these medium-potential soils. Particular effort is made to ensure deep preparation on virgin soils, in order to improve the physical and chemical properties before planting new vines. Polkadraai's changing cultivation conditions necessitate variation in viticultural practices: from low, untrellised bush vine to upright vertical trellises.

Best known for its solidly structured red wines, Polkadraai hosts many of the classic French varieties. The wines have a moderate alcohol (Alc. 13% by Vol. +) and a distinct spiciness, often combined with scents of herbs. Shiraz is very popular with spicy and powerful wines from Saxenburg as well as biodynamic producer Reyneke. This spiciness also shows strongly in the Shiraz and Zinfandel wines

from Zevenwacht as well as the Cape blend (Shz / Cab S) from Nico van der Merwe. The Bein Merlot is inspired by the famous Chateau Petrus, in the classic restrained style with a more powerful mid-palate than generally found in South Africa. De Toren's Fusion V is a blend of the classic five Bordeaux varieties, showing scents of herbs. Amani cellar, situated on an isolated sandy patch, produces fruity Chardonnay and Merlot.

DRIVING ROUTE: POLKADRAAI

The Polkadraai Pocket is located west of Stellenbosch. From the intersection of the R44 and Dorp Street, drive west and join the R310 (Adam Tas Road) leaving the town in a westerly direction. About four kilometres out of town, the R310 turns left (south) towards the N2 freeway, and from there, the M12 continues in a westerly direction.

The Polkadraai Pocket starts about 11 kilometres outside Stellenbosch. When you reach the Polkadraai farm stall on the right, turn left onto Vlaeberg Road opposite the farm stall. A few metres down the road, on the left hand side, is the boutique winery, Raats Family Wines. The two Raats brothers are nurturing Chenin Blanc and Cabernet Franc vines as they believe that, since no New World country has yet taken "ownership" of these varieties, South Africa may well be the one to specialise in Chenin Blanc and Cabernet Franc.

Rejoin the M12, turn left and head west for a kilometre as the road rises again. On the crest, turn right at the sign indicating Bein Wine. Just off the M12, take the first right turn. You are driving parallel to the M12 in the direction of Stellenbosch. The second building (on the right) hosts the quaint boutique winery of Bein Wine, exclusively producing Pomerol-style Merlot.

The M12 rises over the last hill to a spectacular view of Somerset West, False Bay and the suburbs of Cape Town. Follow the road down the hill to the entrance of Saxenburg on the right. A miniature game reserve flanks the driveway to the cellar, with small antelope roaming in camps. Producer of many fine wines, Saxenburg also boasts a restaurant, Guinea Fowl, famous for its fish dishes and its own cookbook. Saxenburg focuses on the production of single varietal wines and its range includes a sparkling and a sweet dessert wine. Winemaker Nico van der Merwe also has his own label, Nico van der Merwe Wines. Wines are sold privately as there is no visitor facility at present.

Polkadraai farm stall sells strawberries and other fresh produce from the area. You can pick your own strawberries during the early summer months.

GPS waypoints	
Bein Wines	S33 57.729 E18 44.061
Nico van der Merwe Wines	S33 56.827 E18 43.149
Raats Family Wines	S33 58.252 E18 44.845
Saxenburg	S33 56.827 E18 43.149

Travelling tips	
Restaurants:	
Guinea Fowl restaurant +27 (0)21 906 5232	
Interests:	
Polkadraai farm stall (strawberries) +27 (0)21 881 3303	

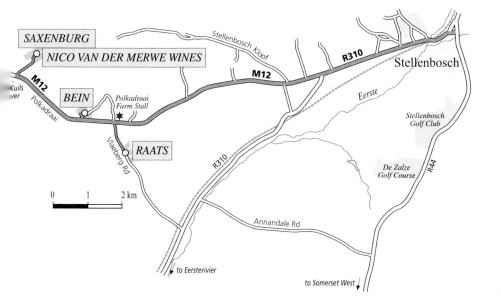

Chenin Blanc

The dominance of Chenin Blanc in the Cape was originally the result of its easy cultivation and suitability for brandy. As other varieties became popular, Chenin Blanc decreased significantly (32 per cent total vineyard plantings in 1990 to only 18 per cent in 2002). The wines lacked distinctive varietal character and aging potential. Improved viticulture (restricted yields, old bush vines) and vinification (natural fermentation, use of wood, lees contact) show its true varietal character: delicacy with concentration. Many of the new styles are capable of aging and show floral, citrus and honey aromas. Key producers are De Trafford, Raats, Post House, Ken Forrester, Kanu, Hildenbrand.

Traditional viticulture – Chenin Blanc bush vines

Raats Family Wines *Polkadraai Pocket*

The aim of Raats Family Wine is to craft world-class wines from Chenin Blanc and Cabernet Franc. While its own vineyards develop, grapes are sourced from selected sites. Trellised Chenin Blanc (ex Bottelary) on sandstone and gravel soils give citrus and mineral characters with high natural acidity, while mature bush vines (30 y, ex-Helderberg) on clay soils give mid-palate weight and structure. The canopy of the Chenin Blanc is opened during the season, increasing filtered sunlight while still offering protection from sunburn, permitting development of tropical and white fruit flavours in the grapes. A selection of yeasts, fermentation in barrel and lees contact yields a spicy, full-bodied white wine. To achieve dense colour and overcome uneven ripening, the Cabernet Franc is allowed only one bunch per shoot. The grapes are given cold maceration (7 days) and fermented dry with regular pump overs to extract maximum colour. Eighteen months maturation, using only 20 per cent new wood, results in a full, structured herbaceous palate of red fruits and silky tannins.

> 🛈 Chenin Blanc, Cabernet Franc 🍇 Chenin Bl, Cab F
> 🕐 by appt 📞 +27 (0)21 881 3078 ✉ braats@mweb.co.za
> 🍷 white 4 – 6 y, red 6 – 10 y ▪ Cab F 01, 03; Chenin 02, 04, 05

Nico van der Merwe Wines *Polkadraai Pocket*

Nico van der Merwe's Mas Nicolas is a smoulderingly dense wine of Polkadraai Shiraz and Simonsberg Cabernet Sauvignon. Mature Shiraz vines (30 y+), cultivated on dry land in decomposed granite, yield the deeply coloured and concentrated spicy fruit. Cabernet Sauvignon gives structure to the blend. Hand-harvested grapes are fermented *sans* sulphur in open-top vessels. Regular punch downs and extended skin contact (up to 3 weeks) ensure maximum extraction for complexity. After pressing, free-run and press juice are combined and the young wine is transferred to barrels for maturation. Components are blended and bottled without filtering or fining. Van der Merwe believes Cab / Shiraz is the Cape Blend and, without Pinotage, can deliver the elegance and richness of Cape *terroir* fruit. The seamless white blend (Sauv Bl / Sém) shows gooseberries and peaches with subtle oak. The Sémillon (ex-Schaapenberg) is oak fermented and matured on its lees, while the unwooded Sauvignon Blanc adds a crisp, fresh acidity.

> 🛈 Mas Nicolas (Cab S / Shz) 🍇 Cab S, Merlot, Shz, Sauv, Sém
> 🕐 tasting by appt 📞 +27 (0)21 903 9507
> ✉ wilhelmshof@xsinet.co.za 🍷 10 y ▪ 00

Bein Wine *Polkadraai Pocket*

Bein Wine Cellar, located on a hillside overlooking False Bay, produces exclusive quantities of wine from a tiny Merlot vineyard of 2.2 hectares. The site is particularly suited to Merlot with highly weathered granite and a gentle south-facing hill, facing the ocean about 10 kilometres away. The early morning mist and cool air from the ocean ensures a slower, extended ripening period, allowing the ripening of fruit flavours and tannins without dramatic increases in sugar levels and potential alcohol. The flagship Merlot is made from a single block and blended with a small percentage of Cabernet Sauvignon, depending on the vintage. The wine, made in the classic Pomerol style, has tremendous fruit concentration and elegance with the alcohol level purposefully kept down. A higher than usual fermentation temperature of 30°C is used to concentrate flavours in the wine and 12 months oaking in a combination of new (40 per cent) and older French barrels presents a well-rounded tannin structure to the elegant wine.

> 🛈 Bein Merlot 🍇 Merlot 🕐 by appt only
> 📞 +27 (0)21 881 3025 ✉ lib@beinwine.com
> www.beinwine.com 🍷 5 – 8 y ▪ 03, 05
> 🛈 one of the smallest production cellars, great views

Saxenburg *Polkadraai Pocket*

Africa was still a wild and untamed place when Joachim Sax first settled on the hills above the Kuils River, some 30 kilometres east of the Dutch settlement at the Cape of Good Hope. In 1693 Sax was one of only 350 free burghers (free farmers) granted land by Governor Simon van der Stel. He set about planting vines, and built the original manor house in 1701. Four years later, the farm was sold to Olaff and Albertus Bergh. Saxenburg developed from these early pioneers.

Almost three centuries passed before this historic farm was acquired by the Bührer family from Switzerland. Along with their close working team, they have revived the proud family tradition of Saxenburg's historic past. Fulfilling a wish to have a sister vineyard in France, the family acquired the 16th century Chateau Capion near Montpellier (Languedoc) in 1996, where the same passion and single-minded dedication see fine wines being grown.

Situated between the Atlantic and Indian Oceans, Saxenburg enjoys moderate climatic conditions aided by cool ocean breezes during the summer months. Ninety hectares (of 200) are cultivated. Vines are planted on the surrounding hills with aspects from south-west to north-west, on fertile, decomposed granite and red gravel soils. The maritime influence and prevailing winds (south and south-west) create cool ripening conditions for the grapes without damaging the young shoots. Maximising this cooling effect, heat-sensitive grapes like Sauvignon Blanc, Chardonnay and Merlot are planted on the cooler southern side of the farm, while varieties with greater heat requirements (Cabernet Sauvignon, Shiraz) are planted on the warmer south-western side, receiving more sunlight hours.

The lower relative daytime temperatures result in slower, more even ripening of grapes and a higher level of natural acid at harvest. Vineyard management is focused on restricting vigorous growth and achieving more concentration in the grapes. Vines are trellised and planted to a higher density of 3, 600 vines per hectare on the fertile soils. Supplementary irrigation is only applied in very warm conditions to prevent damage to the plants. Summer pruning, leaf removal and suckering improve airflow around the vines to reduce humidity and disease in the canopy. The dense wines reflect the maturity of the vines (12 y+), with the exception of Chenin Blanc, which is almost 30 years old and used for non-*Botrytised* dessert wine.

59

Harvested grapes are fermented in open-top vessels *sans* sulphur. Selected yeast cultures and a high fermentation temperature (30°C) are used, particularly on the Shiraz, resulting in deeply coloured wines. Another two to four weeks of maceration is allowed after fermentation is completed to ensure that the colour and flavour components are stabilised and excessive tannins are precipitated out. Malolactic fermentation is completed in barrel (only from selected blocks) and in tank before the wines are matured for 18 months, using only about 40 per cent new wood. A percentage of American oak (up to 40 per cent) alongside the French oak gives a slight vanilla note and sweet tannins. The wines are generally powerful and dense with high alcohol levels, requiring some cellaring.

Tranquillity – a small pond (Top)
Attention to detail (Centre)
The celebrated Guinea Fowl restaurant (Left)

Saxenburg Shiraz Select ● Shz, Cab S, Sauv Bl, Merlot, Pinotage, Chard, Chenin Bl, Viognier, Malbec, Cab F
Mon – Fri 9 – 5 Sat 9 – 4 Sun 10-4 (closed Sun – Tues in winter), publ hols 10 – 4. Closed Easter Fri, Dec 25, Jan 1
+27 (0)21 903 6113   +27 (0)21 903 3129   info@saxenburg.com, www.saxenburg.com ● 10 y+ ● 91, 93, 98, 00, 01, 03
restaurant and lapa, olive oil, venue: conference, weddings, small game park, French sister chateau wines available

STELLENBOSCH KLOOF POCKET

The Stellenbosch Kloof Pocket is nestled in a valley on the south-facing side of the prominent Bottelary Hills. The climate is similar to that of neighbouring Polkadraai, but the valley floor (at 200 m above sea level) is bordered by two parallel ranges of hills, with each range reaching an elevation of 400 metres above sea level. The Pocket thus has aspects which vary considerably. South-facing aspects are directly exposed to False Bay and its summer sea breezes, cooling the vineyards significantly. Northern aspects and the valley floor are sheltered and consequently warmer.

Terroir in this Pocket is characterised by varying elevations, with vines located on altitudes from 60 to 400 metres above sea level. Soils are predominantly yellow to reddish-brown and well drained with high potential. As a granite derivative, these soils have a favourable physical structure and good water and nutrient retention properties. More humid conditions exist on lower slopes, planted to drought-sensitive varieties such as Merlot. These varying conditions necessitate variation in viticultural practices: from low, untrellised bush vine on the well-protected valley floor to vertical trellises on the exposed south-facing slopes.

White wines from Stellenbosch Kloof show white fruit and floral aromas and have great finesse, whereas the reds are more robust. Jordan Winery's range of aspects delivers an elegant Chardonnay and a drier style, non-*Botrytised* Noble Late Harvest. Although Kanu is known for its superb Chenin Blanc and *Botrytised* Noble Late, its (Cab S / Merlot) blend also follows this tannic trend, as does the red blend from Bonfoi (Cab S / Merlot / Shz). Cabernet Sauvignon dominates the powerful red blends from this valley. Merlot,

Shiraz and even a combination of these two are used as blending partners, adding spicy notes and softening the tannic structure of Cabernet Sauvignon. DeWaal (Cab S / Shz / Merlot), Jordan Winery (Cab S / Merlot), Overgaauw (Cab S / F / Merlot) and newcomer Boschkloof (Cab S / Merlot) all produce red blends with an abundance of fruit, structured tannins and longevity. Boschkloof also produces a single varietal Shiraz, with powerful upfront fruit and black pepper. The indigenous South African variety, Pinotage, nestles in one of the oldest blocks on DeWaal Wines' farm. These vines produce highly aromatic grape flavours and densely structured Pinotage wines. Overgaauw's port from the traditional Portuguese varieties offers great intensity and promises long development.

DRIVING ROUTE:
STELLENBOSCH KLOOF

The Stellenbosch Kloof Pocket is located to the west of Stellenbosch. Leave the town on the R310, driving west towards Cape Town. About four kilometres out of town, the R310 turns left (south) towards the N2 freeway. From there the M12 continues in a westerly direction. About three kilometres further, passing Neethlingshof's fountain on the right, the road reaches a nadir and Stellenbosch Kloof Road turns off directly to right. Exercise caution as pedestrians frequently cross the road and speed limits are enforced by roadside cameras.

Make your way along the secluded valley. White-washed walls announce the entrance to the first winery on the route, Overgaauw. An historic building houses the tasting room with wrought-iron lace work on the veranda, a reminder of the Victorian area. Behind the cellar, you can see the gentle south-facing slope where Overgaauw's red varieties are cultivated on dry land, producing concentrated wines. Overgaauw was the first producer to bottle a single varietal Merlot wine in 1982. It is the only cellar in South Africa which produces Sylvaner as a single varietal wine.

Driving further along Stellenbosch Kloof Road, you will see neatly laid-out vineyard blocks arranged along the north-south-facing slopes that characterise this Pocket.

Only a few hundred metres further, the road forks. Take the right fork to visit DeWaal Wines. Pass the manor house (circa 1791) to the tasting room and cellar. DeWaal's famous Top of the Hill vineyard gave its name to the tree visible from the tasting room patio. Picnics can be arranged at this stunning location overlooking the valley.

The road leads deeper into the valley, surrounded by trellised vineyards facing north, south and east, making the most of sun exposure in this cool valley. Jordan Winery's single vineyards that produce the Nine Yards Chardonnay, as well as the Mellifera Riesling, are visible high on the ridge behind the cellar. Take a picnic basket to enjoy under the trees. To the far left, vineyards cling to steep hills in the Jonkershoek valley and the equally steep Helderberg Mountain to the far right.

Return to the M12, turn right and continue in a westerly direction to visit Kanu, home of champion Chenin Blanc. The road rises over a hill and, just short of the crest, signs indicate a turn-off to Kanu. Turn right at the imposing entrance guarded by the mythical bird of bounty and follow the road downhill. It forks left to the tasting room. Kanu has been an integral part of South Africa's Chenin Blanc revolution. Previously an over-produced, under-valued variety, Chenin was mainly used for juice production or distillation, but a few producers have nurtured Chenin Blanc from relative obscurity to recognition as a noble wine.

61

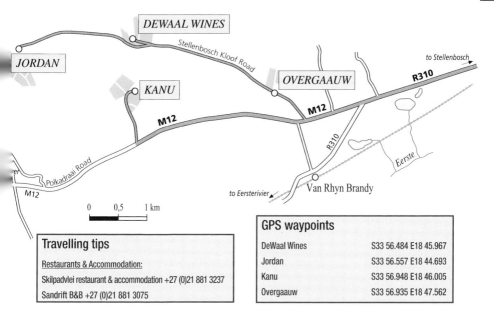

Travelling tips

Restaurants & Accommodation:

Skilpadvlei restaurant & accommodation +27 (0)21 881 3237

Sandrift B&B +27 (0)21 881 3075

GPS waypoints

DeWaal Wines	S33 56.484 E18 45.967
Jordan	S33 56.557 E18 44.693
Kanu	S33 56.948 E18 46.005
Overgaauw	S33 56.935 E18 47.562

Contours – the vineyard rows of Jordan winery

DeWaal Wines *Stellenbosch Kloof Pocket*

Five generations of the DeWaal family have owned the Uiterwyk property. The 200-year-old cellar, renovated in 1998, creates high quality, enjoyable wines at affordable prices. One hundred and twenty hectares of vines are cultivated on a high planting density (5, 000 vines/Ha) in order to reduce growth vigour on the fertile soils as low yields and old vines (up to 60 years old) increase fruit concentration. Pinotage, Shiraz and Viognier are grown on poor, north-facing gravel soils with high clay content. Sauvignon Blanc, Merlot and Cabernet Sauvignon are planted on slightly richer granite soils on south-facing slopes, optimising cooler conditions. The flagship vineyards yield only two tons per hectare. The Pinotage and Cape Blend are fermented at high temperatures (30°C) and mature for 15+ months in 100 per cent new French oak barrels, producing intensely structured wines with silky tannins and upfront fruit. White varieties are cold fermented, retaining white fruit and floral flavours, with the highly aromatic Viognier carrying a touch (15 per cent) of oak.

[i] Top of the Hill Pinotage (sgl vineyard), DeWaal Cape Blend (Pinotage/Merlot/Shz) [icon] Pinotage, Shiraz, Merlot, Viognier, Sauv Bl [icon] Mon – Fri 9 – 4:30 (Oct – Apr) Mon – Fr 10 – 12:30 2 – 4:30 (May – Sept) Sat 10 – 4:30 (year round). Closed Easter Fri/Sun, Dec 25, 26, Jan 1 [icon] +27 (0)21 881 3711 [icon] +27 (0)21 881 3776 [icon] info@uiterwyk.co.za www.dewaal.co.za [icon] 10 y+ [icon] 01, 03, 04 [i] one of oldest Pinotage vineyards

Overgaauw *Stellenbosch Kloof Pocket*

A hundred years ago, Abraham van Velden bought a piece of land from his grandfather and named it Overgaauw. Today, the fourth generation of the Van Velden family cultivates the 70 hectares of vineyards. South-facing slopes provide decomposed granite soils of medium growth vigour and a standard planting density (3, 400 vines/Ha) is used. Red and white varieties are placed on south-facing slopes, where the cooling influence of the ocean provides slow, even ripening. Only Pinotage is cultivated as bush vines for greater flavour concentration. Red wines are fermented at lower temperatures (26°C) with extraction achieved through extended maceration of up to one month. Completing malolactic fermentation, the wines are matured for 18 months in 100 per cent new oak barrels, resulting in powerfully structured wines. Tria Corda is only released in the best years. Chardonnay is lightly wooded while Sauvignon Blanc shows rich tropical fruits and a restrained alcohol content of 12 per cent.

[i] Tria Corda (Cab S / F /Merlot) [icon] Cab S / F, Merlot, Shz, Chard, Sauv Bl, Pinotage, Sylvaner [icon] Mon – Fri 9 – 12:30 2 – 5 Sat, publ hols 10 – 12:30 Closed Mar 21, Easter, Dec 25, 26, Jan 1 [icon] +27 (0)21 881 3815 [icon] +27 (0)21 881 3436 [icon] info@ overgaauw.co.za www.overgaauw.co.za [icon] reds 5 – 8 y, port 8 y+ [icon] 74, 76, 82, 89, 95, 01, 03 [i] charming old-style tasting room

Jordan Winery *Stellenbosch Kloof Pocket*

The family-owned Jordan property is situated at the upper end of the Stellenbosch Kloof where it joins the Bottelary ridge at 400 metres above sea level. One hundred and five hectares of trellised vines are cultivated on wind-protected slopes. The judicious use of drip irrigation in dry seasons aids in extending ripening periods and naturally controls potential alcohol levels.

A western slope is home to the Cobblers Hill vineyard, planted to Cabernet Sauvignon, Merlot and Cabernet Franc. Additional Cabernet Sauvignon is planted on sun-exposed northern slopes in deep gravel soil, and Merlot on eastern slopes in deep clay-loam. The white varieties are planted on cooler south and east-facing slopes. Natural farming practices include the use of organic mulches to reduce soil water loss and cover crops to ensure a healthy soil structure.

Fruit for the flagship range is harvested from mature vines and red varieties are fermented in overhead cone-shaped stainless steel fermentation tanks, draining directly into the press. The wines undergo spontaneous malolactic fermentation in small French oak barrels, where they mature for up to two years. Barrel-fermented white wines receive a shorter time in wood, with barrel-rolling to create a less oxidative *bâttonage* effect. The Nine Yards Chardonnay (15 y, single vineyard) matures in French oak for 12 months, resulting in a full-bodied, rich wine. Named after the Cape Honey Bee inhabiting the hives on the farm, Mellifera (Noble Late Harvest) is made in a drier style with aromas of dried apricots and peaches and a well-structured acidity adding to the elegance.

The Jordan cellar

ⓘ Cobblers Hills (Cab S / Merlot / Cab F), Nine Yards Chardonnay, Mellifera NLH 🔴 Cab S, Merlot, Cab F, Merlot, Shz, Chard, Sauv Bl, Chenin Bl, Riesl ⏱ Mon – Fri 10 – 4:30, Sat 9:30 – 2:30, Sun 10 – 2:30. Closed Easter, Dec 25, Jan 1 ☎ +27 (0)21 881 3441 📠 +27 (0)21 881 3426 ✉ info@jordanwines. com www.jordanwines.com 🍷 white 2 – 8 y, red 5 – 15 y 🍾 95, 98, 99, 01, 03, 04, 05 ℹ annual open day, summer picnics, cellar tours during harvest, proteas and natural fynbos, tours by appt

Kanu *Stellenbosch Kloof Pocket*

Kanu is regarded as one of the pioneers of award-winning, world class Chenin Blanc. Its label displays the southern African legend of a mythical bird of promise as all who fell under its shadow would be blessed with a bountiful harvest.

Fifty hectares of vines are cultivated on east and south-facing slopes on decomposed shale soils. The elevation (100 – 200 m) and prevailing south-easterly winds from False Bay (5 km) moderate the daytime temperatures. Vines are trellised to spread the canopy and allow airflow as well as to protect the shoots from the prevailing winds. Very old Chenin Blanc bush vines (ex-Bottelary, 28 years; and Koelenhof, 48 years) are cultivated without any irrigation to produce extremely low yields of highly aromatic grapes.

White grapes are fermented cold (12 – 14°C) to retain the varietal flavours and natural acidity. Free-run juice of both the Chenin Blanc and Chardonnay is naturally fermented at slightly higher than normal temperatures (14 – 17°C), oak maturation adds to the aromatics and weight of the wines.

Winemaking for red varietals focuses on maximum colour and flavour development with the use of cold maceration. Eighteen months of oak maturation blends harmoniously with the fruit structure to ensure wines that are in perfect balance and have the ability to age. Grapes for the noble late harvest receive overnight skin contact to develop varietal character and fermentation is stopped at the desired sugar level. Oak maturation gives structure to this luxuriously textured wine, which shows tropical fruit with a *Botrytis* overlay and an invigorating acidity (8.7 g/l).

Sunset over Kanu

ⓘ Chenin Blanc Wooded, Kia-Ora NLH, Shiraz 🔴 Cab S /F, Shz, Merlot, PV, Viog, Sauv Bl ⏱ Mon – Fri 10 – 5 Sat 9 – 1 (Oct – Mar); Mon – Fri 10 – 4:30 (Apr – Sept) Closed publ hols ☎ +27 (0)21 881 8140 📠 +27 (0)21 881 3514 ✉ info@kanu.co.za, www.kanu.co.za 🍷 5 – 10 🍾 01, 03 ℹ Gift shop, cheese bar for farm-style products, functions venue

STELLENBOSCH WEST POCKET

The Stellenbosch West Pocket is located about eight kilometres to the west of the town. The topography of the Pocket constitutes soft, undulating hills of 60 to 300 metres above sea level (on the back of Bottelary Hill), flattening out to less than 20 metres at Vergenoegd, close to False Bay.

Aspects here are not very prominent, except at Neethlingshof and Asara, which have higher-lying vineyards (over 300 m) on mostly south to south-east facing slopes. The strong locational advantage here is the close proximity to the ocean (10 km), ensuring a relatively cool and temperate meso-climate, conducive to the slow, even ripening of grapes.

In the geological past, this area was inundated by the sea several times, resulting in viticulturally problematic soils. The soils are generally sandy or gravelly material on clay, derived from granite and shale and thus prone to extremes of wet and dryness. These difficult soil conditions result in very moderate growth and production in the vines, producing similar wine character over seasons. Rootstocks adapted to shallow and wet soil conditions are used in the lower-lying areas,

while on elevated sites vineyards are relieved of this problem. Complementary viticultural approaches characterise the diversity of this Pocket. Vineyards vary from small, untrellised bush vines to trained vines on high trellises. Vineyard block layout utilises the cool south-westerly sea breeze that occurs in summer afternoons using mainly south-west to north-east row directions. This allows the airflow to move down the rows, cooling the vines and reducing the relative humidity around the canopy to control fungal diseases.

Stellenbosch West produces very fruity white wines, whereas the reds are diverse in weight, ranging from the big, serious wines to more flashy and sleek examples. Neethlingshof and Spier produce larger ranges including several varietal wines with structured Cabernet Sauvignons as well as Noble Late Harvest wines with dense richness. Vergenoegd and Asara both produce powerful Cabernet-Merlot blends with a fine tannin structure requiring maturation. The Cabernet-based blend from Meerlust shows somewhat more restraint and elegance, as does its aromatic Pinot Noir. An interesting new boutique winery, The Foundry, makes a spicy and dense Shiraz and silky, perfumed Viognier to add to the focused diversity of the Stellenbosch West Pocket's wines.

Picture perfect – sunset over Vergenoegd Estate

Steeped in history – Meerlust Estate circa 1968

DRIVING ROUTE: STELLENBOSCH WEST

The Stellenbosch West Pocket lies to the west of Stellenbosch village. Take the R310 (Adam Tas Road) leading west from Stellenbosch in the direction of Cape Town. About four kilometres out of town, the R310 turns left (south) towards the N2 freeway. From here, the M12 continues in a westerly direction. The Stellenbosch West Pocket includes the first part of the M12 and continues south along the R310.

The soft, undulating hills of this Pocket, similar to those of the Bottelary Pocket, are very noticeable. Light-coloured soils are indicative of high proportions of sand. Due to the underlying layer of clay, the Pocket's vineyards require rootstocks adapted to shallow soils. About 400 metres from the R310 turn-off, along the M12, a local Jet D'Eau fountain

indicates the entrance to Neethlingshof. The driveway up to the cellar and restaurant is framed by old pine trees, leaning in the direction of the prevailing wind. One the most well-known pictures in the area, this driveway has been the background for dramatic black and white photography. From Neethlingshof, turn left and drive back towards Stellenbosch until you reach the R310 / M12 intersection. Turn right and continue on the R310 in a south-westerly direction. Small game camps on either side of the road are home to zebra, antelope, wildebeest, ostrich and cows.

Crossing a small railway bridge, a road immediately turns left to Van Rhyn's Brandy Cellar (see section on the Brandy Route). Driving along the R310, you will pass Annandale Road, which leads to the R44, the Pockets located on the foothills of the Helderberg Mountain and the town of Somerset West.

As the road descends a small hill, two dams (one on either side of the road) become visible. The entrance to Meerlust is on the left, masked by a lane of oak trees. Meerlust's history of more than 300 years is clearly visible in the detailed architecture of the historic buildings, which now house the offices and winery. Giorgio Dalla Cia, a legend in the South African wine industry, brought a distinctly European influence to Meerlust's winemaking. New winemaker, Chris Williams, is pushing the boundaries of conventional wisdom with hi-tech analysis and infrared mapping of the farm. Williams' own label, The Foundry, has grown from a humble garagiste operation to an internationally acclaimed winery. Drive the last three kilometres, crossing the bridge over the R102, to Vergenoegd. A low white wall on the left indicates the entrance. A gravel road, accessible to all vehicles, leads to Vergenoegd's Cape Dutch homestead and tasting room. The relaxed, unpretentious atmosphere is a perfect way to end a day spent touring the Winelands.

Travelling tips

Restaurants & Accommodation:

Skilpadvlei restaurant & accommodation +27 (0)21 881 3237

GPS waypoints

The Foundry	S34 01.037 E18 45.405
Meerlust	S34 01.037 E18 45.405
Neethlingshof	S33 56.514 E18 48.093
Vergenoegd	S34 02.041 E18 44.328

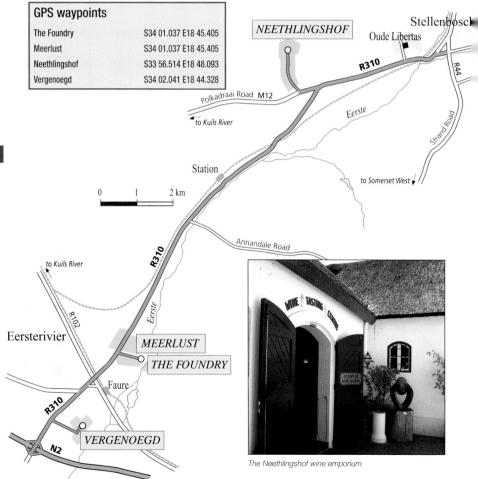

The Neethlingshof wine emporium

Meerlust *Stellenbosch West Pocket*

Johannes Albertus Myburgh bought Meerlust in 1757. His ownership marked the foundation of the Myburgh dynasty. Eight generations of the Myburgh family have farmed Meerlust. The farm, however, dates back to 1693, when the Governor of the Cape, Simon van der Stel, granted the land to Henning Hüsing, who named it Meerlust. From the Manor House to the old slave bell, from the 17th century barn to the cellar with its beautifully moulded staircase, Meerlust is one of the architectural jewels of the Cape Winelands.

Today, 110 hectares of vineyards are cultivated on well-drained granite and shale soils. The prevailing south-easterly wind reduces the average summer daytime temperatures by as much as 5°C. This cooling effect creates slow, even ripening conditions, with grapes retaining naturally high acidity and achieving phenolic ripeness at slightly reduced sugar levels. Meerlust's wines have great maturation potential with adequate acidity and moderate alcohol levels (Alc.14% by Vol.).

The high clay content of the soil retains moisture and nutrients and reduces the vines' crop, further concentrating the fruit. Supplementary irrigation is applied only in extremely hot conditions to prevent permanent damage to the vines. Soil types change over a very short distance on this farm and the diversity of growing conditions requires very careful canopy management in order to achieve a balance between vegetative growth and crop yield. At bunch-set stage, the crop generally averages 10 tons per hectare, but it is reduced to five tons per hectare with multiple green harvests over the growing season. Vineyards are picked several times to ensure that only phenolicly ripe grapes are harvested. Although blocks are replanted with the best material, older 20-year-old blocks still dominate production with their grapes reaching a very high fruit concentration. Grape bunches are hand harvested into small lug boxes to prevent damage and transported to the cellar for vinification.

Chardonnay is whole-bunch pressed and the cleared juice is barrel fermented in heavy toasted barrels. Following alcoholic and malolactic fermentation, the wine is matured on the lees for 12 months, giving a fresh yet creamy wine with aromas of citrus, honey, almonds and white chocolate. Destalked and crushed red grapes are cold macerated for three days to initiate extraction of colour and primary fruit flavours. The must is then inoculated with a selected yeast culture and fermented with regular punch downs and pump overs to ensure proper mixing of skins and juice. All blocks are vinified separately and once pressed, the free-run and pressed wines are matured separately. Malolactic fermentation is completed in barrels to promote integration of the wood and a combination of new and older oak allows extended maturation of 18 months to ensure wines are well integrated and balanced. A fuller style Pinot Noir shows savoury notes with dense, rich tannins while the Merlot's concentrated dark berries and chocolate flavours promise evolution over a decade. The classic Rubicon flagship is rich and powerful with dark fruits, mocha notes and grainy tannins, yet retains a traditional modest alcohol for understated elegance. The wine has great aging potential and requires a minimum of five years to achieve its peak.

A history of wine and architecture (Top)
Cellar detail on staircase (Centre)
Detail continued on outbuildings (Left)

Rubicon (Cab S / Merlot / Cab F) Pinot Noir, Chard, Cab S, Merlot, Cab F, Petit Verdot Mon – Fri 9 – 4, Sat 10 – 2, tour groups by appt only +27 (0)21 843 3587 +27 (0)21 843 3274 info@meerlust.co.za www.meerlust.co.za red 10 y+, white 5 y 86, 91, 95, 98, 01 traditional architecture

The Foundry *Stellenbosch West Pocket*

The Foundry, another garagiste that has grown into a serious producer, was established with the vision of producing excellent wine, reflecting the character of its source vineyards. Syrah is sourced from a neighbouring vineyard, planted on low vigour, well-drained, granitic soils. The cultivation conditions and crop reduction at *veraison* reduces growth vigour, decreases berry size and concentrates flavours with a high skin to juice ratio. Viognier is sourced from a vineyard on shale soils (Wellington Pocket), which is exposed to warm growing conditions. Winemaking is very natural: partially crushed berries, small stainless steel fermenters, natural yeasts and gentle pressing provide great depth and body while the tannins remain smooth. Extended barrel maturation using micro-oxygenation stabilises the colour and tannins. The wine is bottled without any fining or filtration. Viognier is cool fermented in older French barrels using natural and inoculated fermentations to add further complexity. Only half of the wine undergoes malolactic fermentation and lees maturation to soften the crisp acidity.

Syrah / Shz, Viog / by appt only
+27 (0)82 599 0491 / +27 (0)21 843 3274
thefoundry@mweb.co.za www.thefoundry.co.za
up to 12 y / 01, 03 / located on the Meerlust estate

Vergenoegd *Stellenbosch West Pocket*

Vergenoegd (Dutch for "well satisfied") has been farmed by the Faure family for six generations. It was one of the first estates to bottle its own wine in 1972. The Cape Dutch homestead (circa 1773) is an historic monument. Eighty hectares of vines are cultivated only three kilometres from the ocean and receive the full cooling benefit of the prevailing winds off False Bay. The soils vary from alluvial loam to sand on a clay base with calcareous rock. Drainage systems improve the aeration of vine roots on these extremely low aspects (9 m). Attentive vineyard management opens canopies to increase airflow and thereby reduce the humidity and subsequent disease incidence. Red grapes are macerated and fermented in rototanks to ensure proper mixing of skins and juice. Extended maturation (20+ months) in 300 litre French oak barrels gives the flagship blend a rich and powerful tannin structure which deserves maturing. The wines are only released after three years.

Vergenoegd (Cab S / Merlot / Cab F) / Cab S/F, Shz, Merlot, PV, Malbec, Tinta B, Touriga N / Mon – Fri 8 – 5 Sat 9:30 – 12:30. Closed publ hols / 27 (0)21 843 3248
+27 (0)21 843 3118 / enquiries@vergenoegd.co.za
www.vergenoegd.co.za / 10 y+ / 72, 74, 82, 84, 95, 99, 00, 03
older vintages available, tours by appt, restaurant

Neethlingshof *Stellenbosch West Pocket*

A unique kilometre-long pine avenue leads to Neethlingshof. The farm has a history spanning more than 300 years. Planting started in 1692, followed by a wine cellar (circa 1802) and manor house (circa 1814). Two hundred and twenty hectares are cultivated with vines, using vertical trellising and dense panting (4, 000 vines/Ha) in fertile decomposed granite soil to control vigorous growth. South-facing slopes, directly exposed to the nearby ocean, with an elevation of 100 to 300 metres above sea level, create cool ripening conditions, while frequent mists assist in *Botrytis* formation for Noble Late Harvest production. Red grapes are macerated and fermented in rototanks (mixing skins and juice) for improved colour extraction. Laurentius is matured for 12 months with 60 per cent new oak adding spice and toasted flavours to the fragrant black fruit nose. The wood-fermented Chardonnay matures on the lees and in bottle before release, producing a fleshy, luxurious wine. The flagship varietal wines are all from single vineyards.

Laurentius (Cab S/Merlot/Malbec), W Riesling NLH
Cab S/F, Merlot, Malb, Pinotage, Chard, Shz, Sauv Bl, W Riesl, Gewürz, Viog, Sém / Mon – Fri 9 – 6:30 (Mar 1 – Nov 30 closes at 5), Closed Easter Fri, Dec 25 / +27 (0)21 883 8988
+27 (0)21 883 8941 / info@neethlingshof.co.za
www.neethlingshof.co.za / red 5 – 8 y, Laurentius 10 y / 96, 99 , 01, 03 / cellar & farm tours by appt, 2 restaurants; venue: tour groups, play area for kids, open tractor tours.

Ripening Cabernet Sauvignon grapes at Meerlust

BOTTELARY POCKET

The Bottelary Pocket is situated on the northern slopes of the Bottelary range of granite hills, located about 12 kilometres to the north-west of Stellenbosch.

The meso-climate varies within the Bottelary Pocket as vineyards on higher elevations and plateau positions benefit from air movement which cools and dries the vines, while lower-lying vineyards experience warmer conditions. Although granite is the main soil parent material, significant portions of shale also occur, resulting in soil variation between sites. At higher altitudes, soils are typically yellow to reddish-brown, well-drained and favourably structured. Often in association with some stony or gravelly soils, these structured soils allow for extensive vine root development and a far greater water retention capacity throughout the vine's growing season.

Towards the valley bottom, the soils become more duplex and sandy. These soils tend to retain more water during spring and dry out in late summer, requiring more managerial skills in terms of viticultural practices and soil water regulation.

Situated in this Pocket is the north-south running valley of Koelenhof, a wide, open basin with soft, undulating hills at 120 – 200 metres above sea level. It is a relatively cool area due to air from the sea funnelling inland during summer, creating favourable ripening conditions. The soils are almost exclusively derived from shale, with structured medium vigour soils on the lower slopes changing to more gravelly soils on a clay-base on the convex hillside positions. On the flat valley bottom, the clay base is covered with sand. These sites are prone to excessive wetness.

The Bottelary Pocket is characterised by vineyards on northern slopes as well as on the valley floor. In the shallow, layered soils, vines are planted on ridges to increase soil volume with scions grafted on specific rootstocks which are adapted to shallow soils. On the hills, a selection of red and white vines is cultivated on warmer and cooler slopes, depending on the aspect. The north and west-facing slopes favour Shiraz and Pinotage, producing excellent red wines with firm tannins and dark fruit.

Most Pinotage, as well as many Chenin Blanc vineyards, are cultivated as bush vines as this reduces water requirements.

69

Hillside vines – Bottelary vineyards produce some of the best Pinotage wines

These plants have shorter shoots which are less prone to wind damage. The bush vines in particular give highly concentrated fruit with Pinotage showing more of its Pinot-like character. Bush vines are generally not irrigated, while new plantings of high-trellised vines (particularly white varieties) receive supplementary irrigation to assist in the root development of the young vines.

Shiraz in Bottelary tends to have less pronounced white pepper and spicy notes, showing more sour-cherry and plum fruit backed by savoury and beef notes. Frequently oaked with a percentage of American oak, the wines show definite vanilla sweetness and dark chocolate aromas.

Bottelary can be described as Pinotage headquarters, with excellent examples from Bellevue, Kaapzicht, Mooiplaas and Beyerskloof. Bellevue produced the first commercial Pinotage in the country. The farm's unique *terroir* shines through in the unmistakeable cassis and blueberry flavours on the nose, as is also evident on its Malbec.

Cabernet Sauvignon also fares well with structured single varietal examples from Goede Hoop and Hartenberg, and Cabernet blends from Mulderbosch and Hazendal. A good example of a blend containing Pinotage is Kaapzicht's Steytler Vision with up to 40 per cent Pinotage.

Mooiplaas produces delicate Sauvignon Blanc from a cool hilltop vineyard, while the aromatic Sauvignon Blancs from lower-lying vineyards on Mulderbosch and Villiera are more structured. The first Cap Classique (bottle-fermented sparkling wine) in South Africa was produced by Simonsig, with Villiera's Chardonnay MCC joining the top ranks with bone-dry richness and fine acidity.

DRIVING ROUTE: BOTTELARY

The Bottelary Pocket is situated to the north-west of Stellenbosch. From the town, drive towards the N1 freeway, in a northerly direction. At the fourth set of traffic lights, turn left to the R304. As the Bottelary Pocket consists of an L-shaped area, meso-climate varies with the location of vineyards. Elevation and aspect also vary greatly. The rolling hills provide sites ranging from plateau positions which benefit from cooling summer sea breezes to lower-lying, north-facing vineyards experience warmer conditions where the truly South African variety, Pinotage, has found a home.

About five kilometres out of town, the first two wineries' white-walled entrances lie side-by-side to the left. Take the first entrance left and drive along a gravel road to Beyerskloof. The image of a red Pinotage vine leaf, which has become synonymous with Beyerskloof, is featured on the walled entrance. A new tasting facility has been erected, also housing a small shop with wine, selected branded clothing, wine gadgets and Pinotage foodstuffs. From Beyerskloof, take the next left entrance from the R304 to visit Mulderbosch. Mulderbosch's white wines in particular are recognised for their ability to age well.

From Mulderbosch, drive about three kilometres north to the sign for Bottelary Road (M23) and turn left. Notice the range of granite hills to the left. Pass the Devon Valley Golf Course as you drive east. About six kilometres from the turn-off, a cluster of pine trees and a white-walled entrance with a variety of flags announce the entrance to Bellevue. Turn right and follow the gravel road around the winery to the tasting room, in the historic cellar. Bellevue proudly cultivates one of the oldest blocks of Pinotage (planted 1953) still in production. It was planted only one year ahead of the Pinotage blocks on Kanonkop which made the Paul Sauer wine famous.

Further along Bottelary Road, turn left to Fischer Road to visit Goede Hoop (Eng. Good Hope), another family-owned winery. Follow the gravel road along the hillside to the entrance on the left. The old farmhouse, circa 1880, is now home to the third generation Bestbier winemaker and his family.

A stone's throw further along the Bottelary Road is Groenland (Eng. Green Land), also a family-owned winery. Turn left at the oasis of lush trees set between surrounding vineyards to the cellar and tasting room. Groenland recently started production under its own label, previously selling grapes to other producers.

The route continues west on Bottelary Road to a cluster of gum trees on the left. Turn left and follow the gravel road past sandy vineyards into a shallow horseshoe shaped valley to Mooiplaas Estate. The Roos family has lovingly restored the old stables into a charming tasting room. A large tree on the patio is beautifully decorated every festive season. Mooiplaas's vineyards are located on slopes that virtually surround the cellar and produce elegant red and white wines.

GPS waypoints

Bellevue	S33 52.788 E18 45.821
Beyerskloof	S33 53.418 E18 49.526
Goede Hoop	S33 54.552 E18 45.227
Groenland	S33 53.772 E18 44.045
Mooiplaas	S33 55.260 E18 44.417
Mulderbosch	S33 53.326 E18 49.441

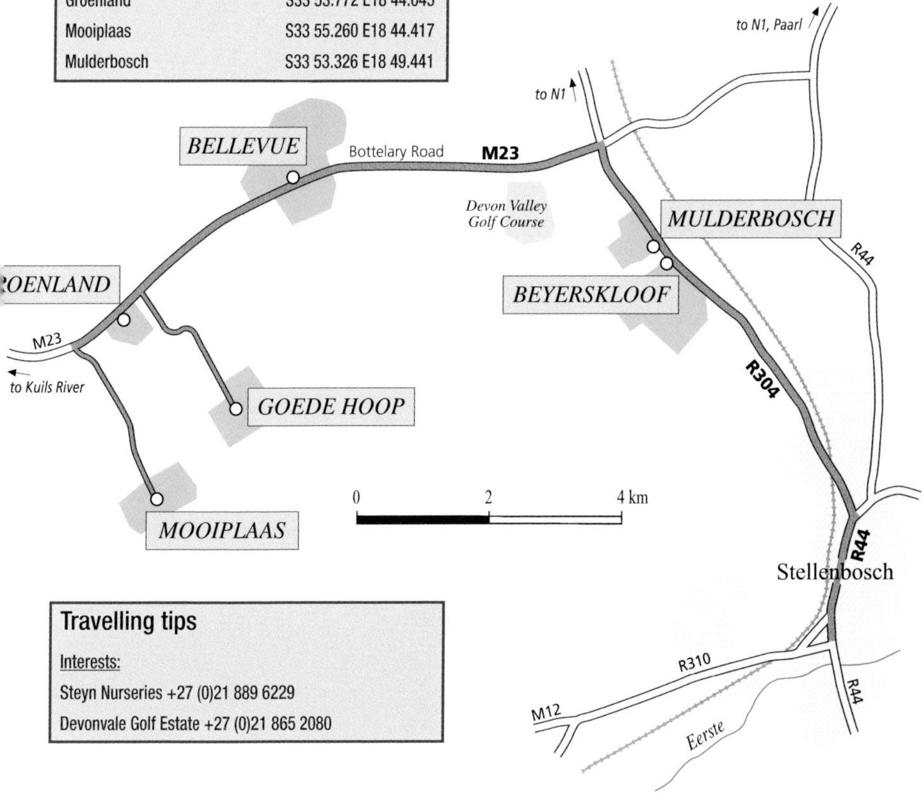

71

to N1, Paarl

to N1

BELLEVUE — Bottelary Road — M23

Devon Valley Golf Course

MULDERBOSCH

R44

ROENLAND

M23

to Kuils River

BEYERSKLOOF

R304

GOEDE HOOP

0   2   4 km

MOOIPLAAS

R44

Stellenbosch

Travelling tips

Interests:

Steyn Nurseries +27 (0)21 889 6229

Devonvale Golf Estate +27 (0)21 865 2080

R310

M12

R44

Eerste

Groenland *Bottelary Pocket*

The Steenkamp family have farmed Groenland (Eng. Green Land) since 1932. During their tenure, they have created a beautiful oasis with lush gardens shaded by willows. Even though 150 hectares of the surrounding Bottelary Hills and valleys are cultivated to vines, the family selected only a small portion of these extensive plantings for their 2002 maiden vintage.

Red varieties are cultivated on west and north-facing slopes in heavy, deep red soils. The heat-sensitive white varieties are planted on cooler sites in the alluvial and sandy soils of the valley floor. Vines are exposed to long sun hours and strong winds. As a result, they are trellised to avoid excessive exposure to sun and wind damage. Like other producers in this Pocket, about 65 per cent of production is dedicated to red cultivars with mature vineyards (10 y+) achieving great flavour concentration and density.

Grapes are hand harvested, destemmed and crushed before fermentation in open cement tanks. Cooling ensures fermentation temperatures are kept below 28°C to achieve proper extraction. Wine is pumped over selectively to prevent over-extraction and harsh tannins. Once alcoholic fermentation is completed, the young wine is drained off and the skins are lightly pressed. The free-run and press wine is blended to ensure structure and longevity in the wine. Shiraz is matured in American oak, adding typical vanilla and roasted coconut flavours to the wine's natural spiciness, while the more fruit-driven Cabernet Sauvignon and Merlot wines are matured in French oak. The wines are fruit driven and powerful with elevated alcohol levels.

Winter splendour – cover crops at Groenland

Shiraz Cab S, Shiraz, Pinotage, Merlot, Sauv Bl, Chard, Chenin Mon – Fri 10 – 4, Sat, Publ hols 10 – 1. Closed Easter Fri, Sun, Dec 25, Jan 1 +27 (0)21 903 8203 +27 (0)21 903 0250 steenkamp@groenland.co.za www.groenland.co.za 8 y 97, 98, 02 BYO picnics, conference and reception facilities, meals by appt

Mooiplaas *Bottelary Pocket*

Mooiplaas, established in 1805, lies in the horseshoe-shaped basin of the Bottelary Hills. An old stable now serves as a rustic tasting room. One hundred and twenty-five hectares are cultivated on elevated slopes (130 – 380 m) above sea level. Sauvignon Blanc is planted on the hilltops, benefiting from cooling breezes. Warmer north-west and east-facing slopes with low-vigour soils are planted to red varieties, satisfying their higher heat requirements. White grapes are picked in the early morning and fermented through a reductive process with dry ice and cold temperatures (12°C) to preserve their pronounced methoxypyrazines aromas (grassy, herbaceous). The wine is left on the lees without any sulphur additions for extended periods to develop more succulent, tropical fruit flavours. Red varieties are cold macerated before fermentation with regular punch-downs to extract colour. Maturation in French oak for up to 24 months with 60 per cent new wood delivers savoury notes to these elegantly structured wines.

Sauvignon Blanc Sauv Bl, Pinotage, Cab S, Shz, Chenin Bl, Merlot Mon – Fri 9 – 4 Sat, Publ hols 10 – 2. Closed Easter, Dec 25, 26, Jan 1 +27 (0)21 903 6273 +27 (0)21 903 3474 info@mooiplaas.co.za www.mooiplaas.co.za 3 y 03 BYO picnic, conservation area, rustic tasting room with artefacts

Vineyards nestle on the valley floor

Chardonnay

Chardonnay was first brought to South Africa in 1920, but the first clones were virus infected; growth was weak, production was limited and ripening difficult. Clone choice is critical and both Old World (citrus and peach) and New World (melon and butterscotch) styles are produced. Natural fermentation allows for a more precise expression of the individuality and locality of the variety. The diverse *terroir* generates three Chardonnay styles: wooded (100%), semi-wooded and unwooded. Cooler climate Chardonnays show a stronger acid structure and are better able to integrate increased percentages of (new) oak. Chardonnay is generally trellised with good concentration and ripeness. Key producers are Glen Carlou, Durbanville Hills, Hamilton Russell Vineyards, Jordan, Mulderbosch.

Chardonnay grapes

Barrel fermentation air-trap

Mulderbosch Bottelary Pocket

Mulderbosch is accepted to be among the best South African white wine producers and its wines, produced in limited quantities, have the ability to age remarkably well, particularly the white wines.

Twenty-seven hectares of vines are cultivated on the east-facing hills in granite and shale soils. The elevation (300 m) and prevailing south-easterly winds from the Atlantic Ocean moderate the daytime temperatures. In these favourable conditions, vines yield a limited crop (5 tons per hectare) of aromatic fruit. Cabernet Sauvignon, Sauvignon Blanc and Chenin Blanc are planted to bush vines, as these require less water and are less affected by the prevailing winds. The bush vines on these particular sites produce high extracts, great complexity and a good sugar-acid balance.

White grapes are pressed and the clear juice is cold fermented. Chardonnay Barrel Fermented is produced from a single vineyard. This naturally fermented wine balances the creamy texture of lees maturation with a crisp acidity and fresh citrus fruit. Sauvignon Blanc receives a few days lees contact after cold fermentation, strengthening the varietal character and adding weight to the wine. The Sauvignon Blanc remains unwooded, showing ripe tropical fruit and a distinctive mineral character. The Centauri blend (Cab S/F, PV) is made only in exceptional vintages and 18 months wood maturation blends seamlessly with the concentrated fruit structure.

Grapes for the flagship red wine, Shiraz, are sourced from Stanford; and this spicy wine shows meaty undertones and a dense mouthfeel. The red blend, Faithful Hound, completes malolactic fermentation in tank and, unusually, components are blended before barrel maturation to allow a longer integration time for the blended product.

Imposing entrance at Mulderbosch

Sauvignon Blanc, Chardonnay Barrel Fermented, Shiraz, Cab S/F, Merlot, Malbec, PV, Sauv Bl, Chard, Chenin Bl, sales Mon – Fri 8 – 5, tasting by appt only, +27 (0)21 865 2488, +27 (0)21 865 2351, info@mulderbosch.co.za, www.mulderbosch.co.za, reds 8 y+, whites 4 y+, white 97, 01, 03; red 98, 01, 03, visits by appointment only

Pinotage

In 1924 an experiment by Professor Abraham I Perold with Hermitage (Cinsaut) and Pinot Noir created South Africa's national grape, Pinotage. Intending to create an offspring which would combine the best character traits of both parents – the classic Burgundy Pinot flavours and the easy-to-grow, disease-resistant quality and taste of Rhône Valley Cinsaut – his experiment yielded seed which he planted, but soon the seedlings were forgotten. The seedlings would have been lost were it not for a young lecturer, Dr Niehaus, who saw a team of gardeners working in Perold's former residence. Knowing about the plants, he swiftly rescued them. These were re-established in the Elsenburg Agricultural College nursery by Perold's successor, CJ Theron. The rescue prompted Perold to propagate the new variety enthusiastically.

The uniquely shaped Pinotage leaf

The first recognition of a Pinotage wine came in 1959 when a Bellevue red wine (made only from Pinotage) was voted champion wine at the Cape Wine Show. The achievement was repeated in 1961 by a Pinotage from Kanonkop Estate. Stellenbosch Farmers' Winery (now Distell) was first to use the name Pinotage on a label in 1961. These successes and the robust and early-ripening character of this variety inspired many farmers to plant Pinotage.

Poor publicity from a group of visiting British Wine Masters in 1976 caused widespread uprooting of the variety as it was said to have no future. A few producers, however, convinced of Pinotage's potential, stubbornly and courageously continued to search for ways of improving the grape quality as well as how best to vinify Pinotage. It took some years before another wine competition re-energised the Pinotage industry. The Diner's Club Winemaker of the Year focuses on a specific varietal or wine category. The 1987 competition was dedicated to Pinotage. Four years later, another success came as Kanonkop's Beyers Truter was named International Winemaker of the Year at the 1991 International Wine and Spirit Competition. Truter was the first South African winemaker to win this prestigious competition. All the more fitting that he did so with South Africa's own wine variety.

In South Africa, most Pinotage is cultivated as bush vines, as this form seems to produce the premium wines. Bush vines produce an average yield of 32 – 52 hectolitres per hectare or 5 – 8 tons per hectare. Pinotage may also be trellised, however, only low trellis systems are used, bringing the grapes closer to the surface of the soil to increase radiant heat. Trellised, Pinotage may yield up to 10 tons per hectare of excellent quality grapes. Pinotage is an early ripener and can be harvested a little earlier than most other red varieties.

Optimum flavour development is achieved at high alcohol levels. Medium-bodied wines are generally produced at between 12.5 and 13.5 per cent alcohol, while a full-bodied wine may reach 15 per cent alcohol or even higher. A percentage of new wood gives good integration of wood flavours and structure to full-bodied Pinotage wines. Maturation takes six to eight months (medium-bodied wines) up to 12 to 14 months (full-bodied wines). Modern Pinotage regulates its inherent astringency well and offers dark plum and raspberry fruit. Pinotage can produce wines in both the light, dry and fruity style as well as the oaked, powerful and enduring style. A new classification of Cape Blend, with a percentage of Pinotage, is under debate. Key producers are Beyerskloof, L'Avenir, Kanonkop, Camberley, DeWaal, Seidelberg, Tukulu.

Goede Hoop Estate *Bottelary Pocket*

Three generations of the Bestbier family have farmed Goede Hoop since 1928. The entire estate is situated on the slopes of the surrounding Bottelary Hills and 80 hectares of vines have been planted on slopes facing north and north-west. Elevations range from 100 to 350 metres above sea level. The highest sites benefit from greater air movement and subsequent cooling and are planted to white varieties. Red varieties are situated on lower altitudes in warmer ripening conditions, which benefit colour and tannin development. The annual rainfall of 600 – 900 mm and the high moisture retention of decomposed granite soils allow for dry-land cultivation. Hand-harvested grapes are sorted, destemmed and crushed in open vats. Natural fermentation with regular pump overs and extended maturation (18 months) in older barrels add to the complexity and savoury notes of red varieties in particular. The Sauvignon Blanc receives lees contact and the wood-fermented Chardonnay is matured in oak for 10 months, both yielding powerful and aromatic yet fresh wines.

[i] Cabernet Sauvignon [■] Cab S, Shz, Merlot, Pinotage, Carignan, Chard, Sauv Bl [○] Mon – Thurs 10 – 5, Fri 10 – 3. Open publ hols [☎] +27 (0)21 903 6286 [✉] 27 (0)21 906 1553 [✉] goede@adept.co.za www.goedehoop.co.za [E] white 3 y+, reds 8 y+ [■] 99, 00 [i] tours, meals, refreshments by appt, BYO picnic, conference venue

Bellevue *Bottelary Pocket*

The Morkel family of Bellevue has been in residence since 1861. They crushed their maiden vintage under their own label in the restored historic Cape Dutch farm in 1999. One hundred and ninety hectares of vines are cultivated along a valley floor and on various slopes. The low potential soils require supplementary irrigation. Pinotage is cultivated as bush vines, mostly on high-lying areas, expressing more Pinot Noir characters. Heat-sensitive varieties are planted on exposed hillslopes to maximise cool afternoon breezes. Mature vines, together with the slightly denser planting, lead to more concentrated flavours while controlling growth vigour on the higher potential valley floor soils. The PK Morkel Pinotage, from a single vineyard, is fruit driven with strong wood flavours. The red wine ferments below 30°C, with extended skin contact to extract colour and flavour and give complexity to the wines. The wines are matured in 100 per cent new French oak barrels, which contribute to the intensity and filling mid-palate.

[i] PK Morkel Pinotage, Tumara (Cab S / F / Merlot / Malbec / PV) [■] Pinotage, Cab S/F, Merlot, Malbec, PV, Shz [○] Mon – Fri 10 – 4, Sat, non-religious hols 10 – 3 [☎] +27 (0)21 865 2055 [✉] +27 (0)21 865 2899 [✉] info@bellevue.co.za www.bellevue.co.za [E] 8 y [■] 03, 04 [i] oldest commercial Pinotage block planted 1953

Beyerskloof *Bottelary Pocket*

An historic circle, broken over a hundred years ago, was finally restored when Beyers Truter bought a farm which belonged to the Beyers family for five generations. A direct descendant, Truter became the sixth generation to own this property.

On the primary property's shallow, gravelly soil, the planting of almost 5, 000 vines per hectare (almost twice the norm) optimises this small 8.5 hectare pocket of land. Row direction is an important factor for heat management and is aligned east-west, with Cabernet Sauvignon and Merlot vines maximising long sunlight hours for the greatest colour development and optimising the prevailing winds to dry and cool the vines. All the vines are vertically trellised to spread and thin out the canopy with more leaf surface exposed to direct sunlight and bunches protected from burn damage.

Cabernet Sauvignon and Merlot grapes are harvested, vinified and matured together to achieve the best possible integration of the fruit structures. This blend is matured in 100 per cent new oak for two years before bottling. This results in a highly structured and powerful wine, needing decanting in youth.

An additional 77 hectare produces Pinotage, Cabernet Sauvignon and Merlot. Using slopes facing in various directions, grapes are cultivated at an elevation of 50 to 100 metres above sea level. Pinotage is fermented at a high temperature (29°C) to produce a scented wine with deep, dark cherry fruit. Pure Pinotage passion is reflected in Pinotage products ranging from Pinotage salami to Pinotage frozen yoghurt, Pinotage Sparkling Brut and even Pinotage dessert wine. A true Pinotage lover's paradise.

Amongst the Pinotage vineyards

[i] Beyerskloof (blend: Cab S / Merlot), Pinotage Reserve [■] Pinotage, Cabernet Sauvignon, Merlot, Cinsaut [○] Mon – Fri 8:30 – 4:30, Sat 10 – 2. Closed Sun, Easter, Dec 25, 26, Jan 1 [☎] +27 (0)21 865 2135 [✉] +27 (0)21 865 2683 [✉] wine@beyerskloof.co.za www.beyerskloof.co.za [E] 10 y+ [■] 91, 94, 95, 98, 99, 05 [i] cellar tours, harvest experience (in season, booking req.), coffee shop

BLAAUWKLIPPEN ROAD POCKET

The Blaauwklippen Road Pocket is located on the R44 south towards the town of Somerset West. This wide valley runs in an east-west direction.

Vineyards are established mainly on the west-facing foothills of the Stellenbosch Mountain as well as the most northern foothills of the Helderberg Mountain. The soils of these foothill are mainly derived from shale and granite respectively, often covered by a mantle of colluvial sandstone material, its calcium carbonate content neutralising the acidity of the granite. The soils found at elevations of approximately 150 – 250 metres become more duplex and sandy in the lower-lying areas.

Although the Helderberg Mountain partly restricts the airflow from False Bay, the Blaauwklippen Road Pocket still benefits from its cooling effect, especially vineyards situated at higher elevations which are slightly more exposed. These vineyards also benefit from the cooling effect of the harsh synoptic south-easterly winds that often tumble down the mountain slopes during early summer.

These winds make a positive contribution to the quality of grapes from this area, as they curtail excessive early season growth on the generally high-potential soils of this Pocket. By limiting excessive vine growth and balancing it with grape production, vines tend to produce naturally smaller berries of high concentration. This in turn leads to greater skin to juice ratios and subsequently increases colour and flavour extraction during vinification.

Vineyards are planted from the fertile high foothills down to the poorer valley floor and growth vigour varies accordingly. The small percentage of vines on the east-facing slope (at Kleine Zalze across the lowest point) receive early morning light and the white varieties benefit from the drying effect and reduced occurrence of *Botrytis* infections.

Bush vines make an important contribution as many older blocks are still cultivated this way. On very fertile soils, vines are trained on trellises of 1.2 to 1.8 metres, creating a vertically extended canopy which reduces leaf density and increases airflow. The classic noble varieties are well represented here, as well as some blocks of Chenin Blanc, Viognier, Petit Verdot and Mourvèdre.

The red wines show velvety tannins and nutty flavours. These wines generally have a powerful structure and dense fruit aromas. Cabernet Sauvignon in particular shows pencil shavings, mintiness and a mineral finish in the varietal wines (Waterford, Kleine Zalze, De Trafford, Graceland and Blaauwklippen). These Cabernet Sauvignon characteristics are slightly quietened in the blends from Dornier and De Trafford, as Merlot and Cabernet Franc add their respective aromas. Vriesenhof, on the other hand, uses Pinotage as the main blending partner for its Enthopio. Its Pinot Noir shows strong Burgundian earthy savoury and berry notes. Other interesting red wines from the Pocket include the smoky Shiraz from Stellenzicht and the Blaauwklippen Zinfandel with sappy, cranberry fruit. Chenin Blanc and Sémillon are favoured white varietals. The unwooded Chenin Blanc from Kleine Zalze (from bush vines) produces a very appealing fragrant floral nose with fresh acidity. Sensitive oaking on De Trafford's Chenin Blanc and Stellenzicht's Sémillon give these aromatic white wines a full and complex structure.

Colluvial / Colluvium: unconsolidated deposits of soil or rock fragments which accumulate at the foot of slopes.

DRIVING ROUTE:
BLAAUWKLIPPEN ROAD

The Blaauwklippen Road Pocket is situated on the foothills of the Stellenbosch Mountain. Take the R44 south towards Somerset West. As the road rises past the Stellenbosch Golf Course, turn left onto Paradyskloof Road. The road winds through a quiet residential area. Turn left at the T-junction and immediately right as the road rises over the hill past a tree in the middle of the road. Residences make way for vineyards. Take the first gravel road to the right to visit Vriesenhof Vineyards. Rugby legend,

Jan Boland Coetzee, is championing Pinotage as a blending partner with other red varieties in a Cape Blend. From Vriesenhof's winery, the road continues to the studio of Dylan Lewis, a celebrated South African sculptor, with works exhibited both locally and internationally. The bronze casting events have limited space and studio visits are by appointment. The narrow road leading to the studio is suitable for standard-sized vehicles only.

Return to the R44 on the same route and continue a few hundred metres to the traffic lights on the crest. Turn left onto

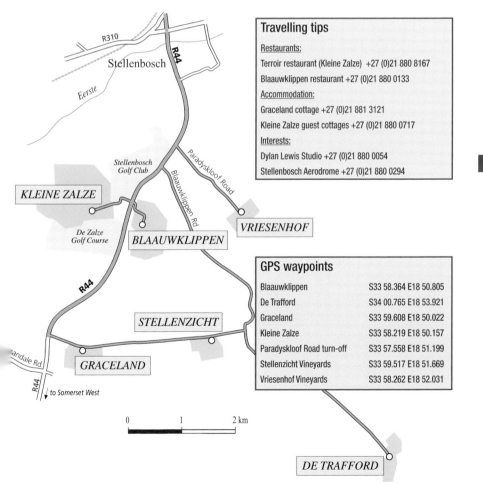

Travelling tips

Restaurants:
Terroir restaurant (Kleine Zalze) +27 (0)21 880 8167
Blaauwklippen restaurant +27 (0)21 880 0133
Accommodation:
Graceland cottage +27 (0)21 881 3121
Kleine Zalze guest cottages +27 (0)21 880 0717
Interests:
Dylan Lewis Studio +27 (0)21 880 0054
Stellenbosch Aerodrome +27 (0)21 880 0294

GPS waypoints

Blaauwklippen	S33 58.364 E18 50.805
De Trafford	S34 00.765 E18 53.921
Graceland	S33 59.608 E18 50.022
Kleine Zalze	S33 58.219 E18 50.157
Paradyskloof Road turn-off	S33 57.558 E18 51.199
Stellenzicht Vineyards	S33 59.517 E18 51.669
Vriesenhof Vineyards	S33 58.262 E18 52.031

Blaauwklippen Road, a petrol station and small shopping centre are located on either side of the turn-off. Vineyards cover the lower foothills. This area is also renowned for horse breeding and stabling. You will frequently meet riders along the way. About three kilometres further, a gravel road turns off to the left. The road snakes higher into this narrow valley. The rugged mountains, pristine vineyards and expansive lawns make this one of the most exquisite areas of the Winelands. Pass Mont Fleur Conference Centre, take the left fork through a small gate and drive the last few metres of steep incline to De Trafford winery. Architect-turned-winemaker David Trafford and his family tend some of the steepest vineyards in South Africa to make powerful red wines as well as one of the few examples of delicate straw wine.

Retrace the route to the turn-off at the gravel road. Turn left onto the gravel road. The next winery, Stellenzicht, is on the left. A pioneer of Shiraz in South Africa, Stellenzicht's dramatic 1994 Shiraz and, more recent, 2002 vintage from a mature vineyard named Plum Pudding Hill, have set a benchmark for this variety. Drive two kilometres down the gravel road to the next winery, Graceland Vineyards, on the left. Buzz the intercom at the gate for access and follow the very narrow farm road to the office. Graceland's limited quantity of powerful red wines is in high demand. Its use of stylish tissue paper wrapping is a visual feast. Continue on the gravel road to the T-junction with the R44 about 300 metres further. Here you can only turn left. A set of traffic lights and a fairly large intersection with an access road to a local shopping mall provide a place to turn around.

Driving north on the R44 (in the direction of Stellenbosch), the road rises to meet the town. Near the crest, two grand ladies await. Kleine Zalze and Blaauwklippen, on either side. Turn left at the signs for Kleine Zalze and left again to the security area. From there it is a few hundred metres to the visitors' area and restaurant, aptly named Terroir. There is also a pristine 18-hole golf course and a luxury guest house.

From Kleine Zalze, cross over the R44 to Blaauwklippen's imposing entrance of white-washed walls and flags. Signs indicate the visitors' area. Adjacent to the tasting room is a restaurant, deli and gift shop offering great gift ideas. A stroll around the exquisite gardens provides many photographic opportunities as sculpted lawns meet historic Cape Dutch architecture.

Traditional architecture – Cape Dutch at Blaauwklippen

A view from the top – Blaauwklippen Road Pocket

De Trafford *Blaauwklippen Road Pocket*

The Trafford family's winery is set spectacularly in the heights of the Helderberg Mountain. A small cultivation of five hectares is established on north-facing slopes, elevated higher than 320 metres above sea level. This secluded valley is well protected from prevailing winds, and enjoys mountain airflow from the steep slopes as well as the cooling effect of higher elevations. Merlot is planted closer to the river on clay soils as it requires more water. Shiraz is sited on higher slopes in poor soil to control its growth vigour. Grapes are harvested at high sugar levels and undergo spontaneous fermentation, adding to the complexity of the wines. Components for the powerful Elevation 393 red blend (Cabernet Sauvignon/Merlot/Shiraz) are individually oaked and bottled without fining or filtration after 22 months. The *Vin de Paillé* is a sweet straw wine made from Chenin Blanc, sourced from a neighbouring farm on the valley floor.

[i] red blend, Vin de Paillé [symbol] Cab S, Merlot, Shz, Chenin Bl
[symbol] Fri, Sat 10 – 1 [symbol] +27 (0)21 880 1611
[symbol] info@detrafford.co.za www.detrafford.co.za [symbol] 10 y [symbol] 98, 00, 01, 03, 04 [i] family artwork on labels of each vintage, secluded valley scenery

Stellenzicht Vineyards *Blaauwklippen Road Pocket*

First established in 1692, the Stellenzicht farm received its name in 1981, literally "view of Stellen (bosch)". With a long history of winemaking, the 1994 Syrah set a new benchmark, taking laurels in a national taste-off. Eight-five hectares of vines are grown on west and north-west-facing slopes on medium fertility soils of decomposed granite and sandstone. Elevation (100 – 400 m above sea level) as well as the close proximity to the ocean provide a cooling effect to the trellised vineyards. Sémillon free-run juice (from a mature, low-yielding vineyard, 4.4 ton/Ha) completes alcoholic and malolactic fermentation in new oak, with eight months of *bâtonnage* while maturing in barrel. This process results in a waxy wine showing citrus fruits, vanilla and smoky oak. Warm fermentation and extended barrel maturation (20 – 30 months) yields powerful and structured red wines. The mature (16 y) single vineyard still produces a prominent ripe, smoky Shiraz wine with high alcohol content (Alc. 15.8% by Vol.).

[i] Syrah [symbol] Cab S / F, Merlot, Malbec, Shz, Pinotage, PV, Sauv Bl, Chard, Sém [symbol] Mon – Fri 9 – 5 Sat, Sun, Publ hols 10 – 4. Closed Easter, Dec 25, Jan 1 [symbol] +27 (0)21 880 1103/4
[symbol] +27 (0)21 880 1107 [symbol] info@stellenzicht.co.za
www.stellenzicht.co.za [symbol] Syrah 10 y, Sém 7 y + [symbol] Shz 94, 98, 99, 01. Sém 98, 99, 02, 03 [i] label features a Golden Triangle (ref to Helderberg area)

Graceland Vineyards *Blaauwklippen Road Pocket*

Graceland, a boutique cellar, is located at the foot of the Helderberg Mountain. Elegant packaging in purple tissue and wooden boxes presents the new flagship blend, known as Three Graces. A new single vineyard Cabernet Sauvignon, Beehive, has also arrived to much enthusiasm.

Ten hectares of red varieties are planted on cool south-facing slopes – an interesting change from the norm, as reds are usually planted on north-facing slopes to maximise sun exposure. The structured soils of sandstone on decomposed granite allow for good drainage and adequate air circulation at root level. Vines are slightly water stressed in the dry summer months, reducing berry size and increasing the skin to juice ratio. Vines are planted to a very low planting density of 2, 850 vines per hectare on the steep slopes.

Careful canopy management sees the removal of excess leaves and shoots to open the canopy, increasing sunlight and airflow to ensure good colour development and to dry the grapes. This practice reduces disease and promotes fertility in the buds. Vineyards are harvested several times, selecting only fully ripened grapes.

Grapes are fermented in open-top cement tanks and several daily punch-downs ensure sufficient skin to juice contact for colour extraction. Extended barrel maturation of 20 months gives the blend a pronounced wood character, but the slow, controlled oxidation integrates and softens the tannins. The classic styled Three Graces, a seamless blend of Cabernet Sauvignon, Merlot and Shiraz, is structured and dense, needing several years to develop.

The Graceland Vineyards cellar

> 🚹 Three Graces (Cab S / Shz / Merlot) 🍇 Cab S, Merlot, Shz
> 🕐 by appt only 📞 +27 (0)21 881 3121 🖨 +27 (0)21 881 3341
> ✉ graceland@iafrica.com www.gracelandvineyards.com
> 🍷 7 y 🔖 98, 01, 03 ℹ B&B cottage

Vriesenhof Vineyards *Blaauwklippen Road Pocket*

Jan Boland Coetzee produces three diverse wine ranges under the labels Vriesenhof, Talana Hill and Paradyskloof. His belief that Pinotage creates its finest expression in a blend gave birth to the new Enthopio (Greek "Indigenous") blend. Forty hectares of vines are planted on south-facing slopes in fertile granite and shale soils, at varying elevations (200 – 240 m). Coastal breezes from False Bay moderate the climate and vineyard management focuses on protecting heat-sensitive grapes while ensuring sufficient exposure for its red varieties. While most varieties are planted in an east-west row direction to reduce direct sunlight during the day, Cabernet Sauvignon is planted along a north-south axis to capture the maximum sunlight. This ensures proper ripening and colour development.

The Pinot Noir, planted on south-facing slopes, receives fewer hours of direct sun and the tops of its high canopy are bent at an angle to give protective shade during the summer. Trellised vines are planted at a density of 4, 700 vines per hectare to restrict vigorous growth with the exception of a hilltop Pinotage vineyard, where low bush vines and rich shale soil enhance its fruity flavours.

Hi-tech equipment blends seamlessly with traditional methods of punch-downs and natural alcohol and malolactic fermentation. Components of the Kallista and Enthopio are blended before maturation and age for 15 to 20 months as completed wines. The Pinot Noir is matured exclusively in Burgundian barrels, supporting typical farmyard and cherry aromas. Talana Hill, a tiny 7.2 hectare south-west-facing vineyard hosts two single-vineyard wines: a Chardonnay and a Merlot/Cabernet Franc blend.

The Vriesenhof manor house

> 🚹 Kallista (Cab S / F) 🍇 Pinotage, Pinot Noir, Cab S /F, Merlot, Chardonnay
> 🕐 tasting Mon – Fri 8 – 4, Sat 9 – 2. Closed publ hols
> 📞 +27 (0)21 880 0284 🖨 +27 (0)21 880 1503 ✉ info@vriesenhof.co.za
> www.vriesenhof.co.za 🍷 10 y+ 🔖 82, 89, 91, 92, 95, 03, 05
> ℹ tours, meals and refreshments by appt

Blaauwklippen *Blaauwklippen Road Pocket*

Blaauwklippen was established in 1690 when the first owner, Gerrit Visscher, of German descent, developed the first plantings. Situated on the slopes of Stellenbosch Mountain, Blaauwklippen's west and north-facing slopes provide grapes for the flagship wines while a percentage of grapes are sourced from neighbouring farms to complement its own production.

The farm has a rich history and legend has it that Cecil John Rhodes bought the farm in 1869 and sold it on the same day. Three centuries later, Blaauwklippen is once again in the hands of German owners.

Today Blaauwklippen cultivates 77 hectares and the majority of the vines are at least 25 years old. The older vines produce six tons per hectare, while the new, young vines are cropped at only four tons per hectare. The new vines are also planted on a higher trellising system, lifting the canopy off the ground to increase airflow under the grape zone.

The average planting density of 2, 800 vines per hectare has been increased to 6, 500 vines per hectare on the mountain slopes. Red wines make up approximately 90 per cent of production. Zinfandel, an American cultivar, is grown on bush vines to increase fruit concentration. It is planted, together with Shiraz and Cabernet Sauvignon, on the lower west-facing slopes of the mountain in sandy soils with a granitic component. These soils seem to influence the floral and fruit expression in wines. Grapes are also sourced from neighbouring vineyards. Merlot excels on the south-facing slopes, with sea breezes tempering the hot summer days.

The flagship, Zinfandel BVS (Blaauwklippen Vineyard Selection range), has been the leading label for this variety over the past decade in the Cape. A philosophy of "less is more in winemaking" has taken hold, with the wine range streamlined to two tiers. Spontaneous fermentation (using naturally occurring yeasts and bacteria) is used for both the alcoholic and malolactic stages of the winemaking process. The successful implementation of this high-risk technique is testimony to the quality control in the cellar. Executed correctly, it develops a completely different range of flavours in wine, supporting the development of spicy and dried fruit flavours.

The flagship Zinfandel is matured in French oak, steering away from the sweetness and vanilla characters of American oak. By using old barrels like many neighbouring cellars, maturation is extended to 16 months. Blending the Cabriolet (Cab S, Cab F, Merlot) is done at the latest possible stage, and each component is matured separately to obtain the most from its own development in wood. The annual blending competition, held publicly, is now in its 22nd year and is still a great favourite with wine enthusiasts.

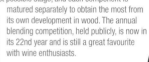

Blaauwklippen offers a wine shop, cellar tours and a restaurant featuring organic produce. Relive a bygone era with horse-drawn coaches around the farm. The Manor House and Werf are magnificent settings for private functions and weddings.

The tree-lined entrance to Blaauwklippen (Top)
Wrought-iron gate detail (Centre)
Classic Cape Dutch architecture (Left)

ℹ️ Vineyards Selection Zinfandel and other reds 🍇 Zin, Cab S, F, Shz, Malbec, Merlot, Mouv, PV, PN, Viog 🕐 Daily 9 – 5. Closed Jan 1
📞 +27 (0)21 880 0133 📠 +27 (0)21 880 0136 📧 hospitality@blaauwklippen.com www.blaauwklippen.com 📧 5 – 10 y
🍷 04 ℹ️ Blending competition, cellar tours, restaurant, cigar lounge, wine shop, conference centre, functions venue

Kleine Zalze *Blaauwklippen Road Pocket*

Wine has been produced on the family-owned wine estate of Kleine Zalze since 1695. For more than 300 years, different owners made wine on this historic property. In the late 1990s the Basson and Malan families took ownership of Kleine Zalze.

Today, 80 hectares of classic grape varieties are cultivated at the foot of the Stellenbosch Mountain. Twenty-six hectares of Cabernet Sauvignon, Shiraz and Merlot are planted on the slightly warmer south-west-facing slopes where they produce bold, fruity wines with great structure. Small parcels of Chardonnay and Chenin Blanc, which require a little more heat for even bud break, are also located on the warmer slopes. The cooler south-facing slopes host 48 hectares of vines. Here Cabernet Sauvignon, Merlot and Shiraz produce elegant, spicy wines. Some Sémillon and Sauvignon Blanc are also planted on these slopes with typical cool climate characteristics. The canopies of vines on the warmer sites are denser to protect grapes from sun damage. The deep red soils of granite and clay are well drained and vines are spaced further apart to encourage root development and subsequent growth vigour. Canopies are vertically spread on the trellis system in order to create a balance between the vine's growth and grape production and to allow grapes to ripen evenly.

The old cellar has been renovated and upgraded to reduce mechanical handling. Natural winemaking methods include whole bunch pressing to reduce harsh tannins in the wine and the use of free-run juice and gentler peristaltic pumping of liquids. A temperature-controlled barrel-fermentation cellar has been installed along with a 1, 000-barrel capacity maturation cellar imbedded in the cool granite earth as well as berry selection by hand on a conveyer belt to ensure only the best quality fruit. The flagship Family Reserve range includes a Shiraz and a Cabernet Sauvignon from single vineyards as well as a Sauvignon Blanc. These varietal wines are only produced from exceptional vintages and are award-winning wines. Red grapes receive three days of cold maceration before fermentation commences with regular pump overs to extract colour and flavour. The wines go through malolactic fermentation in barrel, and are then matured for 18 months in 100 per cent new wood. These labour-intensive practices ensure that wood characteristics are well integrated with fruit flavours. White grapes are pressed and the clear juice is cold fermented to retain its crisp, fruity flavours. Chenin Blanc, from bush vines, is available in both unwooded as well as wooded versions and is produced in an off-dry style (6.5 g/l sugar), producing wines with powerful alcohols of around 14 per cent, neatly hidden within white flower aromas and rich tropical fruit flavours.

The Terroir restaurant, featuring French-Mediterranean cuisine with a local Cape twist, was voted one of the top ten restaurants in South Africa. Kleine Zalze Lodges, a 4-star lodge, is situated adjacent to the first fairway of the world-class De Zalze Winelands Golf Estate and enjoys panoramic views of the Stellenbosch Mountains from a variety of stylishly decorated units.

Kleine Zalze golf and wine experience (Top)
The cellar buildings (Centre)
Hand sorting of individual grape berries (Left)

ℹ️ Family Range: Shiraz, Cabernet Sauvignon (single vineyards) Sauvignon Blanc 🍷 Cab S, Shz, Sauv Bl, Pinotage, Chenin Bl, Chard, Gamay N 🕐 Mon – Sat 9 – 5, Sun 11 – 4. Closed Easter Fri, Dec 25, Jan 1 📞 +27 (0)21 880 0717 📠 +27 (0)21 880 0716 📧 quality@kleinezalze.com www.kleinezalze.com 🍷 White 3 – 4 y, reds 5 – 7 y 🍷 98, 03, 04, 05 ℹ️ tours by appt, restaurant, guest lodge, golf course, play area for children, tour groups, venue: conferences and weddings

ANNANDALE ROAD POCKET

Bordering the Blaauwklippen Road Pocket to the south is the Annandale Pocket. The climatic conditions are very similar to those of its neighbour. However, vineyards are slightly more sheltered from False Bay due to their specific location. Mainly situated on the northern slopes of Helderberg Mountain at elevations of 150 to 300 metres, the vineyards are exposed to the harsh south-easterly summer winds. Most vines are trellised to protect the developing vine shoots.

Ernie Els Wines set on the Helderberg Mountain

The soils are almost exclusively derived from granite, ranging from structured sub-soils covered by sandstone to the coveted yellow to reddish-brown mountain soils. These soils generally have a high potential, but the vines' exposure to strong, cold winds during the early summer months generally give a balanced growth and production by restricting vegetative growth in the vines.

As this Pocket stretches up the Helderberg Mountain, vines are cultivated on both low- and high-lying sites with vigour varying accordingly. Bush vines form a large percentage of the total hectares under cultivation. Trellised vines are trained between 1.2 and 1.8 metres high, creating a vertically extended canopy which reduces leaf density and increases airflow. The classic noble varieties are well represented in this Pocket, as are other varieties such as Chenin Blanc, Viognier, Petit Verdot and Mourvèdre.

The Annandale Pocket is one of the oldest established wine-producing areas in Stellenbosch and, with its highly desirable granite soils and general northern exposure, it became one of the first premium red wine areas. The oldest winery in the Pocket, Alto was one of the first wineries to produce wines

from this area. It still makes wines with Old-World class combined with New-World appeal. The generous fruit flavours of wines from this Pocket effortlessly absorb the high alcohol levels to an elegant finish of silky tannins.

Cabernet Sauvignon and Merlot are firm favourites to produce highly structured blends with some Shiraz, Cabernet Franc, Malbec and Petit Verdot softening the muscular edges of these blends. Highly recommended wines from these varietals are made at Rust en Vrede, Bilton, Hidden Valley, Ernie Els Wines and Helderkruin. Rust en Vrede's reputation is built on a steady Cabernet-Merlot blend, whereas the Ernie Els's blend incorporates other varieties such as Cabernet Franc, Malbec and Petit Verdot as well.

As single varietal wines, the reds produce fragrant red berries and savoury notes while retaining the tight tannin structure, with very impressive examples from Hidden Valley (Cabernet Sauvignon), Annandale (Shiraz) and Bilton (Merlot). High-lying Uva Mira specialises in Chardonnay; the cool ripening conditions yield wine with high natural acidity, fragrant white fruits and restrained alcohol levels, and good structure from the sensitive oaking.

83

DRIVING ROUTE: ANNANDALE ROAD

Annandale Road is the first Pocket south of Stellenbosch at the start of the Helderberg Mountain range. Leave Stellenbosch on the R44 driving towards Somerset West. Just outside the town, at the intersection with Annandale Road, turn left (into Annandale Road) at the traffic lights and drive in the direction of the mountain.

The first winery, Annandale, is on the immediate left. Annandale's owner, South African rugby legend Hempies du Toit, is a man of the earth. His big frame belies the gentle way in which he cares for his vines. The rustic cellar dating back to 1866 is home to a charming tasting room. Leaving Annandale winery, turn left back onto Annandale Road. About two kilometres further, turn right at the signs indicating Ernie Els Wines and Uva Mira. Take the right fork and continue on the tarred road to the heavy wooden gates that guard the entrance to Ernie Els Wines. The friendship between leading sportsman Ernie Els and forerunner in a new generation, wine producer Jean Engelbrecht, led them to combine their efforts in a magnificent estate where "wines are born from

a partnership of minds and hearts". The road to the cellar is a scenic drive, passing a mountain stream and young vine plantings. The striking entrance is adorned by a Koi pond and huge boulders. The tasting room has an exquisite view over False Bay towards Cape Town.

Continue up this road and take the right fork straight up the slopes to Hidden Valley Wines. A young producer, Hidden Valley has already received local and international acclaim with its Pinotage. Return to the fork in the road and this time take the left fork to the gated entrance of Uva Mira. Buzz the intercom for access. Uva Mira's vineyards cling to the steep slopes. The elevation there provides significantly cooler conditions during the warm harvest time.

Return to Annandale Road and take the left fork to Bilton and Rust en Vrede. Previously a fruit and vegetable farm, Bilton has reinvented itself to become a premium Merlot producer. The new tasting facility with deep leather chairs and large fireplace makes for cosy wine tastings in winter. Continue on this road as it passes behind Bilton's cellar to the entrance of Rust en Vrede, marked by white weather-beaten pillars proudly displaying the Rust en

Vine to cellar – transporting grapes by tractor

Vrede name. The road ends in the parking area with a babbling water feature leading to the tasting room and small gift shop. An unrestricted view from the tasting room makes you feel part of the winemaking process. A few photographs, including one of former president Nelson Mandela, subtly hint at Rust en Vrede's illustrious history. Leaving the cellar, you are greeted by one last photo: the grand image of a Rust en Vrede bottle snugly wrapped in the recognisable burnt orange paper, showing only the initials "1694 R&V" which echoes the philosophy of being an Estate of Mind.

For a break from wine tasting, visit Dombeya Farm. At the entrance to the Rust en Vrede estate, take the narrow road which leads to the left. Dombeya specializes in the production of wool, cotton and mohair, which is available from its shop. The Vineyard Kitchen serves a light lunch and snacks in this beautiful tranquil mountain setting.

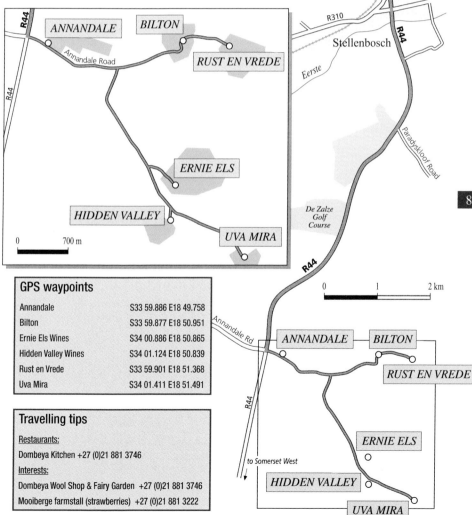

GPS waypoints

Annandale	S33 59.886 E18 49.758
Bilton	S33 59.877 E18 50.951
Ernie Els Wines	S34 00.886 E18 50.865
Hidden Valley Wines	S34 01.124 E18 50.839
Rust en Vrede	S33 59.901 E18 51.368
Uva Mira	S34 01.411 E18 51.491

Travelling tips

Restaurants:
Dombeya Kitchen +27 (0)21 881 3746
Interests:
Dombeya Wool Shop & Fairy Garden +27 (0)21 881 3746
Mooiberge farmstall (strawberries) +27 (0)21 881 3222

85

Hidden Valley Wines *Annandale Road Pocket*

Hidden Valley's exclusive range of red varieties is grown high on the Helderberg Mountain and in nearby Devon Valley. Twenty-eight hectares are cultivated on north-west-facing slopes on the Helderberg property. The elevation (420 m) and exposure to False Bay provide a moderating effect. Consequently, the grapes ripen at lower sugar levels resulting in wines with reduced alcohol.

The Devon Valley property has 25 hectares of vineyards on south-west-facing slopes. Planting density is reduced on the more fertile soils and the vines are trellised. The lower elevation here results in reduced air movement, which increases relative humidity with potentially problematic *Botrytis* and other fungal diseases. To overcome these restrictions, canopies are opened by removing excess leaves and side shoots. This increases airflow and sun penetration to dry the grapes.

Grapes for the Pinotage flagship come exclusively from a 6.3 hectare single vineyard in Devon Valley. These 35-year-old bush vines were rejuvenated by adapting pruning techniques and produce a limited yield of seven tons per hectare. Grapes are hand picked and sorted before being processed at another facility while Hidden Valley's is under construction.

Using open-top fermenters, the wine is pressed after only five days on the skins to limit extraction of grape tannins. Malolactic fermentation is completed in wood with three to four months of lees contact. This further softens and rounds out the mouthfeel. Maturation of up to 10 months gives a well-structured wine with lavender, savoury and olive characters. A limited volume is currently produced, including Pinotage, Cabernet Sauvignon, Shiraz and a Cape Blend.

On the slopes of the Helderberg

Hidden Valley Pinotage | Pinotage, Cab S, Shz, Merlot, PV, Malbec, Mouv, Sauv Bl, Viog | sales by appt | +27 (0)21 880 2646 | +27 (0)21 880 2645 | info@hiddenvalleywines.com www.hiddenvalleywines.com | 5 – 7 y | not available yet | restaurant, olives, cheese, tours by appt

Rust en Vrede *Annandale Road Pocket*

Rust en Vrede is an "estate of mind". First established in 1694, its rebirth in 1978 marked the beginning of a new era in the local wine industry, as the property was the first in South Africa to specialise in the exclusive production of red wine. The original farm buildings and vineyards have been restored to their former splendour.

Thirty-eight hectares of red varieties are cultivated on warm, north-facing foothills, on elevations of 100 to 250 metres. The northern exposure satisfies the heat and sunlight requirements, while the cooling effect of the higher elevations and the close proximity to False Bay slow and extend the ripening period.

The weathered shale and clay soils have a high water and nutrient retention; however, an underlying granite layer provides good drainage, ensuring that the roots are adequately aerated. The trellising system allows adequate airflow under the vines and through the canopy to reduce humidity and fungal diseases.

Grapes are hand picked and only the best berries are selected. High fermentation temperatures (28 – 30°C) with selected yeast, regular pump overs and punch downs assist in colour and flavour extraction, yielding elegant wines of great concentration and complexity. The wines effortlessly absorb maturation in an average of 30 per cent new oak, giving compact yet supple tannins.

The Rust en Vrede Estate is a powerful wine which is matured for up to 20 months in new French and American oak, giving the wine a solid structure with fresh, pure fruit and prominent acidity.

Beautiful outbuildings in the Cape Dutch style

Estate (Cab S / Shz/ Merlot) | Cab S, Shz, Merlot | Mon – Fri 9 – 5, Sat 9 – 5 (Oct – Apr), 9 – 4 (May – Sep), 9 – 4 Publ hols. Closed Easter Fri, Sat, Dec 25 | +27 (0)21 881 3881 | +27 (0)21 881 3000 | info@rustenvrede.com www.rustenvrede.com | 15 – 20 y | 97, 98, 01, 03 | tours during tasting hours, gifts, walks, nature conservation

Ernie Els Wines *Annandale Road Pocket*

Ernie Els, one of South Africa's leading ambassadors and sportsmen and long-standing friend, Jean Engelbrecht, created their signature wine "born from a partnership of minds and hearts". A newly completed cellar high on the Helderberg Mountain is home to the signature wine, the Engelbrecht-Els Proprietor's blend and a lifestyle range, Guardian Peak.

Forty-five hectares of mountain slopes are exclusively planted to red varieties. The northern exposure satisfies their heat and sunlight requirements, while high elevations (250 m+) and afternoon sea breezes create cool, slow ripening conditions. The planting density is low (2, 500 vines/Ha) to discourage excessive growth on the fertile clay soils, with canopies nevertheless vertically extended on trellises to accommodate increased growth. Canopies are opened by leaf and shoot removal, increasing sunlight penetration and air movement through the vines, which dries the grapes and reduces the risk of disease.

Hand-picked grapes are crushed into small, 6-ton open-top vessels and fermented warm (27°C) with selected yeast culture. The small vessels allow easy workability and five daily mixings of skins and juice (punch downs and pump over) ensure maximum colour development during the short alcoholic fermentation of five days. Post-fermentation maceration of five days stabilises the colour and flavour components. Then the skins are pressed and the young wine is transferred to barrel. Malolactic fermentation adds mid-palate weight and softens the wine's acidity. Each component develops a distinct, individual character during extended maturation of 20 months in 100 per cent new French oak. A small portion of unwooded components (5 per cent each Cab F, PV, Malbec) balances a freshness with the dark, rich fruit and dense tannins of the complex Bordeaux-styled blend.

Vineyards orientated for optimal ripening

Ernie Els Signature blend (Cab S / Merlot / PV / Malbec/ Cab F) Cab S / F, Merlot, Shz, PV, Malbec Mon – Fri 9 – 5, Sat 9 – 3 (May – Sept), Sat 9 – 4 (Oct – Apr). Closed Easter Fri, Dec 25, 26, Jan 1 +27 (0)21 881 3588 +27 (0)21 881 3688 info@ernieelswines.com www.ernieelswines.com 8 – 15 y 00, 03 gifts, spectacular views over Stellenbosch area

Uva Mira *Annandale Road Pocket*

Uva Mira is perched high on the slopes of the Helderberg Mountain. Thirty hectares of vines are located at an astonishing 420 to 620 metres above sea level, providing a much cooler climate. Mature Sauvignon Blanc vines (18 y) are planted at the highest point in order to give highly concentrated flavours. The vines are trellised on decomposed granite and clay soils and green harvest restricts yields. Grapes from the single vineyard Chardonnay, with an altitude of 550 metres, are whole- bunch pressed to avoid skin contact and harsh tannins. Fermented naturally in barrel with lees, the grapes produce a rich, citrus and creamy wine with a restrained alcohol content of 13 per cent due to the cool ripening conditions. The Sauvignon Blanc is fermented reductively at low temperatures (12°C) in order to protect its pungent tropical fruit and gooseberry flavours. Red varieties are wooded after both alcoholic and malolactic fermentation are complete. These wines are matured for 18 months in French barrels, giving dense tannins and a dry finish to the aromatic red blend.

Vineyard Selection Chardonnay (sgl vineyard), Uva Mira (red blend: Cab S/ Merlot / Shz) Cab S/F, Merlot, Shz, Sauv Bl, Chard, Viog Mon – Fri 8:30 – 5 Sat 9:30 – 1. Closed Christian hols, Jan 1 +27 (0)21 880 1683 +27 (0)21 880 1682 info@uvamira.co.za www.uvamira.co.za Chard 5 y, red 8 y+ 04 organically grown proteas (seasonal availability), fynbos conservation

Cold Atlantic air – cooling the vineyards

Shiraz

In South Africa, Shiraz (Syrah) produces an inky black texture and distinctive nose of leather, spice and pepper. Warmer areas produce wines with higher alcohol levels, high extract and flavours of sweet chocolate and coffee, while cooler Pockets produce dark, spicy wines with hints of pepper. Grapes are harvested very ripe, to the point where the berry skin starts to wrinkle. Shiraz is generally oak matured. American oak imparts a sweet vanilla character, while French oak enhances the inherent spicy, dark chocolate and smoky characters. Shiraz produces structured single varietal wines and interesting blends with Viognier (perfumed Rhône-style), Mourvèdre, Grenache and other varieties.

Fermented Shiraz grapes ready for pressing

Annandale *Annandale Road Pocket*

The historic Annandale Wine Estate dates back to 1866 and is home to some serious red wines. Springbok rugby legend Hempies du Toit established 45 hectares of vines along west and east-facing foothills of the Helderberg Mountain. Vineyards are cultivated on gravelly granite-based soils, which have a high potential. The crop is limited to 7 tons/Ha by strict canopy management and slightly increased planting densities of 3, 750 vines per hectare, producing concentrated fruit. Vertical trellising protects the vines from the strong prevailing south-easterly wind. Hand-selected grapes are crushed and destemmed before fermentation with selected yeast culture. The extended skin contact creates wines with great extraction and depth. Maturation is extended to 36 months (on the flagship) with a combination of new and older French oak barrels, which delivers elegant, well-integrated wines. Hempies regards walking through the cellar and vineyards as "food for a person's soul".

[i] Cabernet Sauvignon [icon] Cab S, F, Shz, Merlot [clock] Mon – Sat 9 – 5 . Closed Christian hols [icon] 27 (0)21 881 3560 [fax] +27 (0)21 881 3562 [email] annandale@telkomsa.net [icon] 10 – 15y [icon] 99, 01 [i] 17th century rustic cellar, 6 generations of wine tradition

Bilton *Annandale Road Pocket*

Vines were first planted on Bilton's historic property in 1726. The original cellar (circa 1824) still graces the estate. Bilton commands only a small portion of the 105 hectares of vineyards established on various exposures of the Helderberg Mountain. The fertile granite soils necessitate and increased planting density (4, 000 vines /Ha) to temper high vigour growth. Using a standard cordon height, the canopy is vertically extended on a higher trellis to increase the sunlight exposure as the leaf surface receives first light in the late morning due to mountain shadow. This, alongside frequent mountain mists and cool sea breezes, facilitates slow, even ripening of even the delicate Sauvignon Blanc grapes. Red wines are fermented in open-top vessels at high temperatures (28°C) resulting in typical New World fruitiness while retaining some austerity. Maturation is extended to 18 months using older oak barrels and a higher alcohol (Alc. 14,1% by Vol.) goes almost undetected as it fits seamlessly into the fine tannin structure and upfront fruit.

[i] Merlot [icon] Merlot, Cab S, Shz [clock] Mon – Fri 8:30 – 4:30, Sat 9 – 1 (Oct – Apr). Closed public holidays [icon] +27 (0)21 881 3714 [fax] +27 (0)21 8813721 [email] sales@biltonwines.com www.biltonwines.co.za [icon] 6 y [icon] 04 [i] Gluhwein and a winter fireplace, BYO picnics, boules court, walks

HELDERBERG POCKET

The Helderberg Pocket takes its name from the towering Helderberg Mountain. Vineyards here are planted at a relatively high elevation and as the Pocket lies within seven to eight kilometres from False Bay, it enjoys the full benefit of cooling sea breezes.

The soils are mainly derived from granite, although small patches of shale do occur. As with neighbouring mountainside Pockets, the soils are yellow to reddish-brown and well drained with a high potential. The induced growth vigour of the vines is halted by cold and often strong early summer winds, which ensures a good balance between the vigour of the vine and its fruit production. This balance is a requirement for the production of premium quality wine grapes.

The vineyards of the Helderberg Pocket are spread over the foothills with elevations of 60 metres to over 400 metres above sea level. Due to the elevation and subsequent soil variation, vines are cultivated both as untrained bush vines and on vertical trellises. Bush vines are largely concentrated in the lower-lying areas. Large variations in planting density occur due to the steepness of slopes, from as little as 2, 500 vines on the steepest slopes to 4, 500 vines per hectare in lower-lying areas.

This Pocket is well known for its refined white and red wines. The red wines have very prominent blue and black berry aromas, a fine tannin structure and generally a moderate alcohol level. All the noble varieties are represented in this Pocket, as well as a significant portion of Chenin Blanc. Cabernet Sauvignon, Merlot and Shiraz are the favourite red varieties and are represented in blends as well as in single varietal wines.

The spectacular Helderberg Mountain

Grangehurst's weighty red blends benefit from extended oak maturation. By releasing the wines after substantial maturation (3 years) in their own cellar, Grangehurst ensures these wines have attained a degree of accessibility. Interestingly, Cordoba has a Cabernet Franc-based blend with some Cabernet Sauvignon and Merlot adding a mineral tone to the wine.

Vineyards lying on the lower slopes tend to produce more rustic wines, with the old bush vines of Stonewall yielding a highly concentrated Cabernet Sauvignon with typical plum and cassis flavours. Wines from Avontuur, Eikendal, Yonder Hill and Somerbosch show more upfront sweet fruit and choc-mintiness. In line with the substantial wines from this Pocket, JP Bredell produces a spicy Shiraz and fortified red wines from traditional Portuguese varieties.

Lushof's Sauvignon Blanc shows a fresh, light appeal of goose-berries and white fruit with some herbaceous characters, while seriously styled Chenin Blancs are produced at Post House and Ken Forrester. The Chenin Blancs have a definite Old World structure and great complexity with aromas of apple, marzipan, a lime acidity and steely finish.

DRIVING ROUTE: HELDERBERG

The Helderberg Pocket is located on the slopes of the towering Helderberg Mountain and lies just south of the town of Stellenbosch. Take the R44 (south) from Stellenbosch towards Somerset West. About 10 kilometres out of town, you pass a large dam on the right. A few metres further, turn right onto Eikendal Road towards the mountain. Less than one kilometre further is the entrance to the first winery to visit, Grangehurst. This family-owned boutique winery specialises in classic red wines and is one of the few wineries to release wines after three years of bottle aging. The airy tasting room is decorated with stained glass windows and a very interesting wall-mounted corkscrew (locally manufactured).

Along Eikendal Road, old bush vines have been trained to a low trellis system to facilitate picking and canopy management. Even further up the foothills lies Lushof (Eng. Garden of Eden), another family-owned boutique winery. At this high elevation of 350 metres above sea level, Sauvignon Blanc grapes thrive in the cool afternoon ocean breezes.

Return to the R44, turn left and drive south. About two kilometres further, at the Firgrove turn-off (R102 / M6 to Macassar), the foothills of the mountain even out to a gentle slope towards the ocean. Turn right onto Winery Road (R102) and right again on Raithby Road. Less than a kilometre further on is the entrance to Post House Cellar on the right. Previously the official post office of the settlement of Raithby, this property still boasts a bright red post box at the entrance. Owner Nick Gebers not only makes wine, but also lovingly tends his collection of bonsai trees. Right next door to Post House Cellar, is the L'Auberge Du Paysan restaurant, where Alsatian-born owner Frederick Thermann serves French cuisine in a brasserie setting. The high-back chairs and heavy drapes are the perfect background to enjoy a meal with the local wines. Thermann makes his own wines from a tiny two hectare vineyard behind the restaurant.

Return to the R44, turn right and a drive to the last winery on the route. Stonewall takes its name from the low, white-washed wall that encloses the farmyard like a typical French Clos. To return to Cape Town, continue south on the R44 to the N2.

The unmistakeable white wall around the homestead of Stonewall

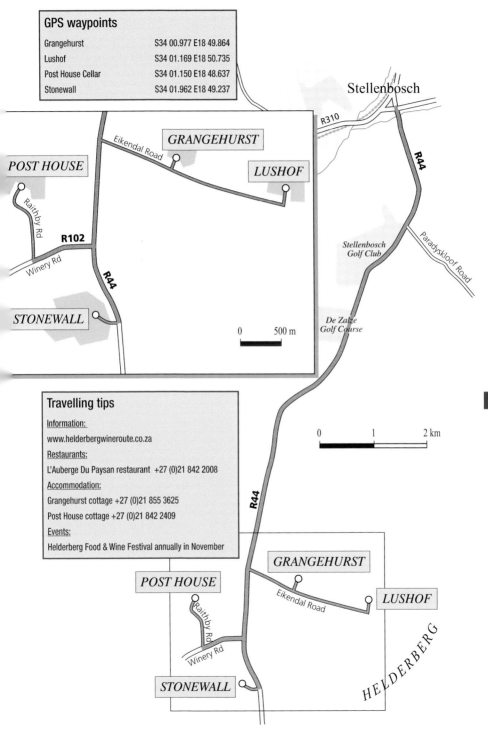

GPS waypoints

Grangehurst	S34 00.977 E18 49.864
Lushof	S34 01.169 E18 50.735
Post House Cellar	S34 01.150 E18 48.637
Stonewall	S34 01.962 E18 49.237

Stellenbosch

R310

GRANGEHURST

Eikendal Road

POST HOUSE

LUSHOF

R44

Raithby Rd

R102

Winery Rd

R44

Stellenbosch
Golf Club

Paradyskloof Road

STONEWALL

0   500 m

De Zalze
Golf Course

91

Travelling tips

Information:
www.helderbergwineroute.co.za
Restaurants:
L'Auberge Du Paysan restaurant +27 (0)21 842 2008
Accommodation:
Grangehurst cottage +27 (0)21 855 3625
Post House cottage +27 (0)21 842 2409
Events:
Helderberg Food & Wine Festival annually in November

0   1   2 km

R44

POST HOUSE

Raithby Rd

GRANGEHURST

Eikendal Road

LUSHOF

Winery Rd

STONEWALL

HELDERBERG

Grangehurst *Helderberg Pocket*

Grangehurst is a specialist red wine producer situated on the lower slopes of the Helderberg Mountain. Most of the grapes are sourced from neighbouring vineyards which are cultivated on a variety of sandy-gravelly soils. An underlying clay layer ensures sufficient water and nutrient retention. Grapes are also sourced from Devon Valley and Stellenbosch Kloof. Grangehurst's own Sunset Vineyard, in the Stellenbosch-Simonsberg Pocket, also provides the cellar with Cabernet Sauvignon, Pinotage, Merlot, Shiraz, Mourvèdre and Petit Verdot grapes. The various vineyards, which benefit from the cool sea breezes from False Bay, comprise both trellised as well as bush vines. Fermentation is done in traditional open-top fermenters with regular punch-downs to extract colour, flavours and tannin from the skins, which are basket pressed. The wines are matured for 12 to 24 months in French and American oak barrels before being blended and bottled at Grangehurst using a gentle gravity flow filling system.

ℹ️ Nikela (Xhosa "Tribute") blend Cab S/Merlot/Pinotage
🍷 Cab S, Pinotage, Merlot, Shz, Mouv, PV ⏰ Mon – Fri 9 – 4, Sat, publ hols "take a chance" 9 – 4 📞 +27 (0)21 855 3625
📠 +27 (0)21 855 2143 ✉️ winery@grangehurst.co.za
www.grangehurst.co.za 📧 Potential: 8 – 12 y 💰 95, 00
ℹ️ self-catering guest cottage

Lushof *Helderberg Pocket*

Lushof celebrated the new millennium with its maiden vintage. Only 12 hectares of vines are cultivated on north and west-facing Helderberg slopes with ample sun exposure. Steep slopes ensure the granite soils are well drained, but planting density has not been decreased in order to control growth vigour on this fertile soil. The high elevation (350 m) and the close proximity of the ocean cool the vineyards for slow, even ripening. Side shoots and excess leaves are removed to increase air circulation and sunlight, which reduces fungal diseases and promotes colour development in red grapes. Young vineyards are harvested several times to ensure that only ripe grapes are selected for vinification. Unwooded Sauvignon Blanc yields granadilla, lime and grass aromas, backed up by lees aging, which gives depth and mellows its crisp acidity. The firm and slightly austere fruit of the red wines (from cool ripening conditions) are tempered by maturation in 30 per cent new French oak, producing attractive mint, chocolate and coffee notes.

ℹ️ Sauvignon Blanc 🍷 Sauv Bl, Cab S, Merlot, Shz, Chard
⏰ Mon – Fri 9 – 5. Closed publ hols 📞 +27 (0)21 855 3134
📠 +27 (0)21 855 3623 ✉️ lushof@icon.co.za
www.lushof.co.za 📧 3 – 4 y 💰 01, 03 ℹ️ tours by appt., view of Robben Island on clear days

Viticultural paradise – the foothills of the Helderberg Mountain

Post House Cellar *Helderberg Pocket*

Nick Gebers built the Post House boutique cellar next to his old farmhouse, which historically operated as a small local post office for the tiny village of Raithby. The old, bright red post box on the farm served as the inspiration for this brand. Thirty-eight hectares of vines are planted on the Helderberg Mountain foothills. Red varieties are planted on gentle west-facing aspects and Chenin Blanc on the cooler south-facing aspect. Marginal gravel and clay soils with high moisture retention result in balanced vines without excessive growth. Situated seven kilometres from False Bay, cool breezes moderate the summer temperatures and the east-west row direction shades the grapes from the hot afternoon sun. Vineyards are trellised, spreading the canopy vertically, and leaves are removed on the south side to allow filtered sunlight through the vines. This assists in the development of tannins and colour.

Grapes are harvested and sorted before being lightly crushed and destalked. Red grapes are naturally fermented in open stainless steel tanks at 28 – 30°C and skins are punched down regularly for optimum colour development. Malolactic fermentation takes place in barrels and the wine is matured for 18 months with rackings to remove unwanted sediment that settles out. Wines are not filtered and receive a gentle egg white fining prior to bottling.

The inky Penny Black blend is Shiraz/ Merlot dominated (32 per cent each) including some Cabernet Sauvignon and Petit Verdot, while a single block of Merlot is vinified separately. White grapes are crushed and receive two hours of skin contact before pressing. The clear juice is naturally fermented in barrel and the wine is left on its lees. This softens the acids and gives weight to the mid-palate of this steely dry wine.

Steady ripening – Helderberg vineyards basking in the afternoon sun

🛈 Penny Black (Shz / Merlot / PV / Cab S), Merlot (sgl vineyard) 🍇 Cab S, Merlot, Shz, PV, Pinotage, Chenin Bl, Viog ⏰ Mon – Fri 8:30 – 5, Sat 9 – 1 ☎ +27 (0)21 842 2409 ✉ ngebers@iafrica.co.za www.posthousewines.co.za 🍷 Chenin 5 y, Reds 8 – 10 y 🏆 99, 00, 01, 03 ℹ bonsai garden, cellar tours, B&B cottage, guests may book hikes and trout fishing

Stonewall *Helderberg Pocket*

In true French Clos style, Stonewall's farmyard is separated from its vineyards by an historic wall dating from the 19th century. Of the 75 hectares of vineyards, Stonewall selects only 10 per cent of the yield for its own label. Planted on north-facing foothills of the Helderberg Mountain, the vineyards are situated in shallow, sandy loam soils. Vines receive supplementary irrigation on the poor sandy soil and naturally produce a low grape yield and harvesting is not requied. The small berries have a higher skin to juice ratio, improving colour and flavour extraction. The close proximity of the ocean and frequent breezes create cool, even ripening conditions. Grapes are hand harvested and fermented with regular punch downs for colour extraction. Once fermentation is completed and the required level of extraction is achieved, the skins are pressed. Malolactic fermentation is completed before wines are transferred to barrels. Fifty per cent new wood and 18 months of maturation yield a concentrated Cabernet Sauvignon from the low-yielding bush vines.

🛈 Cabernet Sauvignon 🍇 Cab S, Cab F, Merlot, Chard, Sauv Bl ⏰ by appt Mon – Fri 9 – 5, Sat 9 – 1. Closed Easter Fri, Sun, Dec 25, 26, Jan 1 ☎ +27 (0)21 855 3675 📠 +27 (0)21 855 2206 ✉ stonewall@mweb.co.za 🍷 6 – 10 y 🏆 03 ℹ historic stone wall dating to 19th century, wine cellar circa 1828

SCHAAPENBERG POCKET

The Schaapenberg Pocket is situated at 100 to 200 metres above sea level around the northern, western and southern slopes of the Schaapenberg Mountain. The very close proximity to False Bay (5 – 7 km) renders relatively cool ripening conditions and both red and white grape varieties achieve excellent flavour concentration here.

Geologically, Schaapenberg is a granitic summit surrounded by shale foothills. Most of the vineyards are situated on the latter, which range from moderate potential, very stony residual soils to high potential and highly weathered yellow to reddish-brown soils which are well drained and favourably structured. Excessive vigour on the latter is curtailed by the strong south-easterly wind during the early summer months.

The strong south-easterly wind not only reduces growth vigour in the vines but also creates great difficulty in canopy management. Detailed attention is given to windbreaks around vineyards and the spacing of trellis wires to protect the young shoots. Alongside the classic noble varieties, some Nebbiolo, Sangiovese, Petit Verdot and Viognier are also cultivated.

The Schaapenberg Pocket is known for its similarly good red and white wines, showing cool climate characters. Lourensford's delicate Viognier has sweet floral aromas, while the white wines from Vergelegen are more powerful. Vergelegen's trademark Sémillon, with insipid waxiness, gives structure and palate weight to the white blend as well as producing a rich reserve wine for aging. Sauvignon Blanc and Chardonnay vineyards on the Schaapenberg show distinct minerality and wet slate character. The red wines of Schaapenberg are Cabernet

Sauvignon dominated, with hugely powerful and dense blends bearing the mark of Old World elegance. However, some fynbos and herb characters show its South African origin. The red wines from Morgenster and Lourensford are more restrained, while Vergelegen's blends are very complex and single varietal reds have graceful elegance.

DRIVING ROUTE: SCHAAPENBERG

Schaapenberg is the southernmost Pocket of the Stellenbosch region. Facing the ocean, this Pocket's vineyards are never far from the cooling ocean breezes. From the starting point in Stellenbosch, drive south on the R44, leaving the town behind. About 16 kilometres from Stellenbosch, turn left at the traffic lights of a large intersection onto Main Road (M9). At the fourth traffic light, turn left onto Lourensford Road. At the following four traffic circles (3 km), take the second exit each time. The impressive gates of Vergelegen (Eng. Far placed) on the right welcome visitors to this internationally renowned winery.

Steeped in history from the Simon van der Stel era, Vergelegen's cellar is anything but old fashioned. Hi-tech equipment and measurements provide detailed information on every aspect, from the soils and vineyards to the grapes, juice and wines in the cellar. Vergelegen also offers a variety of culinary experiences namely: the Camphor Forest Picnic, the Rose Terrace for alfresco meals and the Lady Philips Restaurant for a fine dining experience.

Travelling tips

Restaurants:
Camphor Forest picnic, Rose Terrace, Lady Philips (Vergelegen) +27 (0)21 847 1334

Interests:
Helderberg Nature Reserve +27 (0)21 851 4060

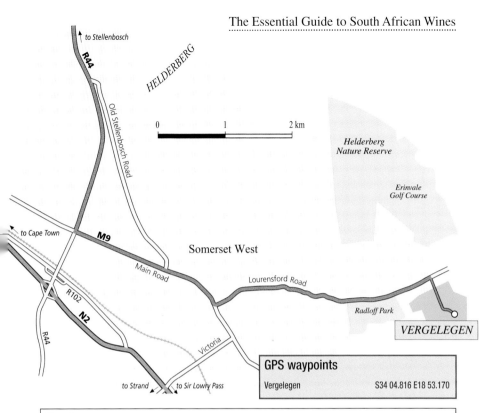

↑ to Stellenbosch

HELDERBERG

R44

Old Stellenbosch Road

0   1   2 km

Helderberg Nature Reserve

Erinvale Golf Course

← to Cape Town   **M9**

Somerset West

Main Road

Lourensford Road

Radloff Park

R102

N2

R44

Victoria

VERGELEGEN

to Strand   to Sir Lowry Pass

GPS waypoints

Vergelegen   S34 04.816 E18 53.170

Vergelegen *Schaapenberg Pocket*

Vergelegen was originally granted to Governor Willem Adriaan van der Stel in 1700 by the Dutch East India Company. A knowledgeable and practical farmer, he soon proved his skills by successfully planting 500 000 vines, camphor trees, fruit trees and vegetables.

Today, Vergelegen is planted to 126 hectares of vines on the slopes of the Hottentots-Holland Mountains in fertile gravel and clay soils. Planting densities have been increased to between 6, 000 and 8, 000 vines per hectare to control vegetative growth. Heat-sensitive white varieties are planted on elevated (220 – 300 m), south-facing slopes to maximise cool ocean breezes from False Bay and a vertical trellis system protects young shoots from the prevailing south-easterly wind.

White grapes are whole-bunch pressed with press and free-run juice fermented collectively providing structure to the wine. Barrel fermented and matured for 10 months, the Sémillon's waxy mouthfeel and the Sauvignon Blanc's melon and citrus tones combine with the spicy, subtle oaking to give a rich, dense blended white wine. Schaapenberg Reserve receives skin and yeast lees contact to soften piercing acidity and the wine shows rare blackcurrant leaf and fynbos notes on a mineral palate. Red grapes are naturally fermented and macerated for three weeks to achieve maximum tannin and colour extraction. Skins are pressed and the young wine completes malolactic fermentation in barrels to soften the acid and add mid-palate weight. The powerful red flagship matures for 24 months in 100 per cent new oak. Its dense fruit balances the strong oaking. Components are blended after 14 months when they have developed their own distinct characters.

Vergelegen's modern cellar facilities

ℹ Vergelegen Red (Bdx blend, Cab S / F / Merlot), Vergelegen White (blend Sauv Bl / Sém), Schaapenberg Reserve Sauvignon Blanc (sgl vineyard) Cab S / F, Sauv Bl, Merlot, Chard, Sém, Shz Daily 9:30 – 16:30 +27 (0)21 847 1334 +27 (0)21 847 1608 info@vergelegen.co.za red 10 y+, white 5 – 10 y 98, 01, 03 , 04, 05 "interpretive centre" depicting the farm's history and self-guided tour to homestead, gifts, tour groups, winery tour, restaurants

STELLENBOSCH-SIMONSBERG POCKET

The Stellenbosch-Simonsberg Pocket is situated along the south-western slopes of the Simonsberg, Skurweberg and Klapmutskop Mountains. Characterised by high-lying sites (200 – 500 m) and soils with a high potential, this Pocket runs over folding slopes creating variations in exposure and cultivation techniques. Although it is located 25 to 30 kilometres from the ocean, the relatively high elevations and south-western aspects ensure that the vineyards benefit from cooling airflow. However, the average summer daytime temperature in this Pocket is slightly higher than for areas to the south of Stellenbosch.

The diverse topography of the foothills and mountainside valleys allows a wide variety of options concerning the choice and placement of grape varieties. Soils here are almost exclusively derived from granite, yielding high potential. These soils are yellow to reddish-brown and acidic but favourably structured with good water and nutrient retention properties.

Excessive growth due to the high potential of the soil is curtailed by strong south-easterly winds which blow during early summer as well as high planting densities (4, 000 vines/Ha+) to create inter-plant competition and restrain growth. As the very strong easterly winds can cause extensive damage to the developing shoots and bunches, vines are trained on a vertical trellis system with the wires offering protection to the young shoots.

Most vineyards are trellised between 1.4 and 1.8 metres with spur pruning vertical positioning shoots. Several plantings of Sangiovese, Mourvèdre, Petit Verdot, Pinot Noir, Viognier, Chenin Blanc and Sémillon are found alongside the classic noble varieties.

In most cases, vine row direction is dictated by the slope, but where possible rows are orientated south-west to north-east in order to utilise the cool summer breezes to moderate the warm days. Windbreaks are used on sites which are exposed to the strong south-easterly winds early in the growing season.

The Stellenbosch-Simonsberg Pocket is primarily suited for red wines and Bordeaux-styled red blends, although exuberantly fruity Chardonnay wines are produced at Rustenberg, Morgenhof and Warwick. Simonsberg *terroir* characteristics include earthy and abundant fruit aromas on red wines and tropical fruit and flinty flavours on white wines. The reds are generally well structured and mature well, usually requiring some time after release to reach their best form.

Pinotage from the Stellenbosch-Simonsberg Pocket has more earthy tones than the wines from Bottelary. L'Avenir, Morgenhof and Kanonkop produce their Pinotage from old bush vines, yielding highly concentrated wines with dense strawberry fruit structure, spicy earthy notes and dry tannins.

The Cabernet Sauvignon-based blends from Muratie, Knorhoek, L'Avenir and Delheim are less overtly powerful, but show dark fruit, cassis and cedar notes. The single varietal wines (Rustenberg, Uitkyk) show a boldly ripe structure, cassis notes and fine tannins. Interestingly Marklew, Knorhoek and Remhoogte include a small portion of Pinotage in their red blends, which have a rich, velvety palate and fine tannins.

Muratie's Pinot Noir is made from the first vines of this variety to be planted in South Africa, more than 75 years ago. The wines show hints of forest floor and delicate red currant with a silky, soft finish.

DRIVING ROUTE:
STELLENBOSCH-SIMONSBERG

The Stellenbosch-Simonsberg Pocket starts a little (5 km) north-east of the town of Stellenbosch. Drive north on the R44 (towards the N1 freeway). Leaving Stellenbosch, the Simonsberg Mountain rises from the east. On the periphery of the town lies the Nietvoorbij Research Centre, where research is done into wine related issues such as vineyard trellising systems, pests, soil analysis and winemaking.

The first winery on the route is Morgenhof, owned by Anne Cointreau-Huchon. Arriving at the gate, you can see the vineyard rows following the contours of the hills. Morgenhof caters for larger groups and have ample tasting facilities as well as a restaurant. The beautiful chapel and gardens remain a choice wedding venue. From Morgenhof, continue on the R44 to the boutique winery of Remhoogte situated on the right, just past a fort-like façade on the left. Remhoogte's vineyards are cultivated high on the foothills of the Simonsberg. World-famous Michel Rolland has teamed up with the Boustred family to produce their wines.

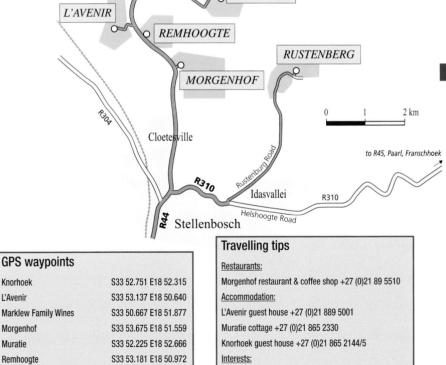

97

A game camp on the property is home to zebra, springbok, eland, black wildebeest and the shy black swan.

On the opposite side of the R44 is L'Avenir, well known for its champion Pinotage. L'Avenir's property saddles an area between Simonsberg and the Bottelary Hills. Pinotage is doing particularly well in lower-lying sites towards the Bottelary Pocket, while Cabernet Sauvignon and Merlot enjoy the foothills of the Simonsberg Mountain.

Over the next hill lies the small, secluded valley of Knorhoek, boasting some impressive wines. At the Knorhoek Road sign, turn right into the valley and follow the road. The left fork leads to Muratie. A wall of remembrance outside the homestead reflects the centuries of owners of this property. Exercise care when driving through Muratie, as the road leads straight through the farmyard where ducks, dogs and wine tasters cross the road. The charming old cellar with low ceilings and thick walls provides wonderful photo opportunities.

Retrace the route back to the fork. The right fork leads further up the valley to Knorhoek winery. Knorhoek (Eng. Growl Corner) has taken its name from "the place

where lions roar". During the pioneering days, feline predators scaled the high kraal walls at night to prey on domestic livestock. The Cape mountain lion became extinct by the late 1700s. However, caracal are occasionally seen on the farm and leopard sightings still occur in the higher reaches of the surrounding mountains, hence the use of the leopard on the Knorhoek estate flagship wine labels.

The road rises to Marklew Family Wines, the Pocket's last winery on the north-western side of Simonsberg. Marklew is a family-owned winery, and the young brother-and-sister team are determined to follow in the footsteps of their acclaimed vinous neighbours.

From Marklew Family Wines, drive back towards Stellenbosch, and turn left onto Helshoogte Road (R310) at the periphery of the town. At the first traffic light, turn left onto Rustenberg Road, and follow the road to the southern foothills of Simonsberg Mountain. At the fork, keep left to visit Rustenberg, the last winery on this route. Magnificent oak trees line the road to the winery and modern tasting facility. A Chartres-style stone labyrinth in the garden offers a moment of quiet introspection, while the lush gardens and pastures make for wonderful walks.

Grand design – classic Cape Dutch architecture set in autumn colours at Rustenberg Estate

Rustenberg *Stellenbosch-Simonsberg Pocket*

Rustenberg is located in the southern Simonsberg amphitheatre. Winemaking started on the farm in the late 1600s, but it was only in 1892 that the first Rustenberg wine was bottled by John X Merriman. Only five winemakers have overseen the crush in the last 100 years, testimony to the commitment and long-term vision of the proprietors. The range of wine includes two single vineyard wines, a regional *terroir* range (incl. John X Merriman blend) and a lifestyle range called Brampton.

One hundred and fifty hectares are now cultivated on decomposed granite with the alluvial component increasing near the Krom River. Cabernet Sauvignon is cultivated in the bowl of the amphitheatre, where warmer air accumulates. On elevated slopes (180 – 480 m), white and red varieties are planted to a slightly lower density, where the vines also benefit from cooler ripening conditions. Mature vines dominate (80 per cent of the vines are 10 – 20 y) resulting in consistent, bold, strong wines. In the single block Cabernet Sauvignon, selected bunches are individually tagged at the onset of the growing season and berries are selected at harvest to create an intense and highly structured wine.

Natural fermentation adds complexity to the wines with the reds fermented at warm temperatures (28°C) with regular pump overs and three to four weeks of maceration to extract and stabilise colour. The Merriman blend includes fruit from 28 parcels and is blended only towards the end of 20 months' oak maturation. Use of large barrels (500l), malolactic fermentation and 14 months' maturation in oak give the Chardonnay a rich and dry mid-palate with subtle wood flavours.

Old casks still bearing the Rustenburg name

ℹ️ John X Merriman (Bdx blend), Peter Barlow (Cab S, single vineyard), Five Soldiers (Chardonnay, single vineyard) 🍇 Cab S/F, Chard, Merlot, Malbec, Mouv, PV, Shz, Viog, Rouss, Sauv Bl 🕐 Mon – Fri 9 – 4:30, Sat 10 – 1:30 (10 – 3:30 Dec, Jan). Closed Easter Fri, Dec 25, Jan 1 ☎ +27 (0)21 809 1200 📠 +27 (0)21 809 1219 ✉️ wine@rustenberg.co.za www.rustenberg.co.za 🗺️ P Barlow, John X 10 y+; 5 Soldiers 4 y ⬛ P Barlow 99, 01, 5 Soldiers 01, 02, John X 97 (magnum), 01, 02 🔖 labyrinth, exquisite garden, dairy viewing

Muratie Estate *Stellenbosch-Simonsberg Pocket*

Established in 1685, Muratie was the first estate to plant Pinot Noir (1927). The winery is set in the historic cellar dating back to the 1930s. Forty hectares are cultivated on gentle north-west-facing slopes in granite soils. The high elevation (185 – 300 m) and afternoon breezes assist in cooling the vineyards. This cooling effect is increased by a higher cordon trellis (1 m), permitting air movement under the vines as well as reducing radiant heat to slow and extend the ripening period. The Ansela wine was named after emancipated slave Ansela van der Caap who married Muratie's first owner more than 350 years ago. Red grapes for the blend are fermented slightly cooler (26°C) to restrict tannin extraction from the skins matured for 12 months with 35 per cent new French oak, giving a discreet tannin backbone to the sultry, dark wine. Intensely aromatic Shiraz shows vanilla notes from American oak and the accessible vintage port is the only one to include Souzão.

ℹ️ Ansela (Merlot / Cab S) 🍇 Cab S, F, Merlot, Shz, P N, Chard, port varieties 🕐 Mon – Fri 9 – 5 Sat Sun 10 – 4. Closed Easter Fri, Dec 25, Jan 1 ☎ +27 (0)21 865 2330 📠 +27 (0)21 865 2351 ✉️ muratie@kingsley.co.za www.muratie.co.za ⬛ Potential: 5 y ⬛ 01, 02, 03 🔖 oldest block of Pinot Noir, charming working cellar (circa 1930s)

Remhoogte *Stellenbosch-Simonsberg Pocket*

Remhoogte's boutique cellar produces French-styled red blends under the guidance of the French viticulturalist (and shareholder), Michel Rolland. Thirty-three hectares of vines have been established on the mountain slope, in fertile, heavy clay soils. A low planting density (2, 800 vines/Ha) restricts growth vigour and vines are trellised with a vertically extended canopy to increase sunlight exposure as well as airflow. The summer south-easterly winds cool and dry the vineyards and lightly stress the vines resulting in greater fruit concentration. To express its dark fruit characters (plum and blackberries), Pinotage is cultivated as bush vines. Merlot is planted on cooler south-facing slopes to avoid water stress. Shiraz is planted on warmer northern slopes giving very ripe fruit. Grapes are sorted before vinification in French oak containers, then the wine completes malolactic fermentation to soften the acid and round off the mid-palate. The wine is matured for 20 months, resulting in an intensely rich wine with a high alcohol content (14 – 15% by Vol.) and fine tannin structure.

ℹ️ Bonne Nouvelle (Cape Blend: Merlot / Cabernet Sauvignon / Pinotage) 🍇 Merlot, Cab S, Pinotage, Shz 🕐 Mon – Fri 9 – 4 ☎ +27 (0)21 889 5005 📠 +27 (0)21 889 6907 ✉️ remhoogte@adept.co.za ⬛ 8 – 10 y ⬛ 03, 04 🔖 game, olive oil, collection of hunting trophies

Morgenhof *Stellenbosch-Simonsberg Pocket*

Morgenhof holds a sense of history (est. 1692) in the French/Old Cape-toned yard with tree-shaded lawns and beautiful Tastevin. Only 70 hectares of this large farm are planted to vines, in deep granite and shale-based soils. The clay component provides good water retention and dry-land cultivation is practised. Vines are trellised to spread the canopy vertically and increase sun exposure. Wider spacing (2, 800 vines/Ha) on steep slopes encourages extensive root development. The Sauvignon Blanc is planted on elevated (400 m) south-facing slopes that benefit from a cooling effect for expression of varietal flavours. Reds are placed on warm northern slopes to fulfil their heat and sun-exposure requirements for ripening. Drought-sensitive Merlot is sited on lower slopes (150 m) in clay soils with ground cover to prevent water loss.

White grapes are pressed and the cleared juice cold fermented (12°C) to preserve delicate flavours. Mature Chenin Blanc vines (mid-30s) provide quince and honey flavours with gentle oaking softening the crisp acidity. The dry MCC is Chardonnay dominated, with a fine mousse after two years lees maturation in bottle.

Reds are fermented warm (28°C) with pump overs for better colour extraction. Complete malolactic fermentation adds complexity. The blend is matured for 20 months in a combination of old and new wood barrels to ensure elegant oaking. Once bottled, the wine is matured further for three years before being released into the market. Fantail Wines targets the younger wine drinker, distinctive as the eye-catching fantail which graces the label.

Peaceful retreat – Morgenhof's formal garden and tower

Première Sélection (Bdx blend Cab S / Merlot / Cab F / Malbec)　Sauv Bl, Chard, Chenin Bl, Cab S /F, Merlot, Malbec, PV, PN　Mon – Fri 9 – 5:30 Sat/Sun 10 – 5 (Nov – Apr); Mon – Fri 9 – 4:30 Sat/Sun 10 – 3 (May – Oct). Closed Dec 25, Jan 1　+27 (0)21 889 5510　+27 (0)21 889 5266　info@morgenhof.com www.morgenhof.com　8 – 12 y　93, 94, 97, 98, 04, 05　restaurant, tour groups, children welcome, helipad, functions venue, formal rose garden

Knorhoek *Stellenbosch-Simonsberg Pocket*

Knorhoek's Van Niekerk family has been in residence for five generations, but only crushed their maiden vintage in 1997. The guest house, originally a clay-and-stone structure housing stables, offers old-world charm. One hundred hectares of vineyards are cultivated on the north and west-facing foothills of the Simonsberg Mountain. The high altitude (200 – 380 m) provides some cooling effect and canopies of east-west-directed rows shade grape bunches during the hottest hours of the day. A low planting density is used on the steep slopes and vines are trellised to protect the grapes from the strong summer winds. In the recently upgraded cellar, winemaking stays traditional, using open-top fermenters and warm temperatures (close to 30° C to prevent the paint-like character in Pinotage) for red wines. The Pantere Cape Blend receives extended maturation (23 months) before bottling, resulting in a dense wine showing rich, sweet berry fruit with a high alcohol content.

Pantere (Cape Blend: Cab S / Merlot / Shz / Pinotage)　Cab S / F, Shz, Merlot, Pinotage, Chenin Bl, Sauv Bl　Mon – Fri 9 – 5, Sat – Sun 10 – 3. Closed Dec 25　+27 (0)21 865 2627　office@knorhoek.co.za www. knorhoek.co.za　5 –7 y　97, 01, 03　restaurant / lapa Sept – May 12 – 4, guest house, conference & functions venue, entertainment, children's facilities, tour groups, walks

Marklew Family Wines *Stellenbosch-Simonsberg Pocket*

Marklew's boutique cellar lies at the foot of the Simonsberg Mountain. Forty-four hectares of varying aspects are planted to vines. Sauvignon Blanc and Chardonnay are cultivated on the highest sites (210 – 290 m), which benefit from greater air movement and subsequent cooler conditions. The trellised vines are cultivated dry-land with the canopies opened to air movement to cool vines and reduce disease. Notwithstanding the area's fertile granite soils, planting density is low on very steep slopes so that the vine canopies can maximise sun exposure. Red grapes are cold macerated to enhance colour and flavour extraction without excessive tannins, and fermented in open-top vessels with regular punch downs. The wines are matured for 11 – 20 months in a combination of new and older wood to achieve a subtle oaking. Capensis, meaning "indigenous to the Cape", is a blend of Cabernet Sauvignon, Merlot, Shiraz and Pinotage, making a powerful yet austere wine. Chardonnay is fermented and matured in oak for five months, giving a hint of wood.

Capensis (Cape blend: Cab S / Merlot / Pinotage)　Cab S, Cab F, Merlot, Pinotage, Shiraz, Chard, Sauv Bl　by appt only　+27 (0)21 884 4412　wine@marklew.co.za www. marklew.co.za　7 – 10 y　03　personal attention, private tastings

L'Avenir Estate *Stellenbosch-Simonsberg Pocket*

The first wines from L'Avenir were certainly "hand crafted" as grapes were destalked by hand on a modest kitchen table. These simple beginnings have evolved extensively and L'Avenir's flagship Pinotage is now regularly awarded local and international honours.

Fifty-four hectares stretch over the lower foothills of the Simonsberg, facing west and south-west, away from the warmer northern exposure. The cooling effect of the south-easterly wind during the afternoon provides a moderate daytime temperature of 21.5°C during the growing season. This slows the ripening period, which contributes to intensely flavoured and structured wines.

The red clay soils have good water retention, supporting the vines throughout the growing season without irrigation. Dry-land cultivation also allows a viticultural practice of lightly stressing the vines during the last stage of ripening, resulting in the production of small berries with an increased skin to juice ratio. Colour and flavour extraction from these berries is easier, requiring less processing (pump over / punch down) to achieve a concentrated wine. The vineyards are planted at an average planting density of 3, 300 vines per hectare on the medium growth potential soil. Pinotage, a middle season ripener, generally favours eastern slopes with deep soils to develop more Pinot Noir style characteristics. L'Avenir, however, cultivates its Pinotage on west-facing slopes, using bush vines, rather than trellised vines, to contribute to a heavier wine with more intense fruit.

The flagship, L'Avenir Icon Pinotage, integrates various vineyard blocks located around the farm. The wine has a high alcohol content (14.5 per cent), but retains a wonderful balance without any fortified character, showing dense red fruits and a tight tannin structure. Each block of red grapes (all varieties) is fermented separately without cooling to ensure maximum flavour extraction. The higher fermentation temperatures (around 30°C) also prevent the feared paint-like character from developing in the Pinotage. A micro-oxygenation system has been added where a controlled dose of oxygen is applied to the wines to assist with the chemical reaction that stabilises tannins and colour. Exclusive use of French oak barrels gives a smoky character to the wine and not the sweet vanilla aromas typical of American oak. Wines from separate blocks are matured separately for 18 months in barrel before the blends are assembled.

White wines are cold fermented, with the Chardonnay matured in oak for 10 months. Malolactic fermentation and *bâttonage* give this wine a weighty mid-palate and mellow savouriness. Sauvignon Blanc and Chenin Blanc are unwooded with fragrant aromas. Ripe fruit and high alcohol levels (13.5 per cent +) give a slight sweetness on the palate. The Cape Vintage port-styled wine combines Portuguese varieties with Cabernet Sauvignon in a dark, rich wine with chocolate and vanilla tones.

The L'Avenir guest house, with individually decorated rooms and luxury facilities, is an ideal place to stay. The beautiful pool and surrounding garden offer tranquillity and peace in the heart of the Winelands. Rooms are fully equipped and a full English or Continental breakfast is included.

Pinotage vines (Top)
Poolside relaxation at the guest house (Centre) Tranquillity at the cellar (Left

Icon Pinotage Pinotage, Cab S, F, Merlot, Chard, Sauv Bl, Chenin Bl Mon – Fri 10 – 5, Sat 10 – 4 Closed Easter Sun, Dec 25, Jan 1
+27 (0)21 889 5001 +27 (0)21 889 5258 info@lavenir.co.za www.lavenir.co.za 5 – 8 y white 01, 03; red 03, 05
luxury guest house, tours by appt, BYO picnics, play area for children, olive products, conference facilities

HELSHOOGTE POCKET

The Helshoogte Pocket is situated on the foothills of the south-western extremities of the Simonsberg and Drakenstein Mountains. Characterised by high-lying sites (200 – 500 m) and soils with a high potential, this relatively small Pocket produces wines with very distinct characteristics.

The location together with pronounced southern aspects create markedly cooler conditions during ripening compared to those of the immediate surrounds of the town of Stellenbosch. The soils are almost exclusively derived from granite, with some mixing of sandstone material at higher altitudes. These highly weathered soils are acid and have high potential. However, due to its favourable structure, good drainage as well as water-retention properties make it desirable for vine cultivation. The cold winds which blow during the early summer months restrict growth and ensure that plants have a balanced yield of fruit.

Rain clouds brought on by the southerly winds provide a high annual rainfall of about 1, 000 mm and run-off water from the mountain slopes increases soil moisture. Frequent mist and constant airflow along the slopes create slow, even ripening conditions for an array of grape varieties.

Due to the intense folding of the slopes, great variation is found in exposure and cultivation. Most vineyards are vertically trellised between 1.4 and 1.8 metres. Row direction is mostly dictated by the slope but, where possible, rows are orientated south-west to north-east to utilise the cool summer breezes. Windbreaks are used on sites which are exposed to strong south-easterly winds early in the growing season.

Wines from the Helshoogte Pocket have the distinct cool climate characteristics of mintiness and berry flavours. White wines are extremely fruity with good palate weight and the reds are less overtly powerful with understated elegance.

Whereas most producers in Helshoogte blend Cabernet Sauvignon and Merlot, the single varietal wines from Thelema and Zorgvliet have elegant fruit with cassis and blackcurrant (Cab S), and leafy and fennel notes (Merlot) respectively. Vuurberg's blend has Cabernet-typical pencil shavings and cassis, while the Merlot adds further complexity. Cabernet Franc is a rising star, joining the red blends from Camberley, Rainbow's End and Delaire, and is produced as a single varietal at Zorgvliet. These wines have the firm tannin structure of Cabernet Sauvignon with slight grassy notes coming from Cabernet Franc.

Shiraz wines from Camberley and Rainbow's End display mintiness and savoury notes. The Chardonnay and Sauvignon Blanc wines from Zorgvliet, Thelema and Tokara show citrus and white fruit on the nose and a high natural acidity due to the cool cultivation conditions. The latter's red wines are light in texture due to very young vineyards.

Tending the season's new growth

DRIVING ROUTE: HELSHOOGTE

Helshoogte Pocket is nestled in the folds of the Simonsberg Mountain, as it runs south towards the town of Somerset West.

From the R44 / R310 intersection in downtown Stellenbosch, drive towards the N1 in a northerly direction, with signs indicating Paarl. At the third traffic light, turn right onto the R310 east out of Stellenbosch towards the Helshoogte Pass. This road traces the perimeter of the town before ascending the spectacular mountain pass.

Vineyards cling to the steep slopes on the left and right as you reach the crest. Notice how the very steep slopes necessitate vines to be planted in small patches. Row directions change from following the contours to following the incline to allow each patch of vines maximum sun and heat exposure. Start the descent into the Banhoek valley. About two kilometres further (10 km from town) is the first winery to visit. Camberley is a family-owned boutique winery overlooking the Banhoek valley with spectacular vineyards. Turn right at the Camberley road sign and follow a narrow dirt road to the entrance with the black gate. Buzz the intercom for access. Walking through the cellar to the wine tasting room, you have a sense of seclusion as you almost become part of this magical process of wine creation. The exquisite rose garden houses a private cottage and is a wonderful, tranquil resting place, complete with fireplace.

Travelling tips

Restaurant:
La Pommier restaurant +27 (0)21 885 1269
Hill Crest Berry Orchard +27 (0)21 885 1629
Accommodation:
Camberley cottage +27 (0)21 885 1176
La Pommier Country Lodge +27 (0)21 885 1269

GPS waypoints

Camberley	S33 55.156 E18 55.948
Rainbow's End	S33 56.424 E18 56.691
Turn-off to Rainbow's End	S33 55.011 E18 55.951
Vuurberg Vineyards	S33 54.392 E18 56.780

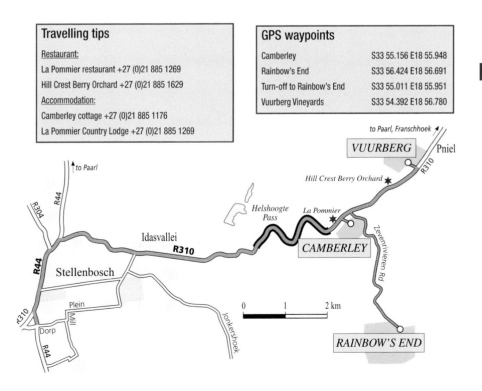

The next winery on the route is Rainbow's End, where architect Jacques Malan and his sons are making some impressive red wines. You may phone the owners to fetch you or attempt the narrow, winding road yourself. From Camberley, turn right onto the R310. Six hundred metres further, turn right onto Zevenrivieren Road (Eng. Seven Rivers). Take a right turn just before the bridge over the small river. Follow the gravel road and turn right again at the first turn-off ascending a steep incline. Keep left at the fork and turn left to the farm gate of Rainbow's End. Pass the office, dam and a small dwelling to the homestead where wine tasting is hosted. The elevated slopes, up to 530 metres above sea level, and varying rock component of the soil allow powerful Shiraz, Cabernet Sauvignon and Merlot wines to be made.

Back on the R310, the road winds down into the Banhoek valley. At the lowest point, a small road turns off to the left to Hill Crest Berry Orchard. Sample fresh berries cultivated in the orchards set high on the mountain at the restaurant. This area is also home to many stables and local riders are frequently seen on their equestrian outings. Please drive cautiously in this area.

Vuurberg is the last stop on this route. Follow the R310 as it rises to the hamlet of Pniel. Less than two kilometres from the Berry Orchard turn-off, you will see a boulder with the words Mountain Wood on the left-hand side of the road. Turn left and buzz the intercom at the gate for access. A narrow, winding road leads up to the flamboyant red winery building.

Lovely spot – Helshoogte provides some spectacular country roads

Vuurberg *Helshoogte Pocket*

Established in 2003, the Vuurberg Vineyards' boutique winery lies on high mountain slopes in the Banhoek valley. A mere nine hectares of vines are cultivated on south-facing slopes of 200 – 500 metres above sea level. The aspect, elevation and regular mountain cloud cover provide cool ripening conditions. The vineyard blocks are planted to only 0.2 of a hectare in extent. This enables row directions to follow the topography, providing canopies with maximum sun exposure and even ripening.

Merlot is planted at an elevation of 200 metres to enable the vines to benefit from slightly increased soil moisture, while Cabernet Sauvignon and Petit Verdot are planted high enough to avoid possible mountain shadows in order to satisfy their higher heat requirements. A clay layer at one metre depth ensures sufficient water retention and vineyards are cultivated on dry land.

Vines are trellised as the high humidity in this region requires the canopy to be opened by leaf removal on the sun-sheltered side. This promotes airflow and drying, which reduce the incidence of fungal diseases. A standard planting density of 3, 200 vines per hectare is used on the lower blocks, but is halved (1, 600 vines/Ha) on the very steep slopes higher up.

Following harvest and sorting, grapes are cold macerated to extract colour and tannins and partially natural fermented to give a diversified flavour profile. After 12 months of oak maturation, the blend is compiled and matured for a further six months. The flagship blend, Vuurberg 2003 blend, has a stylish velvet texture and dense dark fruit, with the highly structured Merlot adding further complexity to this powerful wine.

The steep slopes at Vuurberg

ⓘ Vuurberg blend (Merlot / Cab S / F) 🍇 Cab S/F, PV, Merlot, Malbec, Viog, Chenin Bl, Roussanne, Grenache 🕐 Fri afternoons, phone in advance 📞 +27 (0)21 885 2334 📠 +27 (0)21 885 2714 📧 helshoogte@mweb.co.za 🏭 expected 7 y 🍷 05 ℹ️ spectacular view of Banhoek valley

Camberley *Helshoogte Pocket*

Camberley is situated 270 metres above sea level in the rugged Banhoek Mountains. This gem, with its tranquil garden setting, comprises a mere seven hectares cultivated on warm, north-facing slopes with fertile, red clay soils. In order to reduce vigorous growth, planting density is extremely high, cover crops are planted within the rows and the vines are placed under deliberate water stress during the ripening stage to ensure tannin and fruit ripeness. Grapes are sorted before crushing and cold macerated for 48 hours to extract colour. After alcoholic and malolactic fermentation (softening the acidity) the young wine is matured for 14 months in oak. The blend is a powerful wine with typical cigar box and pencil shavings from the Cabernet Sauvignon. The Merlot vines, in particular, are picked at a very ripe stage to create concentration. The blackberry and slight mintiness, typical characters of the Helshoogte wines, integrate with almond and lavender aromas and very soft tannins.

ⓘ Cabernet Sauvignon-Merlot 🍇 Cab S, Merlot, Shz, Cab F, Pinotage 🕐 Mon – Sat 9 – 5, Sun, Publ hols by appt. Closed Dec 25, Jan 1 📞 +27 (0)21 885 1176 📧 john@camberley.co.za www.camberley.co.za 🏭 8 y 🍷 01 ℹ️ B&B cottage in tranquil garden, olive oil, collection of aeroplane art, art evenings

Rainbow's End Estate *Helshoogte Pocket*

The boutique winery of Rainbow's End exclusively produces red wines. Twenty-three hectares of mountain slopes are cultivated to vines in deep, homogenous granite soils. A high stone fraction (up to 70 per cent) moderates soil temperature and restricts growth vigour with vines naturally producing smaller berries with greater fruit concentration. The Merlot is planted on high (530 m) north-facing sites, benefiting from the cooling effect. Cabernet Sauvignon is planted on lower-lying, north-western sites where increased sun exposure ensures proper ripening. Shiraz is planted on cooler east and south-facing slopes, protected from the afternoon sun. A low planting density (2, 600 vines/Ha) allows sufficient space for each plant's development on steep slopes. Hand-harvested grapes are cold macerated and fermented with manual punch downs to ensure optimum colour extraction. Wines are matured for 12 months in French and American oak. The vines produce robust wines and the rustic Shiraz shows savoury and meaty flavours.

ⓘ Shiraz 🍇 Shz, Cab S/F, Merlot, PV, Malbec 🕐 by appt 📞 +27 (0)83 411 0170 / 082 413 7285 📠 +27 (21) 885 1722 📧 hbmeng@iafrica.co.za 🏭 5 y 🍷 04 ℹ️ spectacular scenery, cellar tour, fynbos reserve

The fertile and cool Devon Valley

DEVON VALLEY POCKET

Located to the south-west of Stellenbosch, the Devon Valley Pocket is accessible only by a narrow, winding lane. The valley lies on an axis from north-west to south-east. It is surrounded by the prominent, rounded Papegaai-berg and Bottelary hills, forming a horseshoe of slopes. These hills (240 – 470m) provide a barrier to the prevailing south-easterly winds, but as the valley opens to the south, it benefits from the cooling sea breezes (17 km).

The Pocket has deep, yellow to reddish-brown soils with good water drainage and retention properties. Derived almost exclusively from granite, these soils induce high growth vigour in the vines. The challenge in Devon Valley is to curtail this potentially excessive vigour in order to achieve even growth and a balanced plant. To ensure sufficient water reserves in the soil during the critical ripening phase, especially on sites where no irrigation water is available, low vigour, drought-resistant rootstocks are used. In the shallow soils near the low end of the valley, vines are either planted on ridges, which increase soil volume or they are cultivated untrellised. The smaller untrellised plants require less soil volume.

Although a predominantly red wine Pocket, some excellent white localities do exist, mainly planted to Chardonnay. Popular noble varieties such as Cabernet Sauvignon and Merlot share the Pocket with lesser known varieties such as Petit Verdot, Malbec and Mourvèdre. Cabernet Sauvignon, however, features most strongly in the Devon Valley vineyards. Structured Cabernet Sauvignon-Merlot blends are very popular, with wines from Clos Malvern, Devon Hill, Meinert Wines and Louisvale showing polished tannins and structure on the palate as well as opulent fruit on the nose. Middelvlei, on the other hand, produces single variety Cabernet Sauvignon and an earthy-toned Shiraz.

Devon Valley's narrow winding road

JONKERSHOEK VALLEY POCKET

The Jonkershoek Valley Pocket is set in a relatively narrow valley running in a south-easterly direction between the Jonkershoek and Stellenbosch Mountain ranges (1, 000 m). The vineyards are mainly situated between 200 and 300 metres above sea level on the steep south-west-facing foothills.

This particular topography creates shorter daylight hours as the sun rises late over the Jonkershoek Mountain and sets early behind the Stellenbosch Mountain. The lower sun exposure, together with the synoptic south-easterly winds that funnel down this valley, result in relatively cooler ripening conditions than the meso-climate would indicate.

Annual rainfall in this valley is relatively high at about 1, 000 mm, compared with 713 mm at the Nietvoorbij Research Station in Stellenbosch. A large portion of Jonkershoek's rain occurs during the summer months, due to wind-driven clouds tumbling down the valley.

The parentage of the soils is diverse, with a band of shale running along the lower eastern slopes, topped by granite at the higher elevations. Due to the generally steep slopes, these soils are usually a mix of parent materials with some material from still higher sandstone mountain caps. This results in highly weathered, acid, often stony soils with good drainage properties and moderate to high vigour potential.

In the Jonkershoek Pocket, the combination of complex topography, strong winds and summer rains requires the adaptation of viticulture practices. Vineyards are planted to manage wind effectively and row directions are orientated to allow the wind force to flow down the rows instead

The majestic peaks guarding Jonkershoek

of directly into vines, potentially causing damage. Because soils are relatively shallow on the valley floor, ridges are used to increase soil volume. On the slopes, however, deep fertile soils allow vines to be trained on vertical trellising. The Pocket is host to all the noble cultivars and planting density varies (2, 000 – 4, 000 vines/Ha) on the differing altitudes.

This small valley produces very finely textured reds and delicate whites. Neil Ellis's Sauvignon Blanc has a definite chalky quality, giving a sleek edge to the gooseberry fruit.

As in many Stellenbosch pockets, Cabernet Sauvignon and Merlot are firm favourites, however, in Jonkershoek these varieties show their greatest expression as single varietal wines. Cabernets from Neil Ellis and Stark-Condé are powerful with elegance and cassis, blackberry and mineral notes, while their Shiraz wines have spicy warmth and smoky characters. These wines have very high alcohol levels (Alc. 15% by Vol. +) and require long cellaring. Merlots in this Pocket have a more fruity style. Le Riche produces several Cabernet Sauvignon-Merlot blends with juicy fruit while Lanzerac produces a single varietal Merlot.

107

Elgin Pocket

Hidden treasure – early morning fog covers the Elgin vineyards

Elgin is unique in the sense that it is geographically and geologically a very clearly defined mountain basin (in the Hottentots Holland Mountain range) at a high elevation of 200 – 300 metres, surrounded by sandstone rims and peaks at 500 – 1, 000 metres above sea level.

Probably the coolest of all the Pockets, Elgin was traditionally a fruit (especially apples) growing region where the viticultural potential has long been realised, but economic considerations kept it from being properly exploited. Recently, the local economic situation changed drastically, resulting in a marked diversification towards planting wine grapes.

Although Elgin receives slightly more sunlight hours during ripening as Constantia, the high elevation and prevailing southerly winds greatly influence the temperature to make it a cool production area. The average

February temperature is a mere 19.7°C, indicating cool conditions during the ripening season and subsequent late ripening of all wine grape varieties.

There are, however, some warmer locations within the Pocket and, with the varying soil potential, great emphasis is placed on proper site selection. There is a marked difference between locations. Higher lying Iona (420 m) is close to the ocean (3 km), which results in significantly cooler conditions and harvest commences two to four weeks later than for other Elgin producers.

Most vineyards are trellised, firstly to vertically elongate the canopy for optimum sun exposure and photosynthesis, and secondly to protect the shoots from the strong prevailing winds. Interestingly, the height of the cordon is varied depending on the meso-climate, bringing the canopy closer to the soil surface to benefit from radiant heat for improved ripening or distancing the canopy to ensure cooler ripening conditions where required.

The geology of the Elgin basin is predominantly shale with small areas of sandstone. The shale soils are characterised by gravelly topsoil on structured clay. The soils are acidic and require the addition of lime, as well as deep soil preparation to eliminate the chemical and structural limitations of the subsoil. Annual rainfall is more than 1, 000 mm, with marked summer precipitation from south-easterly blown-in clouds. Irrigation is generally not necessary, even when developing new vineyards.

This young viticultural area is still in the process of determining the best-adapted varieties and viticultural practices for its particular growing conditions. Ample evidence indicates that it is particularly well-suited to the more delicate varieties like Sauvignon Blanc, Pinot Noir and Merlot. Since Elgin's establishment as a wine-producing area, its producers have made great strides in achieving first effort honours. Many of the country's foremost winemakers are moving into the area, buying grapes from established vineyards and developing more viticultural land.

Elgin wines have typical cool climate characteristics, modest alcohol levels and high natural acidity creating freshness. The Pinot Noir and Chardonnay wines are delicately crafted with some earthy and steely notes reminiscent of the Burgundy style. Pinot Noir from Paul Cluver is well structured with cool climate flavours of berries and earthy notes. Natural fermentation enhances the Chardonnay's green lime and toasty flavours. The Sauvignon Blanc wines have sumptuous fruit and good complexity. Sauvignons from Oak Valley and Iona have pronounced gooseberry, green fig and nettle characters.

Soil:	sandstone with granite and shale, gravelly
Climate:	cool, high rainfall, windy, sunlight
White varieties:	Sauvignon Blanc, Chardonnay, Chenin Blanc, Sémillon
Red varieties:	Pinot Noir, Cabernet Sauvignon, Merlot
Wine styles:	red, white, dessert

A highlight of the Pocket is the Riesling Noble Late Harvest from Paul Cluver, utilizing the humid conditions late in the season to ensure *Botrytis* in the vineyards. This wine's rich sweetness is balanced with the Riesling's racy acidity. Typical peach, muscat and pepper notes are absorbed into a honeyed *Botrytis* finish. The wine shows great maturation potential of several years.

The red wines show poise and elegance, also with modest alcohol levels. Iona's Cab-Merlot blend and a single varietal Cabernet Sauvignon from Paul Cluver have less pronounced capsicum (green pepper) and eucalyptus aromas, tending more to dark cherry and savoury notes.

DRIVING ROUTE: ELGIN

The Elgin Pocket is situated in a defined basin in the Hottentots Holland Mountain range. Follow the N2 south from Cape Town, through Somerset West and over Sir Lowry's Pass to the top of the mountain.

About 65 kilometres from Cape Town (45 km from Stellenbosch) you will pass the town of Grabouw, the centre of the apple farming community. A few kilometres further, turn left onto the R321 to the towns of Elgin and Villiersdorp. A little further, just before entering the town of Elgin, turn right at the T-junction to Elgin Station and Oak Valley. A short drive past storage facilities will bring you to the entrance of the first winery on this route, Oak Valley. This 1, 780 hectare property is a major supplier of apples, pears, cut flowers and naturally reared beef cattle. It also boasts 30 hectares of protected-in-perpetuity English oaks and 500 hectares of mountain fynbos reserve. The original cellar was decommissioned in the 1940s. Currently Oak Valley shares cellar space at Paul Cluver cellar. A new winery is planned for Oak Valley's own production.

Return to the N2, turn left and 100 metres further past the Peregrine Farm Stall on the right, turn right to Viljoenshoop. Follow the road between orchards for five kilometres, until you reach the sign "R44 via Highlands". Turn left. Continue for about eight kilometres. Pass over a small bridge in a low-lying area. The road rises and turns to gravel. Continue

east on this road for another four kilometres. On the right, you will see a dam and vineyards. The turn-off to Iona is indicated on the right. Iona was previously a fruit farm, but has been cultivating vineyards with great success.

Follow the road back to the N2 to visit Paul Cluver, the last winery on this route. At the N2, turn right and continue for four kilometres until you pass a large structure on the left – the apple packing stores of the Two-a-day company. Turn left at the large entrance of this complex. Signs indicate the road to Paul Cluver on the right-hand side of the complex. Follow the road, winding past a pond teaming with bird life to the cellar and tasting facilities. The Paul Cluver estate also offers luxurious accommodation and the summer concerts in the amphitheatre are very popular.

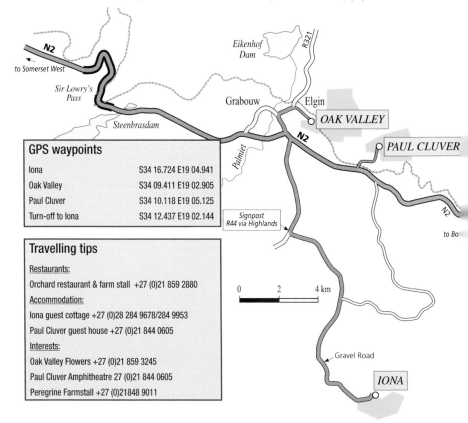

GPS waypoints

Iona	S34 16.724 E19 04.941
Oak Valley	S34 09.411 E19 02.905
Paul Cluver	S34 10.118 E19 05.125
Turn-off to Iona	S34 12.437 E19 02.144

Travelling tips

Restaurants:
Orchard restaurant & farm stall +27 (0)21 859 2880
Accommodation:
Iona guest cottage +27 (0)28 284 9678/284 9953
Paul Cluver guest house +27 (0)21 844 0605
Interests:
Oak Valley Flowers +27 (0)21 859 3245
Paul Cluver Amphitheatre 27 (0)21 844 0605
Peregrine Farmstall +27 (0)21848 9011

Iona Vineyards *Elgin Pocket*

Iona Vineyards, situated high on the Hottentots-Holland Mountain Range, overlooking the Elgin Valley and the Atlantic Ocean in the south, records some of the lowest average temperatures of all South African vineyards. Iona celebrated its maiden vintage in 2001. Twenty-five hectares were established on a relatively flat plain where post-glacial activity deposited gravelly, alluvial soils. The soils are deep (1 m+) and well drained, and a low planting density (3, 000 vines/Ha) discourages extensive root formation and subsequently increased growth vigour. The low average summer daytime temperatures (17.2 °C) and frequent mists require that canopies are opened to increase air movement to combat fungal diseases. Sauvignon Blanc is planted in sandstone soils and the wine has two components based on row direction and sun exposure: east-west rows give green fig and white fruit flavours while fruit from north-south rows show riper tropical fruit. Following harvest, the grapes are cold fermented (13°C) without skin contact, resulting in a steely, mineral character, typical of cool climates. Merlot and Cabernet are cultivated on sites containing more gravel and grapes are tank fermented with regular pump overs to extract colour. Malolactic fermentation is completed in barrel and 14 months maturation in French oak results in elegant, fruit-driven wines with fine tannins.

🛈 Sauvignon Blanc 🏆 Sauv Bl, Merlot, Shz, Cab S, Sém, Chard ◷ Mon – Fri 8 – 5:30. Closed Easter Fri, Sat, Sun, Dec 25, Jan 1 ☎ +27 (0)28 284 9678 📠 +27 (0)28 284 9078 ✉ gunn@iona.co.za www.iona.co.za 🔋 Potential: Sauv 3 y, Merlot 5 – 10 y ■05 ℹ self catering guest house, walks, mountain bike, BYO picnics

Oak Valley *Elgin Pocket*

Oak Valley, family-owned since being purchased by Sir Antonie Viljoen in 1898, made its maiden vintage Sauvignon Blanc in 2003 after supplying many celebrated producers such as Bouchard Finlayson and Rupert and Rothschild. This 1, 780 hectare property boasts 30 hectares of protected-in-perpetuity English oaks and 500 hectares of mountain fynbos reserve. With the original cellar decommissioned in the 1940s, Oak Valley is currently sharing space at the Paul Cluver cellar, but a new winery is planned. Thirty-five hectares of vines are cultivated on steep slopes at 600 metres above sea level. South-facing slopes support low-vigour soils of shale and sandstone where planting density is decreased to 2, 900 vines/Ha. The vines are trellised and canopies are vertically extended to maximise sun exposure and to ensure full ripeness. Cloud cover, mist and rain create cool, even ripening conditions, but the prevailing south-easterly ensures that grapes are dried to prevent *Botrytis*. Oak Valley uses a reductive winemaking process to preserve its herbaceous Sauvignon Blanc aromas. The wine is left on the lees for two months to soften its naturally high acidity. This practice also adds a mid-palate weight, resulting in a full-bodied, dry, minerally white wine.

111

🛈 Sauvignon Blanc 🏆 Sauv Bl, (Merlot blend, Chard & PN to follow) ◷ Mon – Fri 9 – 5 or appt ☎ +27 (0)21 859 4110 📠 +27 (0)21 859 3405 ✉ wine@oak-valley.co.za www.oakvalleywines.com ■3 y+ ■ 03, 04, 05 ℹ English oaks and birding, tours of cut flower production

Paul Cluver *Elgin Pocket*

The Cluver family have farmed this Elgin property since 1896. Nestled in the folds of the Hottentots-Holland Mountains, this estate pioneered Elgin's recognition as an exceptional wine-producing area in the 1980s. One hundred hectares of vines are cultivated in shale and clay soils. The high elevations (300 – 500 m above sea level) and south-easterly winds create cool ripening conditions and, together with shale soils, promote strong minerality and concentration in Chardonnay and Pinot Noir. To ensure proper ripening, red varieties are sited on north- and west-facing slopes to optimise sun exposure. Ripening conditions are further improved by vertically extended canopies, reducing their density and increasing sun exposure. This also reduces disease in the humid environment. Chardonnay is barrel fermented with natural yeasts and matured on the lees (19 months), yielding a spicy wine with green lime flavours and fresh acid promising great aging potential. Eleven months in French oak gives firm but subtle tannins to the dark and aromatic Pinot Noir. Weisser Riesling (for NLH) is harvested at high sugar levels and grapes are macerated overnight giving aromas of peach, mint and muscat. The cleared juice is fermented, resulting in an exciting balance of aromatics, racy acid and honeyed *Botrytis*.

🛈 Chardonnay, Pinot Noir, NHL 🏆 Chard, PN, W Riesling, Cab S, Sauv Bl, Gewurz ◷ Mon – Fri 8 – 5, Sat, Publ hols 9 – 3. Closed Easter, Dec 25, Jan 1 ☎ +27 (0)21 844 0605 📠 +27 (0)21 844 0150 ✉ info@cluver.co.za www.cluver.com ■ white 3 y, red 5 y+ ■03 ℹ BYO picnics, summer concerts, guest house, conservation area, winter gourmet weekends

Walker Bay Pocket

Walker Bay Valley vineyards shrouded in morning mist

The Walker Bay Pocket stretches from the small village of Bot River in a southerly direction to the Hemel-en-Aarde valley outside Hermanus. All these vineyard areas are markedly affected by the maritime influence of the ocean at Walker Bay and surrounded by the Klein Babylonstoren Mountains.

Even more than in the Elgin Pocket, the summer rain originating from clouds driven against the surrounding sandstone mountain ridges by the synoptic south-easterly winds, is a prominent feature in Walker Bay. These summer rains contribute about 50 per cent of the relatively high annual rainfall (up to 1, 000 mm). Because of this, clayey, structured soils in certain sites rarely dry completely and deep soil preparation is required. The mean February temperature at Hermanus is 20.3°C, which is fairly warm. However, the cool, moisture-laden flow from the ocean creates cool ripening conditions. Towards the end of the harvest season, the occurrence of mist allows for *Botrytised* wines in certain vintages. Strong south-easterly and south-westerly winds are common and vineyards are trellised to protect the shoots from damage.

Geologically the area is diverse, with gravelly or stony soils derived from highly weathered granite and shale as well as calcareous, solidified quaternary sand dunes. These marginal soils are a unique feature of this coastal area and, together with the persistent winds, serve to curtail excessive vigour and restrict crop yields for improved grape quality.

The vineyards enjoy various aspects with white varieties south-east facing on the lower-lying sites and reds on the slightly warmer higher slopes. The topography with north and south facing aspects modifies the macro-climate considerably over short distances, allowing a wide range of wine grape varieties to be cultivated.

Wines from the Pocket have pronounced varietal flavours and are complex yet elegant. The generally cool conditions benefit the temperature-sensitive varieties such as Sauvignon Blanc, Chardonnay and Pinot Noir. Sauvignons from Southern Right and Beaumont are powerful with green fig, capsicum and mineral edge. Chardonnay is usually complex and flavoursome with a mineral finish. Good examples are barrel-fermented (and unwooded) wines from Bouchard Finlayson, Hamilton Russell Vineyards and Sumaridge.

Leading Cape examples of Pinot Noir come from Hamilton Russell Vineyards and Bouchard Finlayson. These wines show a luxurious, creamy texture and cherry fruit with very fine tannins. Other interesting examples are Newtown Johnson and Whalehaven whose wines show more forest floor and earthy notes.

Red varieties (Mourvèdre, Malbec, Shiraz, Nebbiolo, Barbera, Sangiovese) are placed on northern-facing slopes to fulfil their heat requirements, producing interesting blends, such as the succulent and exotic Hannibal blend from Bouchard Finlayson, and South Africa's first single varietal Mourvèdre (Beaumont). A few Shiraz wines are also produced, with elegant, spicy examples from Luddite and Beaumont. Newcomer, Hawston Bay Vineyards, has an interesting selection of red varieties coming into production with Shiraz, Mourvèdre, Petit Verdot, Malbec and Cabernet Sauvignon showing great promise.

113

After the harvest – colourful vines in autumn

DRIVING ROUTE: WALKER BAY

Leave Cape Town on the N2 freeway, past Somerset West and over the Hottentots Holland Mountain Range via Sir Lowry's Pass. Descending the mountain on the southern side, take Exit 92 to the small town of Bot River. This turn-off is clearly marked. At the intersection, turn left into the town's main road. A few kilometres further, almost at the periphery of the town, is the entrance to Beaumont on the left. Beaumont's wine cellar dates from the 1920s. Its guest cottages offer tranquil country living. Invitations to its art exhibitions are highly sought after.

Soil:	sandstone with granite and shale, gravelly
Climate:	cool, windy, high rainfall, sunlight
White varieties:	Sauvignon Blanc, Chardonnay, Chenin Blanc, Sémillon
Red varieties:	Pinot Noir, Cabernet Sauvignon, Merlot
Wine styles:	red, white, dessert

Drive back on the main road to the N2. Join the N2 and continue in a south-easterly direction. About five kilometres further, turn right onto Swartrivier Road. Five hundred metres further, turn right to Botriver Hills. This young cellar will specialise in red wines with a small percentage of white varieties.

Return to Bot River and take Exit 92 to the R43, driving in a westerly direction. The road winds in a southerly direction to the costal town of Hermanus. Drive carefully in this area as the road runs through several costal villages and the speed limit changes accordingly. Signage at a large intersection indicates the Hemel-en-Aarde valley to the left. Turn left onto the R320 (27 km from N2). Behind the small shopping centre lies the cellar of Whalehaven. This small winery uses grapes from this valley as well as from Elgin and Stellenbosch to produce its wines.

Drive along the R320 as it makes its way into this beautiful, secluded valley. When you reach the entrance to Hamilton Russell

Vineyards on the right, follow the gravel road to the tasting room, situated a small distance from the main road. You will pass a large dam, and on the rare occasion, you may spot the shy black swan. Peter Finlayson pioneered Pinot Noir in the Hemel-en-Aarde valley before joining Burgundian Paul Bouchard to set up his own winery next door. Today, Hamilton Russell Vineyards specialises in only two varieties: Chardonnay and Pinot Noir.

Continue along the R320 to Bouchard Finlayson, also on the right side of the road. Follow the road to the thatched tasting room and offices. Here Peter Finlayson's focus remains on Pinot Noir, while he continues to experiment with his beloved Italian varieties, Sangiovese and Nebbiolo.

A great place to purchase wine from all the South African areas and Pockets is the Wine Village at the entrance to the valley. Here you will find one of the most comprehensive collections of South African wines, representing more than 380 wineries.

The Hemel en Aarde road winds away from the sea

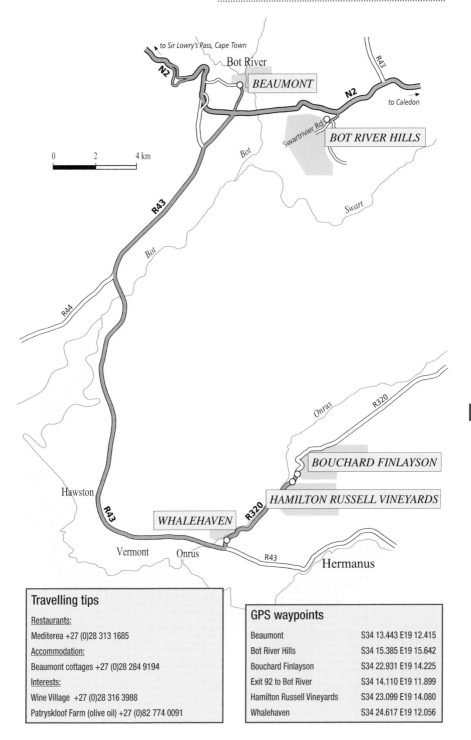

Travelling tips

Restaurants:

Mediterea +27 (0)28 313 1685

Accommodation:

Beaumont cottages +27 (0)28 284 9194

Interests:

Wine Village +27 (0)28 316 3988

Patryskloof Farm (olive oil) +27 (0)82 774 0091

GPS waypoints

Beaumont	S34 13.443 E19 12.415
Bot River Hills	S34 15.385 E19 15.642
Bouchard Finlayson	S34 22.931 E19 14.225
Exit 92 to Bot River	S34 14.110 E19 11.899
Hamilton Russell Vineyards	S34 23.099 E19 14.080
Whalehaven	S34 24.617 E19 12.056

Pinot Noir

Pinot Noir has been quoted as an exasperating variety for growers, winemakers and wine drinkers alike. It is sometimes said to be feminine, alluring or capricious, but mostly it is the pursuit of richness which makes it ultimately satisfy the Holy Grail of winemaking. The first Pinot plantings were based on the Swiss BK5 clone. These vines were prone to leaf roll and did not offer the classic red wine characteristics of Burgundy, but rather presented wines that were weak-coloured and austere, with low extract. In the 1980s, newer, virus-free clones were introduced and vines were pruned to the French double guyot method. This marked a change in vine cultivation which proved more productive, with grapes giving better colour, higher tannin levels and the characteristic and robust sweet cherry flavours. Key producers are Meerlust, Rustenburg, Blaauwklippen, Hamilton Russell Vineyards, Vriesenhof.

Beaumont *Walker Bay Pocket*

Beaumont's small traditional cellar dates from the 1920s. The landscape is characterised by rolling hills of shale and alluvial soils in lower-lying areas. The 34 hectares of old vines produce low yields, with red wines accounting for 60 per cent of production. Planting density is increased to 5,000 vines per hectare. White grapes are sited on cooler south-east-facing slopes with reds on slightly warmer elevated slopes. A low cordon (0.5 m) trellising system brings grapes closer to the soil surface, increasing radiant heat and promoting even ripening in this cool Pocket. Prevailing south-easterly and south-westerly winds create predominantly healthy and disease-free growing conditions. Late summer mist allows for *Botrytised* wines in certain vintages. The powerful, structured wines are less fruit driven and have strong mineral characters. Open-top fermenters are still used for reds, while white wines are fermented in a non-reductive style.

[ⓘ] Ariane (red blend), Hope Marguerite (white blend), sweet wine 🔲 Cab S/F, Malbec, Merlot, Mouv, Pinotage, Shz, Chard, Chenin Bl, Sauv Bl, Sém 🕐 Mon – Fri 9:30 – 12:30, 13:30 – 16:30, Sat 9:30 – 1. Closed Easter Sat, Sun, Dec 25, Jan 1 ☎ +27 (0)28 284 9194 📠 +27 (0)28 284 9733 ✉ beaumine@netactive. co.za www.beaumont.co.za 🍽 8 – 9 y 🍷 95, 97, 00, 01, 04 ⓘ guest cottages, jewellery exhibits, old winery artefacts

Botriver Hills *Walker Bay Pocket*

This new winery specialises in classic French red varieties. Walker Bay is considered one of the Cape's coolest macro-climates and vineyards are situated on north and north-west-facing slopes to take advantage of the sun. When combined with this aspect, the prevailing wind and frequent mists from the nearby ocean create ideal ripening conditions. Higher sandstone slopes (250 m) provide run-off water for the vineyards, but supplementary irrigation is necessary for the young Cabernet Sauvignon and Merlot vines that are planted on low-lying shale soils. The vineyard rows are directed to maximise airflow through the vines. This reduce humidity and disease, while trellising protects the vines from possible wind damage. Shiraz is mainly planted in poor sandstone soils giving elegance, as well as some shale soils which give body and structure. A small parcel of Sauvignon Blanc and Sémillon on a south-facing slope overlooks the ocean. The maiden vintage at the cellar is expected in 2007.

Meticulous preparation in the vineyards

[ⓘ] yet to be determined 🔲 Shz, Mouv, Malbec, P V, Cab S/F, Merlot, Sauv Bl, Sém 🕐 by appt ☎ +27 (0)28 284 2918 ✉ hbv@telkomsa.net 🍽 N/A 🍷 N/A ⓘ lavender fields, blue crane (SA national bird) spotted frequently

Whalehaven *Walker Bay Pocket*

Whalehaven Wines is located at the entrance of the Hemel-en-Aarde valley. This boutique winery sources grapes from three *terroir* areas to make its wines: Walker Bay, Elgin and Stellenbosch. The Chardonnay vines (in Walker Bay) are trellised to protect shoots from the strong prevailing wind as well as to increase sunlight exposure and even ripening. The Chardonnay is wood fermented and matured for 12 months. A combination of French, American and Hungarian oak adds complexity while *bâttonage* gives a creamy and filling mid-palate. Pinot Noir is sourced from cool Elgin vineyards on medium vigour soils. The Pinot Noir is an elegant, dense and restrained wine. Cabernet Sauvignon, Cabernet Franc, Merlot (ex-Stellenbosch) are more herbaceous and show massive tannins. The red wines are warm fermented (28°C) with a combination of punch downs and pump overs to extract colour and flavour. Viognier (ex-Stellenbosch) receives skin contact and is fermented at very low temperatures (12°C) to retain apricot and peach flavours.

[ⓘ] Pinot Noir, Chardonnay 🔲 PN, Chard, Cab S / F, Viog, Merlot 🕐 Mon – Fri 9:30 – 5 Sat, non-religious hols 10:30 – 2, Sun 10:30 – 4:30 (summer). Closed Easter Fri – Sun, Dec 25, Jan 1 ☎ +27 (0)28 316 1633 📠 +27 (0)28 316 1640 ✉ wine@whalehavenwines.co.za 🍽 2 – 5 y 🍷 97, 00, 04 ⓘ BYO picnics

Hamilton Russell Vineyards *Walker Bay Pocket*

Hamilton Russell Vineyards is nestled in the lower Hemel-en-Aarde valley. The farm was established in 1975 and pioneered wine production in the Walker Bay appellation. The lovingly restored schoolhouse and an historic farm workers' cottage now house the offices and tasting room.

While most of the property's sandstone soils are covered with indigenous fynbos, 52 hectares of Chardonnay and Pinot Noir vineyards are limited to a bank of stony, clay-rich Bokkeveld shale-derived soils. The clay with its extremely high internal surface area increases the potential for cation exchange and indirectly results in tighter structured more minerally wines.

Organic farming of the soils and a permanent cover crop encourages beneficial microbiological activity in the soil, improving its structure and the root development of the vines. The vineyards are cultivated on north-east-facing slopes, and are planted at densities in balance with the vigour of the specific site. Low overall vigour requires particularly low yields to achieve balance with the canopy mass and yields are generally below 30 hectolitre per hectare.

The close proximity to the cool Atlantic Ocean, only three kilometres away, provides a constant flow of cool air into the valley and average maximum temperatures during the hottest summer months only reach 25°C. This creates ideal slow ripening conditions for the heat-sensitive Burgundian varieties. A range of cliffs at the top of the estate, overlooking the Hermanus coastal plain and Walker Bay, protects the property from the strong south-easterly wind in summer. Vines are trellised for optimal vertical shoot positioning and timely suckering ensures open canopies and beneficial air movement, which reduces the risk of fungal diseases in the high humidity surroundings.

Once the grapes reach *veraison* (the first signs of colouring in the bunches), green harvesting removes all excess bunches to balance the yield with the canopy vigour. This facilitates achieving full physiological ripeness at high natural acidity and low pH with flavour concentration and length. At harvest, grapes are hand sorted to remove any rot and under-ripe or over-ripe bunches – both in the vineyard and at the cellar on a sorting table.

Cleared Chardonnay juice is fermented from start to finish in small tight-grained French oak barrels. Pinot Noir grapes are punched down three times a day during a week-long cold soak prior to fermentation and then gently pumped over during active fermentation. The wine is pressed off the skins as soon as fermentation is complete to prevent the extraction of harsh tannins. The wines are aged in Burgundian barrels for 10 months, using one-third new oak to ensure a subtle, balanced presence of oak character. A tight, dry, mineral character complements the Chardonnay's varietal fruit. The Pinot Noir has a certain tightness and length to balance its richness and texture. Not overtly fruity, soft and sweet, it generally shows a dark, spicy, complex primary fruit perfume.

The beautiful barrel cellar is worth a visit (Top)
Permanent cover crops (Centre)
A fine balance in planting densities (Left)

Pinot Noir, Chardonnay | PN, Chard | Mon – Fri 9 – 5, Sat 9 – 1. Closed Easter Fri, Sun, Dec 25, 26, Jan 1 | +27 (0)28 312 3595 | +27 (0)28 312 1797 | hrv@hermanus.co.za | 15 – 20 y | 00, 01, 03, 05 | underground barrel cellar, Estate olive oil, fynbos honey, mountain fynbos reserve

Bouchard Finlayson *Walker Bay Pocket*

Peter Finlayson is aptly described as the pioneer of Pinot Noir in the Hemel-en-Aarde valley and, for that matter, South Africa as a whole. After a dozen years of working with this variety on neighbouring Hamilton Russell, Finlayson joined Burgundian Paul Bouchard to set up the boutique winery of Bouchard Finlayson, nestled in the secluded Hemel-en-Aarde valley. Established in 1989, the estate is conveniently situated an hour's drive (about 120 km) from Cape Town, just outside the charming and popular seaside village of Hermanus.

Bouchard Finlayson boldly broke away from establishing a traditional Cape Dutch-style winery and today the luxurious facilities welcome visitors. With its thatched roof and pre-dominating white walls, the Bouchard Finlayson winery – which is elegantly featured on its label – maintains a Cape feel while the ornate gables, towering walls and high ceilings so typical of Cape Dutch architecture give way to clean lines and low-slung walls. A pitched roof supports vast thatch overhangs which form a wrap-around veranda which protects the building and cellar from the harsh heat of the midday sun. Since its maiden vintage of 1991, the small cellar has been dedicated to the production of Pinot Noir, Chardonnay and Sauvignon Blanc. Sangiovese, however, and a handful of Tuscan and French varieties are also under exploration – Sangiovese, Nebbiolo, Barbera and Mourvèdre.

Located only six kilometres from the Atlantic Ocean, the 125 hectare farm enjoys a maritime climate. The sheltering Galpin Peak (810 m) and the Tower of Babel (1, 200 m) trap cloud cover and moisture from the prevailing cool Atlantic sea breezes which in turn promote slow-ripening, flavour-rich grapes from even the most sensitive varieties. Bouchard Finlayson's soil is predominantly shale and its duplex structure, consisting of stony gravel and fine clay shale, ensures good moisture retention, while gentle slopes drain excess water to aerate the vine roots.

Only 19 hectares are planted to vines with 50 per cent devoted to Pinot Noir – the variety for which the valley is most acclaimed. Viticultural practices are based on the Burgundian philosophy of high density planting, with 9, 000 vines planted per hectare. This encourages greater surface to leaf exposure and restricts root growth, improving fruit concentration, while ensuring equitable sunlight exposure to the vines, which are planted on gentle west-facing slopes in a north-south direction. Vineyards are trellised and green harvesting is practised annually to remove underdeveloped or damaged grapes. Fully ripened grapes are harvested by hand, with more than one pass through the same vineyard not uncommon. The estate's 200-ton winery focuses on Pinot Noir and Chardonnay and, in a daringly different style, a Sangiovese blend.

Grapes for the Galpin Peak Pinot Noir are crushed and destemmed before inoculation with selected yeast cultures for alcoholic fermentation in open-top vessels. Fermentation temperatures are kept well below 30°C to preserve the truffles and forest floor aromas of the Pinot Noir in particular. Regular pump overs and slight aeration of the fermenting wine ensures a deep colour and rich mouthfeel. The fermented wine is matured in small Burgundian barrels for about 10 months. About 30 per cent new wood is used to prevent the subtle varietal flavours from being overpowered by the wood. In the best vintages, however, a Tête du Cuvée Galpin Peak Pinot Noir is made from selected barrels and matured for 14 months in 80 per cent new wood, resulting in a dense wine with fine-laced tannins.

Proximity to the ocean (Top)
Early morning tending of the vines (Left)

Tête du Cuvée Galpin Peak Pinot Noir, Galpin Peak Pinot Noir PN, Sauv Bl, Chard, Sangiovese, Nebb, Mouv, Barbera, Shz Mon – Fri 9 – 5, Sat 9:30 – 12:30 + 27 (0)28 312 3515 +27 (0)28 312 2317 info@bouchardfinlayson.co.za www.bouchardfinlayson.co.za 5 – 20 y PN 97, 01, 05. Chard 00, 03 spectacular views, groups by appt

The Cape's first Sangiovese blend, Hannibal, was born from experimental varieties and incorporates Sangiovese, Pinot Noir and small amounts of Nebbiolo, Barbera, Shiraz and Mourvèdre. The blending of Sangiovese and Pinot Noir is unique. Fermentation temperatures are slightly increased (28°C) to bring out the varietal character of the Tuscan varieties and the components are individually oaked for 14 months before blending. Although an elegant blend, the wine shows deceptively substantial power. Red wines are bottle matured for 12 months before release onto the market.

Once harvested, white grapes are destemmed and lightly pressed to remove juice from the skins. The cleared juice is fermented at low temperatures (13 – 16°C) to preserve the varietal flavours. Missionvale Chardonnay is the white flagship wine and takes its name from the historical site where Moravian missionaries established a hospice in the region. One hundred per cent barrel fermented, it also undergoes malolactic fermentation in the barrels. The wine is kept on the lees for five to nine months with regular *bâttonage* softening the wine's acids and giving weight to the mid-palate. The unwooded Chardonnay and Sauvignon Blanc are made in a riper, more tropical fruit style and are bottled without malolactic fermentation.

For certain wines, grapes are selected from within the region – one such contracted vineyard is Kaaimansgat (Crocodile's Lair). Situated in a blind valley high in the Cape Coastal Mountains, the Chardonnay grapes are grown in the cool region of Villiersdorp on non-irrigated slopes at an elevation of 700 metres above sea level. This wine has typical gravelly tones and lemon fruit. Partially oaked, it carries a slightly higher alcohol (Alc.14% by Vol.) with grace.

High-trellised Nebbiolo vines (Top)   The trademark Bouchard Finlayson cellar architecture (Below)

119

Franschhoek Pocket

The picturesque Franschhoek Valley

The narrow Franschhoek Valley is enclosed on three sides by towering mountains: on the south-west the Groot Drakenstein, on the south-east the Franschhoek and on the north-east the Wemmershoek Mountains. The mountain peaks rise as high as 1, 700 metres above sea level, with the valley floor far below, at an elevation of less than 300 metres. These mountains create shaded periods which directly influence viticultural practices and winemaking in the valley.

This prominent valley (about 5 km wide) stretches in a north-westerly to south-easterly direction and is mainly drained by the upper reaches of the Berg River, flowing to Paarl, Swartland and eventually into the Atlantic. The climate is typically Mediterranean, with an annual rainfall in excess of 800 mm. The enclosed nature of the valley combined with the average February temperature of 23.5°C indicates that it is a warmer region, comparable to the greater Stellenbosch area.

The geology is predominantly sandstone (ca. 500 – 400 Ma) with some shale around the southern extremes of the valley and small outcrops of granite towards the North. The soils are sandy and alluvial along the river banks, changing to yellowish-brown, well-drained and light-textured soils on the higher-lying mountain foothills. The sandy nature of the soil necessitates irrigation on all but some of the heavier-textured, dark soils close to the river course.

The changing aspects provide various sites for cultivation and vines are planted from the valley floor to elevations as high as 600 metres above sea level. Due to these variations, soil depths and types vary. Vine spacing ranges from 2, 500 vines per hectare on the steep slopes, and almost doubles on the flat soils of the valley floor. Some small bush vines still exist, although new plantings are trellised to spread the canopy vertically for a greater leaf surface to be exposed to the sun.

The two mountain ranges in the northern part of the valley decrease the daylight hours with the early onset of mountain shadow in the south-east end of the valley. Viticultural practices are adapted to accommodate this loss of sunlight by high trellising. The range of soils and relatively high rainfall permit production of a wide variety of wines, with particular attention to Chardonnay and Cabernet Sauvignon. Shiraz and Merlot are also well represented while Chenin Blanc is becoming more popular for vinification in a more serious wooded style.

A gargoyle protecting the cellar at Plaisir de Merle

Franschhoek's white wines are very fruity, particularly Chardonnay and Sauvignon Blanc. On the south-facing slopes these white varieties are very popular with La Petite Ferme and Cape Chamonix producing Chardonnay wines with chalky and mineral tones. Towards the centre of the valley, Chardonnay shows tangy citrus and tropical fruit with structured examples from Glenwood, Mont Rochelle, La Couronne and Rickety Bridge. A fine example of single varietal Sauvignon Blanc from this area comes from the Boschendal cellar that, together with Akkerdal, has proved the extremely versatile character of Sauvignon Blanc in white blends. These blends tend to show more earthy lime and citrus flavours with a smooth finish.

The red wines from the Franschhoek area are medium textured with concentrated fruit (dark berries, plums), generally soft and ripe tannins and gentle minty undertones. Merlot produces ripe fruit with savoury notes and a herbaceous finish with examples from Dieu Donné and Akkerdal. Franschhoek seems favourable for Shiraz with the wines showing attractive violet and smoky beef characteristics with a lengthy finish. Single varietal wines are produced by La Motte, Lynx, Stony Brook and Boekenhoutskloof.

In the western area of the Franschhoek Pocket, towards the entrance of valley, the soil and differences in aspect are reflected in the wines. The red wines can be characterised as medium bodied with silky tannins and expressive fruit while the white wines are generally pleasantly perfumed and very accessible. Cabernet Sauvignon is especially popular, showing dense dark berry fruit and firm tannins, with powerful single varietal wines coming from Graham Beck Wines, Plaisir de Merle and Boschendal.

Classic flagships in the form of red blended wines from Boschendal, Graham Beck, Plaisir de Merle and Akkerdal show velvet fruit supported by sensitive oaking with a firm tannin backbone. Classic noble varieties are blended with newcomers such as Mourvèdre, Malbec and Pinotage.

Soil:	sandstone with shale, granite sites, sandy and alluvial by river, yellow-brown in foothills
Climate:	warm, abundant rainfall, mountain shadow
White varieties:	Chenin Blanc, Sauvignon Blanc, Chardonnay
Red varieties:	Cabernet Sauvignon, Merlot, Shiraz, Pinotage
Wine styles:	red, white, sparkling, dessert, fortified

DRIVING ROUTE: FRANSCHHOEK

Follow the N1 northbound in the direction of Paarl. About 60 kilometres from Cape Town, take Exit 55 to Paarl / Franschhoek. At the intersection, turn right onto the R101 and drive south-west for two kilometres. About 1.2 kilometres further, turn off left onto the R45 towards Franschhoek.

The first winery on the route is Plaisir de Merle. Take time to stroll through the grounds and request to view the line house, one of only two remaining examples in South Africa. The cellar is surrounded by a Koi-filled moat, complete with a working water mill.

Follow the R45 in a westerly direction. On the left is Bien Donne, venue for many local agricultural events, including the popular annual Cheese Festival during March. About 150 metres further, turn-off onto the R310 to Stellenbosch via the scenic Helshoogte Pass. Boschendal's grand property is only a few hundred metres down the R301. This winery boasts an impressive list of wine styles to suit almost every palate. Enjoy a leisurely wine tasting and a light lunch in dappled sunlight under the oak trees.

Return on the R310 to the turn-off onto the R45, and continue eastwards. Only a few kilometres further is the cellar of Graham Beck Wines Franschhoek. The entrance to the cellar is guarded by two bronze cat sculptures by the internationally acclaimed South African sculptor, Dylan Lewis. His works are in great demand around the world and can be viewed at this studio outside Stellenbosch (see Blaauwklippen Road Pocket in Stellenbosch).

Continue on the R45, crossing the Berg River. The Berg River hosts the gruelling annual canoe race of the same name which draws top canoeists from around the world. Take the R301 turn-off on the left towards Wellington, to Lynx Wines. The entrance to the cellar is on the left. This interesting boutique cellar produces New-World super-ripe Shiraz.

A wild rose bush and a black sign in the shape of a horse on the right announce the entrance to Akkerdal. Pieter Hanekom has created a fantastical mix of French, Spanish and Italian varieties.

Further towards Franschhoek, the entrance to La Motte on the left is adorned by bougainvillea – a stunning sight in full bloom. La Motte's grand tasting hall is also the venue for classical concerts in the summer months under the auspices of South African vocalist, Hanneli Koeglenberg née Rupert.

As you enter the town, the turn-off to Dieu Donné from the Main Road is clearly indicated. Turn left and follow Uitkyk Road towards the mountain. The road continues past a small stream and crosses a stone bridge. Dieu Donné's cellar and tasting room are perched high on the slopes of the mountain and provide a stunning view with plenty of photographic opportunities. The fireplace makes for great winter's day visits, while summer days are

Quiet Franschhoek main road

GPS waypoints

Akkerdal	S33 52.707 E19 02.843
Boschendal Wines	S33 52.646 E18 58.356
Dieu Donné Wines	S33 53.799 E19 07.776
Graham Beck Wines Franschhoek	S33 52.815 E19 01.444
La Motte	S33 52.908 E19 04.043
La Petit Ferme	S33 55.040 E19 08.181
Lynx Wines	S33 52.347 E19 02.658
Plaisir de Merle	S33 50.518 E18 57.500

Travelling tips

Information:
www.franschhoekwines.co.za

Restaurants:
French Connection +27 (0)21 876 4056
La Petite Ferme restaurant +27 (0)21 876 3016
Le Quartier Français restaurant +27 (0)21 876 2151
Reuben's +27 (0)21 876 3772

Accommodation:
La Petite Ferme guest cottages +27 (0)21 876 3016
La Couronne Hotel +27 (0)21 876 2770
Le Quartier Français +27 (0)21 876 2151

Events:
Annual Cheese Festival in March

Interests:
Museum (Boschendal) +27 (0)21 870 4200
Huguenot Fine Chocolates +27 (0)21 876 4096
Dewdale fly fishing +27 (0)21 876 2755
Kei Carpets +27 (0)21 876 2192
Truckles Traditional Cheese +27 (0)21 876 4928

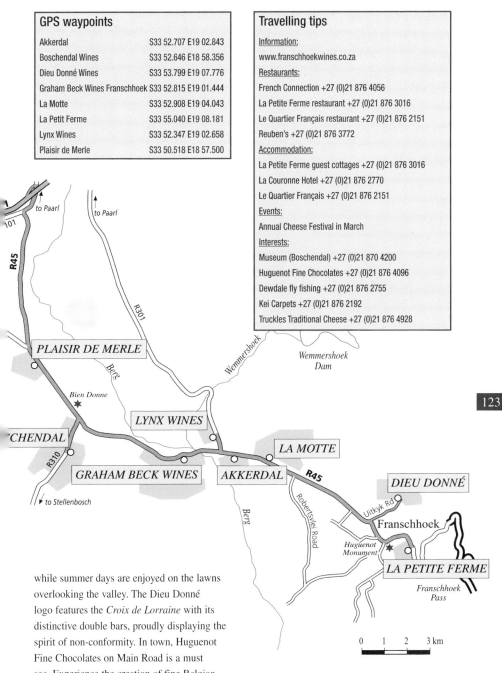

123

while summer days are enjoyed on the lawns overlooking the valley. The Dieu Donné logo features the *Croix de Lorraine* with its distinctive double bars, proudly displaying the spirit of non-conformity. In town, Huguenot Fine Chocolates on Main Road is a must see. Experience the creation of fine Belgian chocolate with a tour and tasting. Bookings are essential.

Restaurants and cafés line the streets of the town and are best explored on foot. The French Huguenot Monument, situated to the east of the town is well worth a visit.

Heading left at the intersection (north-east) up the Franschhoek Pass on the R45, the entrance to the last winery on this route, La Petit Ferme, lies slightly disguised on the right. Drive very carefully and be aware of traffic descending the pass. La Petit Ferme's small winery is adjacent to its celebrated restaurant, where magical dishes are paired with its wines. The terrace offers magnificent views of the valley and the rolling lawns make for a perfect summer picnic. Book well in advance for weekend dining.

La Motte *Franschhoek Pocket*

Although initially established in 1695, French Huguenots planted the first vineyards at La Motte in 1752. The beautifully preserved manor house (circa 1751), historical cellar (circa 1782) and water mill (circa 1741) have all been declared national monuments. Eighty hectares of irrigated vines are cultivated on varying altitudes, from the valley floor to the slopes of the Drakenstein Mountain (206 m). The different soil profiles all hold a high sand percentage which ensures good drainage. Vines are trellised and canopies protect developing bunches from harsh sunlight. Grapes are also bought from Darling, Paarl, Wellington and Walker Bay. Red grapes are partially natural fermented with extended maceration, ensuring wines with ample body and structure. Malolactic fermentation and maturation in French and American barrels give smoky and spicy notes. Chardonnay is partially barrel fermented and 12 month maturation in French oak yields a spiced, citrus wine with silky consistency.

Shiraz | Cab S, Merlot, Shz, Sauv Bl, Chard | Mon – Fri 9 – 4:30, Sat 10 – 3. Closed Sunday, Publ hols, Dec 25 | +27 (0)21 876 3119 | +27 (0)21 876 3446 | cellar@la-motte.co.za www.la-motte.co.za | 5 – 10 y | 88, 91, 95, 96, 98, 04 | summer garden restaurant, food & wine experience, classical music concerts

La Petite Ferme *Franschhoek Pocket*

The small boutique winery of La Petite Ferme cultivates only 14 hectares of densely planted vines (5, 000 vines/Ha) on steep north-facing mountain slopes, in shallow shale and gravel soils. The elevation (220 m) and mountain shade during morning hours create cool growth conditions. White varieties are planted on the highest sites and canopies are kept closed on the west side to protect fruit from sun damage. Red varieties are sited on lower slopes and canopies are opened to maximise the long, warm afternoons and ensure proper ripening and colour development. White wines are made from a very reductive process and fermented at a low 9 – 12°C to protect delicate floral aromas. Partially natural fermented Chardonnay completes malolactic fermentation in barrel, softening the acid to a full, rich wine. The flagship Sauvignon Blanc is flinty and mineral with granadilla fruit and lively acid. The wine is matured on yeast lees adding mid-palate weight. Shiraz, Chardonnay and Merlot are all from single vineyards.

Sauvignon Blanc | Sauv B, Merlot, Sém | tasting by appt | + 27 (0)21 876 3016 | +27 (0)21 876 3624 | info@lapetiteferme.co.za www.lapetiteferme.co.za | Sauv 2 – 4 y; reds 5 y | Merlot 02, Chard 01, Sauv Bl 04 | restaurant, own cookbook, luxury guest suites, gift shop

Fine dining – La Petite Ferme Restaurant perched high in the Franschhoek Pass

Akkerdal *Franschhoek Pocket*

The small family winery of Akkerdal cultivates an unusual blend of French, Spanish, Italian and South African varieties. Vines are cultivated on the riverbanks of the Berg River in sandy and alluvial soils, changing to yellowish-brown, light textured soils. Good drainage allows slight water stress in the dry summer months, reducing berry size, achieving a better skin to juice ratio and improving colour and flavour concentration. Summer cover crops are planted between vine rows to reduce possible damage caused by excessive light and heat reflected from the sandy surface. The flagship, Wild Boar, is aptly named after the wild boars which created severe vineyard problems for the early French Huguenots. Grapes are fermented in open-top fermenters at a lower 24 – 28°C, resulting in a natural reduction of excessive alcohol. Each of the components is fermented and matured separately and, once completed, barrels are selected for the blend. This New World-styled wine shows concentrated fruit with soft tannins.

⬛ Wild Boar (Malbec / Mour/ PV / Temp / Barb / Cab F)
⬛ various ⬤ Sat 9 – 1, Mon – Fri 8 – 5 by appt 🖊 +27 (0)21 876 3481 📠 +27 (0)21 876 3189 📧 wine@akkerdal.co.za www.akkerdal.co.za 🍷 5 – 9 y ⬛03 ⓘ self-catering guest house, wild boars spotted on occasion

Dieu Donné Vineyards *Franschhoek Pocket*

Nestled high in the Franschhoek Mountain, Dieu Donné winery boasts a spectacular vantage point. Translated literally Dieu Donné means "God given" or "Gift from God". Forty-two hectares of steep south-west-facing slopes are cultivated. The aspect and elevation create a dramatic cooling effect with summer daytime temperatures varying within 4°C from the lowest (360 m) to the highest (580 m) sites. This, together with the rocky granite soils, allows grapes to retain naturally high fruit acidity. To accommodate the steep slopes, planting density has been slightly decreased to 3, 800 vines/Ha (in reference to the rest of the farm) and vines are trained on a vertical trellis system, spreading the canopy to improve sun penetration and ventilation. High fermentation temperatures (28°C) followed by extended maturation in French barrels produce a full-bodied, earthy Merlot with ripe, silky tannins. The white wines, fermented at a very low temperature (13°C), show a delicate floral bouquet and refreshing acidity. Most of the varietal wines from Dieu Donné are from single vineyards.

ⓘ Dieu Donné Merlot (sgl vineyard) ⬛ Merlot, Cab S, Pinotage, Shiraz, Sauv Bl, Chard, MCC, NLH ⬤ Mon-Fri 9 – 4, Sat, Sun 10:30 – 4. Closed Dec 25, 26, Jan 1 🖊 +27 (0)21 876 2493 📠 +27 (0)21 876 2102 📧 info@dieudonnevineyards.com www.dieudonnevineyards.com 🍷 reds 10 y + ⬛97, 99, 03 ⓘ fireplace, tours, picnics and cheese platters on terrace(by appt), food and wine pairing events

Graham Beck Wines Franschhoek *Franschhoek Pocket*

Graham Beck Franschhoek and Robertson create a synergy of one brand made by two wineries. Each maintains a distinct yet complementary identity. Grapes are cultivated on properties in Stellenbosch, Franschhoek and Robertson. In Franschhoek, 100 hectares are planted in alluvial soils, also home to The Old Road Pinotage single vineyard (6 Ha).

Varietals for the Joshua blend (Shz, Viognier) are sourced from the Stellenbosch and Franschhoek properties. Grapes are harvested, crushed and fermented together to produce a Côte-Rôtie-styled wine. Recent vintages were ripe with cherry and roasted spice flavours.

The Coffeestone single vineyard (Cab S) is located in Stellenbosch, a mere two kilometres from the ocean, on a north-facing slope in granite and gravel soils, with a coffeestone layer one metre below the surface. Mature vines (15 y) yield only four tons per hectare in an ideal macro-climate created by the vineyard's high elevation and its close proximity to the sea. South-east to north-west row directions maximise airflow to prevent fungal diseases in these humid conditions. The vineyards are harvested several times to select grapes for this flagship wine.

Fermentation takes place in open vessels, with regular pump overs to ensure gentle extraction. Maturation in barrels (up to 20 months) with 75 per cent new French oak, yield a powerful wine with soft tannins.

In a pioneering spirit, components for the William blend (Cab S / Pinotage) are sourced and vinified at the Robertson and Franschhoek cellars respectively. A combination of French and American oak adds vanilla and smoky notes to the savoury finish.

Vines closely follow the contours

ℹ️ Coffeestone (Cab S), Joshua 🍷 Cab S/F, Shz, Merlot, Pinotage, PV, Viog, Sauv Bl ⊙ Mon – Fri 9 – 5, Sat 10 – 3. Closed Easter Fri, Sun, Dec 25, 26, Jan 1 📞+27 (0)21 874 1258 📠+27 (0)21 874 1712 ✉ market@grahambeckwines.co.za www.grahambeckwines.com 🔌10 y+ 🏆 98, 00, 03, 04 ℹ️ newly opened tasting facility, sculptures, tours by appt

Lynx Wines *Franschhoek Pocket*

Lynx Wines and its immaculate vineyards are set between citrus orchards, paddocks and stables on a lush Wemmershoek farm. Of the 11 hectares that are cultivated, 15 per cent are selected for the Lynx label. Alluvial, sandy soils on the valley floor have poor water retention and the young vineyards (5 y) are irrigated. The Shiraz's growth vigour is controlled on the poor soils by strict irrigation and induced water stress, naturally reducing berry size and improving colour development of the wine. Until vines mature, green harvesting sets a low crop yield. In the low-tech cellar, grapes are fermented in open-top cement tanks with maceration before and after fermentation (4 weeks in total) extracting maximum colour. Twelve month barrel maturation yields aromatic wines which are bottle aged for six months before release. Super-ripe Shiraz shows spicy and gamey notes with a powerful alcohol content (Alc.15.3% by Vol.), while the Cabernet Sauvignon and Bordeaux blend are more restrained with a textured palate and elegant, dense tannins.

ℹ️ Shiraz, Xanache (Cab S / F / Merlot) 🍷 Shz, Cab S, F, Merlot, Viognier ⊙ by appt 📞 + 27 (0)21 867 0406 📠 +27 (0)21 867 0397 ✉ winemaker@lynxwines.co.za www.lynxwines.co.za 🔌 8 – 15 y 🏆 04 ℹ️ cellar tour by appt (done by winemaker), self-catering cottages, elegant packaging

Plaisir de Merle *Franschhoek Pocket*

Plaisir de Merle dates back to 1687 when the French Huguenot, Charles Marais, originally named his farm *Le Plessis Marly* after his French home village. During the 1700s, the farm boasted 35, 000 vines, but deciduous fruit became the main crop until its vinous potential was once again recognised in the early 1990s. Today, 450 hectares of vineyards are cultivated on this historic farm, on south-east-facing slopes. High elevations (300 – 350 m) fall in the afternoon shadows from the mountain peaks which mitigate against the generally warm climate. The well-drained granite soils with good moisture retention allow for dry-land cultivation. Grapes undergo cold maceration before and after fermentation for colour extraction and they are fermented at a relatively cool 24 – 26°C. This discourages the extraction of harsh tannins. The wines are generally blended and bottled after being matured for up to 16 months in oak barrels. A blend of six vineyard blocks gives elegance and ripe fruit to the Cabernet Sauvignon, while the red blend (Cab S / Merlot / Shiraz / Petit Verdot / Malbec) is a structured, powerful wine.

ℹ️ Cab Sauv 🍷 Cab S / F, Shz, Merlot, PV, Malbec, Sauv Bl, Chard ⊙ Mon – Fri 9 – 5, Sat 10 – 4 (Nov – Mar), 10 – 2 (Apr – Oct). Closed publ hols 📞+27 (0)21 874 1071 📠+27 (0)21 874 1689 ✉ info@plaisirdemerle.co.za www.plaisirdemerle. co.za 🔌 5 – 8 y 🏆 94, 95, 98, 01, 03 ℹ️ cellar tours by appt, tour groups by appt

Boschendal Wines *Franschhoek Pocket*

Boschendal was established in 1685 when French Huguenot Jean le Long prepared the soil to plant his first vines. A sense of history lives on at the five historic Cape Dutch houses on the farm. The old manor house, converted into a museum, is open to the public. Situated on lower foothills of the Groot-Drakenstein and Simonsberg Mountains and dissected by the Dwars River, Boschendal has east and south-east-facing slopes angling towards the valley floor.

Two hundred and twelve hectares of vines are cultivated on a range of soil types, from the elevated valley floor at 160 metres above sea level (avoiding sandy alluvial river banks) up to the foothills towards the mountain where rich, deep, red soils with a high clay content have higher growth potential and good drainage.

The heat-sensitive Sauvignon Blanc is planted on the highest sites (200 – 390 m) and benefits from the cooling effect. The Shiraz is planted on sites with a higher percentage of rocks, which restricts this variety's vigorous growth, achieving more concentrated fruit. Cabernet Sauvignon and Merlot are planted on east and north-east-facing sites, which provide more sunlight to ripen the red grapes properly. These vineyards supply fruit for the flagship wines, while fruit for the second label wines are sourced from Stellenbosch, Somerset West and Durbanville.

The Sauvignon Blanc grapes are crushed and destemmed after harvest and pressed gently to avoid extraction of any harsh tannins. Only free-run juice is used for the reserve wine, which is made in a reductive process using sulphur and ascorbic acid to protect the juice from oxidation. Cleared juice is fermented cold (14 – 16°C) to preserve subtle floral and fruit aromas and the fermented wine matures on its lees for six months, adding some weight to the palate. The unwooded Sauvignon Blanc shows pungent tropical fruit with grass and gooseberry characters, a fresh wine and rather full compared to other Sauvignon Blancs in the region.

The Shiraz grapes for the premium wine are fermented in open-top vessels at a relatively low (for red wines) fermentation temperature of 25°C with regular pump overs and two weeks maceration to extract maximum colour. The young wine is drained off and skins are pressed. Only a portion of the press wine, which is rich in tannins and highly structured, is blended back with the free-run wine in order to give structure and longevity to the wine. Malolactic fermentation occurs spontaneously and the wine is gently oaked in French barrels (with only 10 per cent new) for up to 18 months.

All premium red wines are bottled and stored for a further two to three years to ensure correct aging before release onto the market. Shiraz shows a smoky bouquet with a 15 per cent alcohol content giving a velvety glow. The Boschendal experience includes a cellar door offering tasting and sales, cellar tours, restaurants, picnics on the lawn and the Manor House museum, which is open daily.

Lovingly maintained Cape Dutch buildings (Top)
The imposing entrance at Boschendal (Centre)
The pavilion as a centre piece in the picnic garden (Left)

ℹ️ Cecil John Rhodes Shiraz Reserve 🍇 Sauv Bl, Shz, Chenin Bl, Chard, Sém, Viog, Cab S/F, Merlot, PN ⏰ Daily 8:30 – 4:30. Closed Easter Fri, May 1, Dec 25 📞 +27 (0)21 870 4200 📠 +27 (0)21 874 1531 📧 taphuis@dgb.co.za www.boschendal.com 📧 Sauv 3 y, Shz 8 y 🍷 98, 01, 03 ℹ️ tours 10:30, 11:30 by appt, restaurant and picnics, tour groups, gifts, conservation area, museum (9:30 – 5)

Paarl

Delightful Paarl – oak trees provide welcome shelter from the afternoon sun

The town of Paarl is situated beneath a large granite outcrop, formed by three rounded domes. The most prominent is called Paarlberg (Afrikaans), meaning "pearl rock", as it glistens in the early morning light, especially after it has rained.

The landlocked Paarl area is large and diverse, situated between Simonsberg to the south, the Hawequa Mountain to the east and Paardeberg to the north-west. The greater Paarl area hosts a mixture of agricultural produce other than wine grapes. The area is also known for its highly sought after table grapes, olives and cheese.

PAARL POCKET

The area around the mountain contains a complex terrain of valley floors, mountain slopes as well as plains. Although Paarlberg is an exposed granite pluton, the soils around it fall into three main groups. Sandstone-derived soils are found along the Berg River, to the east, granite soils on either side of the west and east-facing Paarl Mountain and weathered shale on the north-western side. These soils have varying degrees of wetness, medium to high potential on the yellow to reddish-brown, and medium-textured, well-drained and acid granite soils.

The summer daytime temperatures for the western (23.1°C) and the eastern slopes (24°C) indicate quite warm conditions, especially further away from the mountain and into the valley basin around the town. The summers are long and hot. Even with an annual rainfall of 900 mm, supplementary irrigation is advantageous

Soil:	sandstone, granite, weathered shale
Climate:	warm, abundant rainfall
White varieties:	Chenin Blanc, Sauvignon Blanc, Chardonnay
Red varieties:	Cabernet Sauvignon, Merlot, Shiraz, Pinotage
Wine styles:	red, white, sparkling, dessert, fortified

in reducing the temperature of the plant. In this hot climate, some of the very best wines come from vineyards on higher lying sites as these provide cooler ripening conditions. The variation in ripening temperature allows for the cultivation of a wide variety of wine grapes, including all six noble varieties, strongly favouring Chardonnay and Shiraz. As soil types and topography vary, planting density and trellising (bush vine and vertical trellises) are adjusted according to the location of the vineyard. The favourable *terroir* of this area makes for an array of wines, including white, sparkling, red and port wines.

Preserving history – official historical building plaque

Sémillon, Chardonnay, as well as blends of these, produce a bouquet of fruit flavours with occasional citrus and mineral characteristics, with examples from Nederburg and Seidelberg. The rich sweetness buffed with *Botrytis* and a tang of citrus of Weisser Riesling and Sémillon Noble Late Harvest from Nederburg, in particular, have proved the area's suitability for this style of wine.

Red varieties generally produce a medley of fruit with serious structure and richness in single varietal wines but also in blended wines. Vendôme, Seidelberg and Landskroon produce Cabernet wines, while Shiraz features at Avondale, Coleraine, Domaine Braham and Ridgeback. Robust and rustic styled blends are typical of Black Pearl, Nederburg and Fairview. Port varieties give elegant, creamy, ripe fruit textures in the port wines of this area, with the most well-know example being Landskroon.

The famous annual Nederburg auction is a highlight of the wine calendar in South Africa. Nederburg produces small quantities of wine from selected vineyard blocks to express the varietal characters while other local wineries are subject to a screening process to participate in the auction.

DRIVING ROUTE: PAARL

The Paarl Pocket is situated around the granite outcrop of Paarl, about 55 kilometres from Cape Town (25 km from Stellenbosch). From the N1 freeway, take Exit 47 to the left. At the intersection, turn left onto the R44. Seven kilometres further a sign indicates Black Pearl Wines on the right. This small boutique winery's vineyards grow right next to its fynbos conservation area. From Black Pearl, follow the R44 south, in the direction of the N1 freeway, for about one kilometre. Turn left onto the Suid Agter Paarl Road and continue for 3.8 kilometres to the turn-off to Seidelberg, clearly marked with white walls and flags. Seidelberg not only hosts wine tasting of its *terroir* wines, but also includes a restaurant, a glass blowing studio, walking trails and children's facilities including a petting zoo.

The road continues south-east for four kilometres to a T-junction with the R101. Turn left onto the R101 for a kilometre. Pass under a low bridge (the N1 freeway). Just past this bridge turn right to join the N1 heading north-east. Continue for 2.8 kilometres. Take Exit 59 to the left. At the T-junction, turn left onto the R301 and then the next left onto Arboretum Avenue. Three hundred metres further lies the entrance to the next winery, Vendôme, on the right. Ten generations of the Le Roux family have made wine at this family-owned winery since 1692. The beautiful gabled cellar is still in use today.

Return to the N1 along the same route. At the intersection, turn left to rejoin the N1 north. Continue for four kilometres to Exit 62a and turn left onto Sonstraal Road. Cross over a small intersection and drive along the winding road (4.5 km) to the entrance of the last winery visit, Nederburg. Nederburg became famous for its consistent wines over the years, but has also gained recognition for its annual wine auction. This auction is one of the highlights of the wine industry calendar. In Paarl, visit the KWV (Koöperatiewe Wjinbouers Vereniging) for wine tours through its facilities, including a presentation on barrel making.

Travelling tips

Information:
www.paarlwine.co.za
www.paarlonline.com

Restaurants:
De Leuwen Jagt (Seidelberg) +27 (0)21 863 5222
De Malle Madonna +27 (0)21 863 3925
Marc's +27 (0)21 863 3980
De Oude Paarl +27 (0)21 872 1002
Pontac Manor restaurant +27 (0)21 872 0445

Accommodation:
De Oude Paarl Hotel +27 (0)21 872 1002
Grande Roche Hotel +27 (0)21 863 2727
Pontac Manor Hotel +27 (0)21 872 0445

Interests:
Oude Paarl Belgian chocolate shop +27 (0)21 872 1002
Glass Blowing Studio (Seidelberg) +27 (0)21 863 0330
Drakenstein Olives +27 (0)21 868 3185
KWV Emporium Wine Tours +27 (0)21 807 3008
Paarl Bird Sanctuary +27 (0)21 872 3829/4842
Wynland Ballooning +27(0)21 863 3192

GPS waypoints

Black Pearl Wines	S33 44.166 E18 53.683
Nederburg	S33 43.181 E19 00.141
Seidelberg	S33 45.855 E18 55.128
Vendôme	S33 45.442 E18 58.718

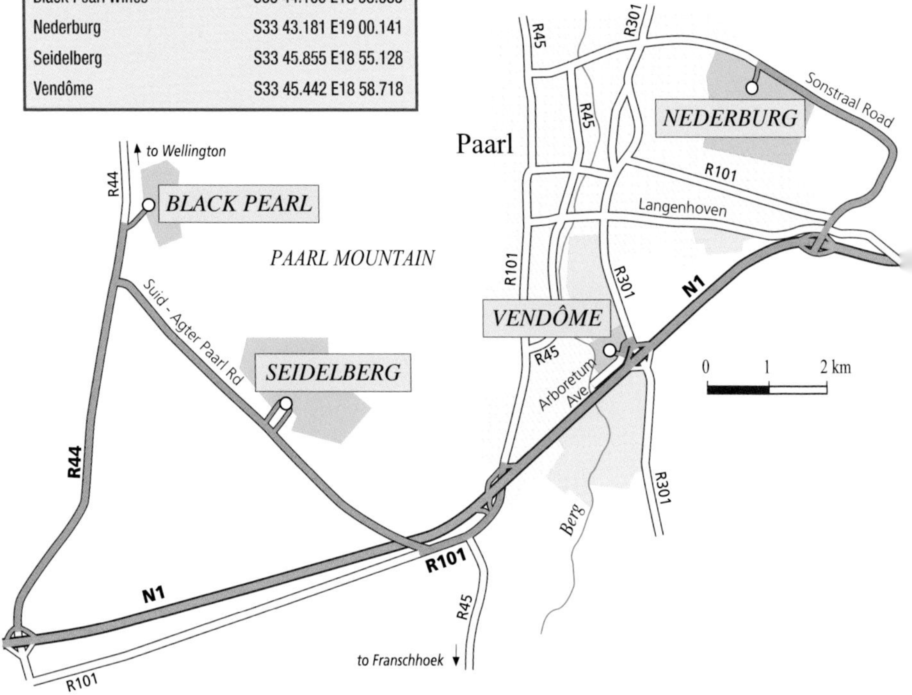

130

Seidelberg Estate *Paarl Pocket*

First established in 1680, Seidelberg was granted by Governor Van der Stel as De Leuwen Jagt, its Dutch name meaning "The lion hunt". Since the construction of the cellar (circa 1700), Seidelberg has produced wines from its own grapes, but it is the latest plantings of Viognier, Mourvèdre and Malbec that inspire wine enthusiasts.

Just over 100 hectares of vines are cultivated on the west-facing slopes of Paarl Mountain. In the relatively hot climate, vineyard management is directed to protect vines from heat and direct sun as well as to conserve as much soil moisture as possible. The granite dome of Paarl Mountain provides some relief from the heat, which collects in the eastern precincts of the low-lying town. For example, the Merlot block on the higher mountain slopes is 5°C cooler than on the Paarl Valley floor as the vineyard is exposed to cooling airflow in the afternoon.

Maintaining water retention in the deep granite-based soils also has a slight cooling effect, while supplementary irrigation is applied during extremely hot conditions. All varieties, except Pinotage, are trellised with the canopies providing sun protection during the heat of the day. The juice and skins of these varieties are also mixed more frequently, vines to give concentrated berry fruit and to reduce the plants' water requirements. Eighty per cent of the farm is planted to red varieties as these are better suited to the soils and climate. The white varieties are planted high on the slopes and benefit from the cooling effect of the higher elevation.

Grapes are hand harvested into small lug boxes to prevent damage, and hand sorted to remove all matter other than grapes. The red grapes are macerated after crushing to assist in colour extraction and then fermented. Both open and closed fermenters are used with some varieties requiring more time to extract colour and flavour. The juice and skins of these varieties are also mixed more frequently, every four hours. Once fermentation is completed, the bulk of the liquid is drained before the skins are pressed. Pressed and free-run wine is then blended to complete malolactic fermentation before barrel maturation. As very little new wood is used, maturation is extended to 14 months using French oak. The exception is Shiraz (a single vineyard wine with a yield of only two tons per hectare) where 30 per cent American oak gives the wine a vanilla note underlying the dense palate. The white grapes are harvested and cold fermented in stainless steel tanks to retain their fruity bouquet. Only Chardonnay is barrel fermented, giving a butterscotch and toasty palate.

Seidelberg also has a popular restaurant and terrace under 300-year-old oaks, a glass blowing studio and gallery, and an art exhibition. Working only with its own vineyards, Seidelberg says: "We resist the temptation to make mass market wines; rather we focus on *terroir*-driven wines to show the uniqueness of Seidelberg." In that spirit, Seidelberg continued to present its 1999 Pinotage, which was rejected 16 times before finally being certified by the local wine certification board as a " typical" *terroir* wine.

Lush gardens surround the manor house (Top)
The unmistakable entrance to Seidelberg (Centre)
Sunrise as experienced on the Estate (Left)

131

🛈 Roland's Reserve range: Merlot, Syrah, Pinotage, Cab S 🍷 Cab Franc, Malbec, Mouv, Sauv Bl, Chenin Bl, Viog 🕐 Mon – Fri 9 – 6 Sat, Sun Publ hols 10 – 6. Closed Dec 25 ☎ +27 (0)21 863 5200 📠 +27 (0)21 863 3797 📧 info@seidelberg.co.za www.seidelberg.co.za
💶 5-7 y 🛏 N/A ℹ️ tours daily, wine blending competition, gifts, farm produce, venue: functions and conference, glass blowing studio, restaurant, hiking trail, conservation area, petting zoo

Nederburg *Paarl Pocket*

Nederburg's wine history dates back to 1791 when Philippus Wolvaardt was granted 49 hectares of land, located at the foot of the Drakenstein Mountain. The farm was promptly planted to vines and within six years the first wine was made. By 1810, more than 63,000 vines were established. Today, Nederburg is one of the most successful premium wine brands, with flagship wines created from a fusion of Paarl and other carefully selected and complementary *terroir* sites.

Sauvignon Blanc grapes are sourced from Darling, Durbanville and Stellenbosch vineyards. Grapes are harvested early in the morning and fermented at 13°C to preserve the herbaceous and tropical fruit flavours. Chardonnay (ex Durbanville, Klapmuts-Simondium) is oak fermented and matured on the lees to yield a discreetly oak-scented wine with citrus notes and minerality.

Shiraz (ex-Philadelphia, Durbanville) is sourced from dry-land, trellised vineyards in decomposed granite soils. The vineyards are situated on south to south-westerly-facing slopes at low altitudes (60 – 80 m) and enjoy the cooling maritime influence. Cabernet Sauvignon (ex-Darling, Paarl and Stellenbosch) is sourced from well-drained, deep red and yellow soils. Red grapes are harvested by hand at relatively low sugar levels (23 – 25° Balling), resulting in restrained alcohol wines. The grapes ferment on the skins for 14 days at 25° – 28°C and are regularly pumped over for colour extraction. Following malolactic fermentation, the young wine is transferred to wood for a 12 to 24 month maturation period. A combination of French, Romanian, Hungarian and American barrels is used for the maturation of the wines.

The entrance to Nederburg

Cab S, Merlot, Shz, Pinotage, Chard, Sauv Bl and others ◯ Mon – Fri 8:30 – 5, Sat 10 – 2 (Apr – Oct), Sat 10 – 4 (Nov – Mar), Sun 11 – 4. Closed Easter Fri, Dec 25, Jan 1 ☎ +27 (0)21 862 3104 +27 (0)21 862 4887 ✉ nedwines@distell.co.za www.nederburg.co.za ▤ white 2 – 3 y, red 5 – 10 y ◼ Reds 94, 96, 01. White 97, 03, 04 ℹ homestead national monument (circa 1800), cellar tour, picnic lunches, tour groups, venue: wedding and conference, conservation area

Black Pearl Wines *Paarl Pocket*

Black Pearl Wines has grown from a true garagiste to a recognised wine producer. This small vineyard of eight hectares is cultivated on the western slopes of Paarl Mountain in shale soils. The mountain provides early morning shade, with the afternoon sun creating warm ripening conditions. Prevailing south-easterly winds relieve the intense summer heat and the trellis system is lifted higher off the ground (1 m) to reduce radiance from the soil surface. The deep, fertile soil has good water retention, allowing dry-land cultivation and a lower planting density is used to discourage growth vigour in the vines. The red blend is named Oro after God Oro, King of the Firmament, who gave a black pearl as a gift to the ocean. A small 4.5 hectare single vineyard provides fruit for the Shiraz. Once fermented, the grape skins are gently pressed in a traditional wooden basket press. The wine matures ini oak and the wine remains unfiltered and unfined. The Shiraz is fruit driven with hints of fynbos and eucalyptus.

Oro (Shiraz/ Cab) Shiraz, Cab S ◯ by appt ☎ +27 (0)21 863 9200 +27 (0)83 395 6999 ✉ info@blackpearlwines.com www.blackpearlwines.com ▤ 3 – 5 y ◼ 04 ℹ indigenous conservation area

Vendôme *Paarl Pocket*

The Le Roux family of Vendôme have been producing wine since 1692. They still produce wine in the gabled cellar and cultivate 40 hectares of vines on south-west-facing slopes. These slopes are in shadow during the early morning hours, moderating the warm daytime temperatures. High planting densities and deliberate water stress (reducing supplementary irrigation) are used to restrict vine growth on the loam, clay and rocky soil. Row direction (east to west) and vertically trellised canopies protect the developing grape bunches from direct sunlight, while maximising airflow through the canopy. Grapes for the Vendôme blend are given cold maceration and ferment naturally at lower temperatures (25°C) before being matured in older barrels. The wine is elegant, showing ripe fruit and mineral notes. The red wines show firm tannins and the unwooded Chardonnay has a racy, lime acidity.

Vendôme (Merlot / Cab S / Cab F) Cab S, Cab F, Merlot, Chard (single vineyard) ◯ Mon – Fri 9:30 – 1 (1 – 4:30 by appt), Sat 9:30 – 12:30. Closed publ hols ☎ +27 (0)21 863 3905 +27 (0)21 863 0094 ✉ lerouxjg@icon.co.za www.vendome. co.za ▤ 7 – 8 y ◼ 03 ℹ cellar tours by appt, venue: conference and functions

VOOR-PAARDEBERG POCKET

The Voor-Paardeberg (Eng. "The front of Horse Mountain") Pocket lies to the south-east of the Paardeberg Mountain. This granite outcrop is located a few kilometres north-west of the town of Paarl. A warmer area, southerly winds prevail throughout the year, helping to cool the vineyards. Summer daytime temperatures are approximately five degrees cooler than in the general Paarl region. Higher up on the slopes, soils are close to pure granite and of higher potential. Lower on the slopes, granite formations mix with varying percentages of clay, which results in medium to low potential soils. Vines are trellised to curtail excessive growth and offer protection against the prevailing winds.

This Pocket has only recently started to vinify grapes under its own labels, making some interesting wines. The hot, dry climate favours red varieties, although high-lying sites allow for the production of white varieties such as the Chardonnay from Détendu. This wine is enlivened by grapefruit aromas, with a fresh restrained finish. Shiraz is the most prominent red variety, with a complex nose and expressive wild flavours in a balance between fruit and spice. Exciting new examples of Shiraz come from Horse Mountain, Scali, Détendu and Armajaro. Fruity, well-structured Pinotage is emerging (Scali), along with interesting red blends (Armajaro).

DRIVING ROUTE:
VOOR-PAARDEBERG

The Voor-Paardeberg Pocket lies 70 kilometres from Cape Town (43 km from Stellenbosch). From the N1 freeway, take Exit 47 to the left. At the intersection, turn left onto the R44. Follow the R44 for 17 kilometres to the turn-off onto Agter Paarl Road to the left. The road ends in a T-junction nine kilometres further. Turn right to visit Armajaro, the first winery on this route. The entrance to the farm is just over the crest on the left, indicated with a sign. Vines were first planted on this farm in the 1700s. The UK-based company Armajaro Holdings has restored the farm to produce quality wine again.

A little further down the road, also on the left, is the next winery, Détendu. The name, meaning "relaxed", aptly describes the atmosphere in the restored cellar. Visits are by appointment only.

133

The Paardeberg offers varying aspects to viticulturists

Only a few metres further, this time on the right, is Scali. This family-owned winery takes its name from the predominant soil type (shale) on the farm. Scali also offers bed and breakfast accommodation and produces its own olive oil.

Continue on the road to Horse Mountain Wines. A gravel road turns off to the left. Buzz the intercom at the gate to enter. Horse Mountain was named after the granite outcrop, Paardeberg, on which it lies. The quagga graces the wine label. The winery is actively involved in a project attempting to breed this species. A group of the animals from the breeding programme can be viewed on request.

Travelling tips

Accommodation:
Scali B&B +27 (0)21 869 8340
Sonop Accommodation +27 (0)21 869 8534

GPS waypoints

Armajaro	S33 35.777 E18 51.038
Détendu	S33 35.813 E18 51.604
Horse Mountain Wines	S33 34.940 E18 51.966
Scali	S33 36.697 E18 51.494

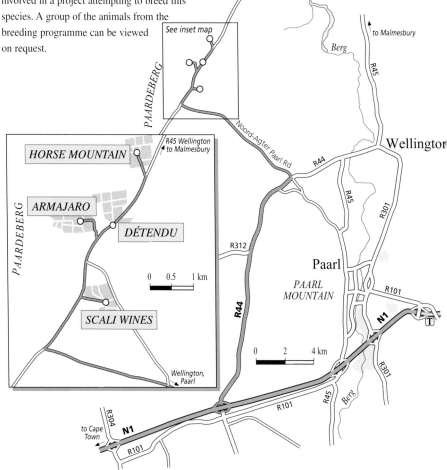

Armajaro *Voor-Paardeberg Pocket*

Armajaro, a UK-based company, bought this historic property where wine grapes and winemaking have been practised since the early 1700s. Vines are cultivated on granitic soils on the south-west and especially the east-facing slopes of the Paardeberg Mountain. Early afternoon mountain shadows and increased rainfall (due to the mountain slopes trapping clouds) moderate the summer temperatures. Lower-lying sites, with more moisture retention and thus slightly cooler, are planted to white grapes. Red varieties are purposefully water stressed on the drier slopes, naturally reducing berry size and concentrating flavours. Shiraz, Mourvèdre and Carignan are cultivated as bush vines, yielding pronounced varietal characters. Grapes are cold soaked before fermentation to extract colour and flavour without harsh tannins. Pressing is done using a traditional basket press and the wines are transferred to larger barrels (300, 500 l) for maturation, imparting gentle oak characters. The wines are made in a minimalistic way to retain the natural fruit flavours associated with this *terroir*.

---

[i] Armajaro, Vondeling (Shz / Mouv / Gren) [icon] Shz, Gren, Mouv, Carig, Cab S, Merlot, Viog, Chard, Chenin Bl [icon] by appt [icon] +27 (21) 869 8595 [icon] +27 (21) 869 8595 [icon] Armajaro@iafrica.com www.armajaro.co.za [icon] 8 y [icon] 05 [i] 430 Ha of natural fynbos

Détendu *Voor-Paardeberg Pocket*

The word Détendu means "relaxed", a fitting *nom de bataille* for this humble boutique cellar on the Klein Vondeling farm spread along the south-eastern slopes of the Voor-Paardeberg Mountain. Fifty-five hectares of vines are planted on high slopes where early evening shadows moderate the heat of the day. Due to a gradual slope, the poor granite soil provides good drainage with vines planted to a low density (2, 800 vines/Ha) to improve concentration. A small portion of the crop is selected for the Détendu label while the balance is sold. Following harvest, grapes are cooled to 4°C and hand sorted to remove any damaged or underdeveloped grapes. Red wines ferment at a cooler than normal 24°C and are cold soaked for another three days to ensure colour stability. Chardonnay receives skin contact before fermentation to add complexity and only 50 per cent is wooded resulting in a crisp wine with a hint of oak.

---

[i] Shiraz, Chardonnay [icon] Chard, Chenin Bl, Shiraz, Pinotage, Merlot, Cab S [icon] by appt [icon] +27 (0)21 863 3282 [icon] +27 (0)21 863 2480 [icon] info@detendu.co.za www.detendu. co.za [icon] 5 – 7 y [icon] 03 [i] Small hands-on cellar, limited production 6, 000 bottles annually, personal attention

---

Horse Mountain Wines *Voor-Paardeberg Pocket*

Horse Mountain Wines cultivates 45 hectares on south-east-facing slopes of fertile, decomposed granite soils at the foot of the Paardeberg Mountain. High vegetative growth is accommodated on a vertically extended trellis system and the well-supported, larger canopy allows for a higher crop yield of 10 tons per hectare without loss of quality. With the south-east aspect, there is less sunlight exposure and thinner canopies provide more airflow, moderating the heat of day. A typical New World approach sees grapes picked very ripe with warm fermentation (28°C), malolactic fermentation in wood and heavy toasted barrels. This results in a wine of high alcohol content with very ripe, upfront fruit. Twenty-five per cent Merlot of lower alcohol content softens the mouthfeel on the Cabernet Sauvignon-dominated blend. Pinotage and Shiraz wines are from single vineyards, and a lifestyle range named Quagga Ridge comprising a trio of red, white and rosé. Interestingly, all Horse Mountain wines are sealed with screw tops.

---

[i] Michele (Cab S/F, Merlot) [icon] Cab S / F, Merlot, Shz, Pinotage [icon] Mon – Fri 9 – 5, Sat 9 – 1. [icon] +27 (0)21 869 8328 [icon] +27 (0)21 869 8329 [icon] wine@horsemountainwines.com www.horsemountainwines.com [icon] 8 y [icon] 04 [i] BYO picnic, supports project to reintroduce the quagga species

Scali *Voor-Paardeberg Pocket*

Five generations have owned Scali on the slopes of Paardeberg. The name refers to the predominantly shale soil on the farm. The decomposed shale and gravel soils have a very low growth vigour and planting density is double the norm (7, 250 vines/Ha) to promote deep root development. Each individual vine is supported by a pole to protect it from the prevailing south-westerly winds, and yields are low at only four tons per hectare. Summer daytime temperatures are warm (26°C) and only the cooler south-facing slopes are cultivated. Winemaking is traditional; grapes are cold macerated prior to fermentation to allow colour and fruit flavours to be extracted. Fermentation (22 – 28°C) is done in open oak fermenters with regular punch-downs. The wines mature in new and older French oak (50/50) for up to 24 months, resulting in full-bodied wines with gentle tannins and ripe berry fruit flavours.

---

[i] Pinotage, Shz [icon] Pinotage, Shz [icon] by appt [icon] +27 (0)21 869 8340 [icon] +27 (0)21 869 8383 [icon] info@scali.co.za www.scali.co.za [icon] 8 y [icon] 01, 03 [i] B&B accommodation, olive oil

135

KLAPMUTS-SIMONDIUM POCKET

The Klapmuts-Simondium Pocket includes the northern and eastern foothills of Simonsberg and the Klein Drakenstein Mountains. The majority of the vineyards are situated on reddish-brown, medium textured, well-drained soils derived from the granite base of the mountain, grading into sandier soils with an alluvial nature on lower slopes. Soils are deep, allowing for extensive root development and excessive growth is a potential problem. The summer daytime temperature is 22.6°C, indicating that this Pocket is warmer than, for instance, some Pockets in Stellenbosch, but receives more abundant rain (annual rainfall 800 mm). Due to the warm climate, sites on the mountain slopes are used for heat-sensitive white grape varieties such as Chardonnay and Sauvignon Blanc with great success.

This area is quite diverse in style, making very juicy whites and very interesting, layered red wines. Favourite varieties are Cabernet Sauvignon, Shiraz and Chardonnay.

Glen Carlou has always been recognised for its intense, rich Chardonnay and seriously styled, charming Pinot Noir and Shiraz wines with their timeless, classic style.

Shiraz from Klapmuts-Simondium has deep, complex layers of fruit, with some savoury and peppery characteristics. Lindhorst, Glen Carlou, Backsberg and Cowlin are the main Shiraz producers in the area. Cabernet Sauvignon and Merlot and blends thereof show cedar, herbal and minty hints with firm acids and good ripe tannins. The blends incorporate Petit Verdot, Cabernet Franc and Mourvèdre. Wineries which produce Cab, Merlot and blends are Glen Carlou, Rupert & Rothschild, Anura and Vrede and Lust.

DRIVING ROUTE: KLAPMUTS-SIMONDIUM

The Klapmuts-Simondium Pocket lies between the towns of Stellenbosch and Paarl, on the Klapmuts Road. Take the N1 freeway towards Paarl. About 40 kilometres from Cape Town, take Exit 47 to the left. At the intersection, turn right onto the R44 and drive in the direction of Stellenbosch. Pass Butterfly World on the left and cross the intersection with the R101. Take the following turn-off to the left onto Klapmuts Road. Look out for Silver Kestrels in this Pocket. They are often seen on overhead telephone lines, hunting for potential prey in vineyards and shrubbery.

The first winery, Glen Carlou, lies about three kilometres further on the north-facing slopes of Simonsberg Mountain. The road rises over a small hill. At the crest, turn right to Glen Carlou's gated entrance and follow the road to the thatched building housing the tasting room and art exhibition. This is where David Finlayson produces his classy Chardonnay, Pinot Noir and Shiraz. Drive cautiously when leaving Glen Carlou as the exit has a blind spot on either side.

About three kilometres further, turn right to Backsberg winery where a lane of trees leads up the mountain slopes. Approaching the entrance to the property, very sandy soils are noticeable. The sand component is particularly important for the steely white wines produced here. It is more prevalent in the lower-lying vineyards. Backsberg's airy tasting room is complemented by the restaurant, appropriately named Tables.

A lane of young oak trees leads up to Drakensig, a winery set high on the foothills of Simonsberg Mountain. Drakensig's boutique cellar produces excellent red wines and

GPS waypoints

Backsberg	S33 49.717 E18 54.919
Drakensig	S33 50.113 E18 56.274
Glen Carlou Vineyards	S33 48.577 E18 54.314
Lindhorst Wines	S33 47.647 E18 56.891

Travelling tips

Restaurants:

Backsberg Tables restaurant +27 (0)21 875 5141

Accommodation:

Lindhorst Cottages +27 (0)21 863 0199

Santé Winelands Hotel & Wellness Centre +27 (0)21 875 8100

Interests:

Dalewood Fromage +27 (0)21 875 5725

Butterfly World +27 (0)21 875 5628

Animal Zone +27 (0)21 875 5063

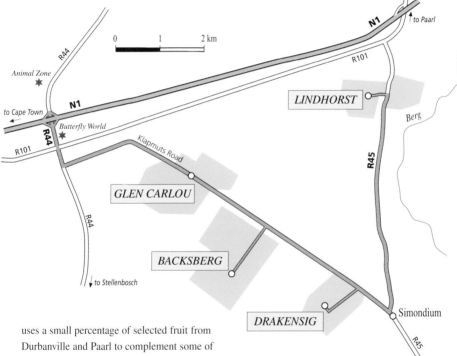

uses a small percentage of selected fruit from Durbanville and Paarl to complement some of its wines. The Shiraz in particular shows the leather, pepper and spicy characters associated with the Paarl area.

At the T-junction, turn left onto the R45, and drive North in the direction of Paarl. About 7 kilometres further turn left at the signs indicating Lindhorst Wines on the left. Another family-owned winery, Lindhorst also offers tastings to interested groups and corporate events in all major centres, game lodges and cruise liners (more details on their website). Lindhorst's self-catering cottage, situated in the heart of a Merlot vineyard, attracts an abundance of bird life and is a great base from which to explore the Winelands.

A sideways view on Simonsberg Mountain

Backsberg *Klapmuts-Simondium Pocket*

The Backsberg Estate was established in 1916 and produces a large range of wine styles. One hundred hectares of vines are cultivated on the northern slopes of Simonsberg Mountain. Red varieties are planted in lighter soils on the lower slopes (190 m) to ensure balanced growth. Heat-sensitive white varieties are cultivated in rich soils on the higher-lying sites, benefiting from the cooling effect. Prevailing south-easterly winds further moderate the daytime temperatures. The vines are trellised to protect young shoots while the canopy shades bunches from the harsh sunlight. Cleared juice from white grapes is cold fermented and the aromatic Viognier shows a rich mouthfeel. The Chardonnay combines rich fruit flavours with oak maturation. The reds are fermented in open-top vessels and macerate for up to eight weeks. This practice ensures deep, dark-coloured wines with rich fruit and soft tannins. The flagship red wine matures in French oak for up to 30 months.

Klein Babylons Toren (Cab S / Merlot, Cab F / PV / Malbec) Cab S/F, Merlot, PV, Malbec, Chard, Viog, Shz, Sauv Bl, Pinotage, Chenin Bl, Sang, Mouv Mon – Fri 8 – 5, Sat 9:30 – 4:30, Sun 10:30 – 4:30. Closed Easter Fri, Dec 25 +27 (0)21 875 5141 +27 (0)21 875 5144 info@backsberg.co.za www.backsberg.co.za 10 y 03, 04, 05 self-guided tours, restaurant (functions and weddings by appt), maze, gift

Drakensig *Klapmuts-Simondium Pocket*

Drakensig means "view of the Dragons" and aptly names this small boutique cellar perched on the northern side of Simonsberg Mountain. The farm comprises only 13 hectares of red varieties planted on east and west-facing slopes in deep, weathered granite soils with little clay and good natural drainage. Vineyard blocks are sited in the mountain's afternoon shadow. Its cooling effect allows even ripening of grapes, while retaining high acid levels. Grapes are fermented in closed fermenters without cold maceration to prevent over-extraction and excessive tannins. After 12 months of barrel maturation, the wine is bottled and rested for a further three months prior to release. The reserve Cabernet Sauvignon, complemented by a small percentage of fruit from the Durbanville Pocket (less than 10 per cent), has a smoky, chocolate character. The use of cooler climate grapes adds a touch of elegance to the fruit-driven wine and reduces alcohol levels. Shiraz, sourced from the Swartland Pocket, shows a structured and smoky mocha palate.

Reserve range – Cab S, Shz Cab S, Shz, Pinotage Mon – Fri 9 – 5, Sat 9 – 1, low season by appt +27 (21) 874 3881 +27 (21) 874 3882 drakensig@mweb.co.za 8 y Cab S 01, Shz 02 olive oil, conference venue (small groups)

Lindhorst Wines *Klapmuts-Simondium Pocket*

The Lindhorst boutique winery is located to the south of the Paarl Mountain where vines are cultivated on east-facing slopes in red soils containing a high percentage of shale. All the vineyards are planted to red varieties with the exception of Viognier which will be used as blending partner for the Shiraz. The 17 hectares are all trellised to ensure sufficient sun exposure for colour development in the reds and cover crops are used to improve the soil's biodynamic content. Due to the warm ripening conditions, all grapes achieve concentration with judicious water management. After harvesting, grapes are sorted and cooled before fermentation with selected yeast cultures. Malolactic fermentation is done in barrel, and with the use of 50 per cent older wood, maturation is extended to 20 months giving integrated and soft tannins. The Shiraz-based blend shows a complex palate of ripe fruit and dense tannins, reflecting the warmer ripening conditions and a slight Rhône edge with the addition of a portion Viognier.

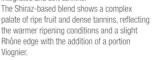

Statement (Shz/Merlot/Cab) Shz, Merlot, Cab S, Pinotage Mon – Sun 10 – 5. Closed Easter Sun, Dec 25, Jan 1 +27 (0)21 863 0199 +27 (0)21 863 3694 info@lindhorstwines.com www.lindhorstwines.com 3 – 8 y 03 meals and refreshments (booking req.), guest cottage in vineyard, children's facilities, gifts, farm produce

Glen Carlou Vineyards *Klapmuts-Simondium Pocket*

For two decades Glen Carlou has been under the meticulous, loving care of the Finlayson family. Its thatched winery, located on the Simonsberg Mountain overlooking the valley towards Paarl, is undergoing a major upgrade. In 2003, the Hess Group, from Switzerland, bought out the family's share. New developments include a production cellar, barrel cellar and art museum exhibiting some of Donald Hess's private collection. David continues as Managing Director and chief winemaker.

Seventy-five hectares of north-east and north-west-facing slopes of Simonsberg Mountain are cultivated on low-vigour gravel soils with a dense clay layer half a metre in depth. Although this clay layer restricts vertical root development, the clay sub-base ensures excellent water retention. The gravel, provides sufficient drainage and air movement, particularly for the Merlot, which is sensitive to excess soil moisture.

In the relatively warm growing conditions of this area, the focus is on vineyard management in order to moderate heat and sunlight and protect grape quality. The vineyard's northern aspect increases sunlight hours and the relative daytime temperatures. Nevertheless, its elevated slopes are exposed to strong south-easterly winds, significantly reducing the heat. The wind, however, requires trellising to protect young shoots and leaves from wind damage. Zinfandel bush vines have recently been placed on a low trellis to maximise air movement and cooling. Pinot Noir vines are planted to a high density of 7, 000 vines per hectare as the vines are generally smaller and inter-plant competition favours greater concentration in the berries. Vigorous vegetative growth is controlled. Leaves are removed as leaf removal and green harvesting of underdeveloped bunches favours the development of the ripening berries. The canopy on the Chardonnay vines is kept slightly denser to protect bunches from sun damage and to retain a crisp acidity and natural minerality. Optimum sugar and tannin ripeness is achieved at a generally lower sugar level and, together with low yields and meticulous sorting, grapes are harvested with ripe flavours and dry tannins without excessive alcohol.

Two new flagships, Gravel Quarry Cabernet Sauvignon and Quartz Stone Chardonnay, will be introduced in the 2006 vintage. Both are from single vineyards. The Chardonnay is barrel fermented using natural yeasts to assist in slow integration between the wine's fruit and wood flavours. The wine undergoes malolactic fermentation and is aged for 10 months on the lees to soften the acidity and to add weight to the mid-palate. The flinty and mineral Chardonnay shows vibrant citrus and tropical fruit aromas and carries its 14 per cent alcohol well. Red wines are fermented in both open-top and closed vessels. Regular punch downs and pump overs are used to mix skins and juice for optimal colour extraction. The Cabernet Sauvignon is matured for two years in 100 per cent new French oak, creating a dense and structured wine requiring further cellaring. Grand Classique uses the five classic cultivars of the Bordeaux blend. The Syrah introduces Mourvèdre and Viognier for a dense Rhône-styled wine. Pinot Noir, leaning towards a New World style, has ripe upfront fruit.

Optimal use of space in the barrel cellar (Top)
Dwarfed by technology (Centre)
Early morning coolness over the vineyards (Left)

Gravel Quarry Cabernet Sauvignon, Quartz Stone Chardonnay PN, Shz, Zinf, Cab S, Merlot, PV, Malbec, Mouv, Chard
Mon – Fri 8:45 – 4:45, Sat 9 – 12:30. Closed Easter Fri, Sun, Dec 25, 26, Jan 1, by appt other publ hols +27 (0)21 875 5528
+27 (0)21 875 5314 welcome@glencarlou.co.za www.glencarlou.co.za Chard (reserve) 10 y ; Red 12 – 15 y+ Chard 90, 95, 96, 01, 02 jewellery, art gallery, friendly dogs

Wellington Pocket

Tasting in the presence of terroir, a soil profile at Nabygelegen

The small town of Wellington lies about 10 kilometres north of Paarl and has emerged as a quality wine-producing area in recent years. This Pocket is also a premier vine nursery area with more that 90 per cent of vines for the South African market being produced here. Vineyards stretch out around the town over alluvial terraces towards the rolling hills and wheat fields of the Swartland. A percentage of vines are cultivated on the foothills of the towering Hawequa and Groenberg (Eng. Green Mountain) Mountains, where small valleys create unique meso-climates with varying sunlight exposure changing viticultural practices.

Although Wellington is generally a warm cultivation area, the foothill sites (at elevations above 200 m above sea level) benefit from wind exposure as well as the collection of moist air flowing down the mountain slopes. These factors create favourable cooler conditions for vine cultivation and ripening

of grapes. A wide range of grape varieties is produced in this area. Annual rainfall for the Wellington area is about 500 mm. The area has a relatively high average summer daytime temperature of 24.3°C. Supplementary irrigation is necessary to ensure stable, sustainable growing conditions for the vines as well as to prevent excessive water stress during ripening. In winter, snow covers the mountain peaks and night-time temperatures are lower than at the coast some 60 kilometres away, which makes for good resting periods for the winter-dormant vines.

The geology changes from shale-based soils on lower elevations, to sandstone and granite on the foothills and mountain valleys to the east. The latter renders gritty, light-coloured, medium textured soils with good water and nutrient retention properties. To the west, fertile alluvial soils are found closer to the Berg River. These soils are mainly used for the vine nurseries.

Chenin Blanc, which constitutes the majority of vineyard plantings, is now making way for classic red varieties such as Shiraz, Cabernet Sauvignon, Merlot and Pinotage. The growing conditions also allow the cultivation of less common varieties such as Mourvèdre, Grenache and Petit Verdot with great success. These varieties render full-bodied, perfumed reds with firm tannins and elegance, both as single varietal and blended wines. White wines are food-friendly with zesty acidity. Hildenbrand's Sémillon and Napier's Chardonnay are good examples of aromatic white wines from this area.

Soil:	shale on low altitudes, granite and sandstone on foothills, alluvial near river
Climate:	warm, moderate rainfall
White varieties:	Chenin Blanc, Sauvignon Blanc, Chardonnay, Sémillon
Red varieties:	Cabernet Sauvignon, Merlot, Shiraz, Pinotage
Wine styles:	red, white, sparkling, dessert, fortified

The Shiraz wines from Wellington are well structured with a broad spectrum of flavours ranging from pepper and savoury notes to red fruit. Producers like Mischa, Hildenbrand, Linton Park and Mont du Toit all offer single varietal Shiraz wines. Cabernet Sauvignon and Merlot wines have a velvety ripe fruit palate with dry savoury tannins with a firm finish, both in single varietal and blended examples. Welbedacht, Napier and Jacaranda are good examples of these. Interestingly, Nabygelegen's Mediterranean blend incorporates Tempranillo and Malbec, adding exotic sweet berry and spice. Diemersfontein enjoys good success with the native Pinotage grape, the wines showing dense fruity sweetness and well-structured tannins.

DRIVING ROUTE: WELLINGTON

Wellington is situated 70 kilometres from Cape Town (41 km from Stellenbosch). From the N1 freeway, take Exit 47. At the intersection, turn left onto the R44. When you reach the town of Wellington (23 km), turn left onto Distillery Road. Landmarks to look out for are the large grey building with pagoda-like tower on the left and the golf course on the right. At the train station bridge, turn right to cross the bridge and head up the Main Road. Pass two sets of traffic lights and the church with its towering spire. At the next traffic circle, take the first exit (left) into Blouvlei Road. Take the left fork, Berg Road, to visit the first winery on this route, Hildenbrand. Hildenbrand is one of the leaders in the revival of Sémillon in South Africa. The estate also offers a guest house, restaurant, olives and olive products. Owner Reni Hildenbrand is an authority on olives and has published a book on the subject.

Berg Road makes a horseshoe back into town and joins Church Street. Turn right onto Church Street and drive in the direction of Bainskloof Pass. Pass Redemption Leathers on the right. A little further, the entrance to Napier Winery turns off to the right. Napier produces a pot-still brandy alongside its range of wines. The farm also offers accommodation in its cottage as well as a conference venue for smaller groups.

From Napier, drive back along the R301 and turn right at Redemption Leathers onto Hill Road. At the T-junction, turn right onto Bovlei Road. It becomes a gravel road. Continue for two kilometres. You will pass Bovlei Retreat, a popular wellness destination. A sign on the left indicates Nabygelegen. The historic buildings have been renovated and now house the tasting room and winery. Indulge in a game of boules (pétanque) on the boules court or book a picnic to enjoy in the lovely garden.

From Nabygelegen turn right onto Bovlei Road, left past the leather shop and back to the R301. Turn right and go back to the town. At the traffic light, turn right onto Main Road. Turn right onto Pentz Street. At the traffic circle, take the first exit to Addy Road. Continue for two kilometres and turn right on Oakdene Road. This road becomes a gravel road. A little further on, you will reach the entrance to Mischa on the left. Be sure to visit the vine nursery, one of the main suppliers to the South African wine industry.

Retrace the route and turn right onto Addy Road. About 5.3 kilometres further on, turn right again onto Oakdene Road. About one kilometre further on, you will see the entrance to Welbedacht on the left. Owned by Schalk Burger, Welbedacht focuses strongly on sport. Its cricket oval hosts many local games.

GPS waypoints

Hildenbrand	S33 39.586 E19 01.754
Mischa Estate	S33 36.296 E19 00.931
Nabygelegen	S33 37.896 E19 03.839
Napier Winery	S33 38.604 E19 02.390
Welbedacht	S33 34.719 E19 01.172
Turn-off to Mischa	S33 37.294 E19 00.184
Turn-off to Welbedacht	S33 34.501 E19 00.367

Travelling tips

Information:
www.wellington.co.za

Restaurants:
Vercilli restaurant +27 (0)21 873 4231
Oude Wellington restaurant +27 (0)21 873 1008

Accommodation:
Bovlei Valley Retreat +27 (0)21 864 1504

Interests:
Scenic drive: Bainskloof Pass
Leather products from Redemption +27 (0)21 873 3197
Wellington wine walk @ tourist info in town

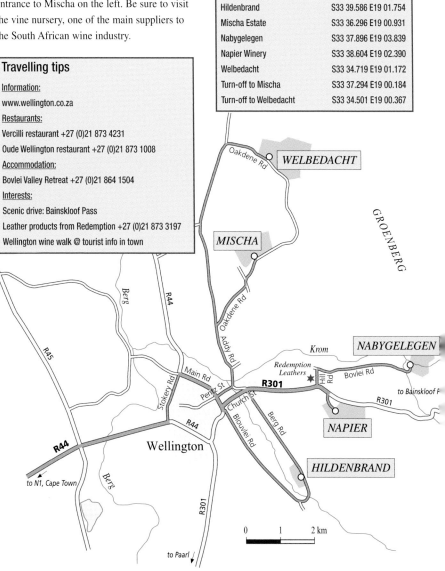

Welbedacht *Wellington Pocket*

Welbedacht, meaning "well thought out", aptly describes the philosophy of this Wellington winery. The farm has been producing grapes since the 1800s and traditionally supplied other wine producers. Its great success with Pinotage, in particular, was the deciding factor in the decision to build a cellar in 2004. Welbedacht crushed its maiden vintage in 2005. The flagship wine was named Cricket Pitch, after the Welbedacht Cricket Oval situated alongside the beautifully restored homestead.

Today 145 hectares of vines are cultivated on the undulating hills of Wellington, at an elevation of 300 metres above sea level. Decomposed granite dominates the high-lying sites with some shale on the lower aspects, providing well-drained soils. Vines are planted to a low density (2, 400 vines/Ha) to allow each plant sufficient soil volume and to encourage greater lateral root development. The greater soil volume and well-developed root system, which increases the supply of nutrients and water to the vine, alongside regulated supplementary irrigation, enables the plants to thrive in relatively hot and dry climatic conditions.

Vine management advocates the "sunlight into wine" principle. The aim is to maximise sunlight exposure and photosynthesis, allowing grapes to reach full ripeness. To achieve maximum sun exposure on the canopy, row directions are orientated from north to south. All the vines are trellised, with the exception of decades-old Pinotage and Chenin Blanc, which are cultivated as bush vines. Mature vineyards make a significant contribution to the high extract achieved in the wines, with most of the red varieties more than 15 years old, and the Chenin Blanc 25 years old.

Grapes are hand harvested and bunches sorted to select grapes for vinification. At the cellar, the grapes are gently destemmed and crushed, with the unfermented red must (skins and juice) cold macerated for five days to maximise colour extraction. The must is inoculated with selected yeast and fermented in open-top fermenters with temperatures peaking at 28°C. On completion of alcoholic fermentation, the young wine is drained off and the skins are pressed in a traditional basket press. The free-run and press wine is matured separately, with a portion of the press wine blended into the wine at a later stage to add structure and body to the final wine.

Malolactic fermentation is completed in barrel, and the wine is matured for 12 months in French oak. Only 25 per cent new wood is used as the Merlot fruit can easily be dominated with excessive new wood. Components of the flagship Cricket Pitch blend are matured separately and blended three months prior to bottling. The finished wine is then rested for another 12 months before release onto the market. The high alcohol content (Alc. 14.5% by Vol.) is neatly hidden in sweet, upfront fruit and firm, elegant tannins. Cleared juice from white varieties (Chardonnay, Chenin Blanc) is barrel fermented and lees matured to provide a silky mouthfeel to the fresh acidity.

The tranquil entrance to Welbedacht's tasting room (Top)
Vineyards are trellised away from the hot soil surface (Centre)
A spectator's view on the barrel cellar (Left)

[i] Cricket Pitch (Merlot /Cab S) 🍷 Cab S / F, Pinotage, Shz, Chard, Chenin Bl 🕐 Mon – Fri 8:30 – 5, Sat 9 – 2, Sun by appt.
📞 +27 (0)21 873 1877 📠 +27 (0)21 873 2877 ✉ info@welbedacht.co.za www.welbedacht.co.za 🔲 expected 5 – 7 y
🔳 N/A 🛈 sport facility (cricket oval), BYO picnic, children's facilities, tour groups, conference venue, mountain biking

Mischa Estate *Wellington Pocket*

Mischa's history started when Kelpie Barns and his wife Yvonne Blake chose to farm outside Wellington. They passed on their knowledge to their son, John, whose success with vine cultivation inspired grandsons Andrew and Gareth to crush their own grapes. The triumphant maiden vintage took place in 1999.

Forty hectares of vines are cultivated with white varieties situated on cooler south-facing slopes and reds on the warmer north-facing slopes. The decomposed granite soil has a very low growth potential and the vines require irrigation in the warm, dry climate. The climate does provide several advantages, however, as there is little disease and early ripening at harvest means late varieties are safely in the cellar before the hotter summer days arrive. Vines are trellised to offer protection against the strong south-easterly wind and the harsh sun. No green harvesting or leaf removal is required and cover crops are used to minimise water loss from the soil surface.

All Mischa's wines are sourced from single vineyards, although these have not been officially registered. The new wine cellar uses state-of-the-art equipment, yet employs the traditional techniques of hand picking, sorting and cold maceration before fermentation in open-top vessels. Gentle pressing is followed by malolactic fermentation in barrels and tanks to create a softening effect on these robust wines. Wines are matured for 12 months in French oak using one-third new oak. The Cabernet Sauvignon is extraordinarily scented with a huge fruit concentration and a moderate 14 per cent alcohol content, while the Shiraz flagship shows minerality on the mid-palate along with rich fruits.

An entrance as beautiful as their wines

ℹ️ Shiraz 🍇 Cab S, Shz, Merlot, Viog 🍷 by appt 📞 +27 (0)21 864 1016/19/20 📠 +27 (0)21 864 2312 ✉️ wines@mischa.co.za www.mischa.co.za ⏰ 8 – 10 y 🍷 00, 02 ℹ️ snacks and meals by appt, walks, mountain biking, vine nursery tours by appt

Hildenbrand *Wellington Pocket*

In 1853 a wine cellar of remarkable size and architecture was erected on the Hildenbrand farm. Today the restored estate runs to multiple agricultural activities including accommodation. Eighteen hectares of vineyards are cultivated on the foothills of the Hawequa Mountain in fertile granite soils. Sémillon and mature Chenin Blanc vines (22 years) are cultivated on west and south-east-facing slopes respectively with less sun hours moderating the heat. Red varieties are planted on less fertile soils to reduce growth vigour and increase fruit concentration. Canopies are opened on the eastern side to increase airflow and sun penetration, while the unopened west side provides protection from the hot afternoon sun. Red wines are fermented warm and are gently pressed to prevent excessive tannins. The bush vine Shiraz has a limited yield of four tons per hectare and matures in Hungarian oak to produce a highly concentrated and aromatic wine with ginger and cinnamon notes. Skin contact and natural fermentation in barrel produces a dense Sémillon.

ℹ️ Shz, Cab S, Chard, Sém 🍇 Cab S, Shz, Chard, Sém, Malbec, Chenin Bl 🍷 Daily 10 – 4. Closed Ester Fri – Sun, Dec 25, Dec 31, Jan 1 📞 +27 (0)21 873 4115 📠 +27 (0)866 700 147 ✉️ info@wine-estate-hildenbrand.co.za, www.-wine-estate-hildenbrand.co.za ⏰ Shiraz 8 y 🍷 02, 04 ℹ️ restaurant, guest house, olives, olive oil, book on olives

Nabygelegen *Wellington Pocket*

Established in 1712, Nabygelegen cultivates 17 hectares of vineyards at the foot of the Limietberg Mountain. The historic cellar (circa 1748) has been rejuvenated to provide a new expression for the wines of this wonderful old farm. Red varieties enjoy warmer north-facing sites of deep granite soils, while Merlot and the white varieties are planted on cooler south-facing slopes. Due to relatively warm ripening conditions, the white varieties are trellised higher off the ground than the reds, with the cordon at one metre to reduce radiant heat. Denser canopies also protect grapes from the sun. Chenin Blanc rows run north-south as well as east-west; the former giving a richer style of wine which is wooded, and the latter a fruitier style, which is used for the blend. Harvesting at slightly lower sugars gives balanced wines, and cold maceration of red varieties allows gentle colour extraction. Twelve months of maturation in older French oak yields an elegant, spicy and savoury flagship blend.

ℹ️ 1712 blend (Cab S / Merlot / PV) 🍇 Cab S, Merlot, PV, Tempranillo, Sauv B, Chenin B, Sém 🍷 Mon – Fri 10 – 5, Sat 10 – 1. Closed Easter Fri, Sun, Apr 27, May 1, Dec 25, Jan 1 📞 +27 (0)21 873 7534 ✉️ sales@nabygelegen.co.za www.nabygelegen.co.za ⏰ 10 y 🍷 03 ℹ️ verjuice, boules court, walks, picnic (booking req.)

Napier Winery *Wellington Pocket*

Napier is named after Sir George Napier, Governor of the Cape of Good Hope (1838 – 1844) who named the town of Wellington in honour of the Duke of Wellington, his commanding officer in the wars against Napoleon. Sir George is also the name given to Napier's vintage pot-still brandy. Napier Winery was established in 1989 under the towering Hawequa Mountains, on land farmed since the late 1600s. The existing Chenin Blanc, Cinsaut and Cape Riesling were largely replaced with noble varietals and the maiden vintage was crushed in 1994. Since 2000, Leon Bester, part-owner, manages the vineyards and cellar.

The vineyards are established on both sides of the Lion Creek River, resulting in warmer north-east and cooler south-west-facing aspects. A constant airflow from the surrounding mountain cools the vines and rows are orientated from east to west to maximise this cooling effect. Vines are trellised and canopies offer bunches protection from sun damage.

Thirty-six hectares of vines are cultivated in decomposed granite soil with an underlying clay layer. Soil close to the river is loamy, wetter with a high potential and is cultivated with Colombar for the pot-still brandy. Drip irrigation allows selected vineyard blocks (80%) to be lightly water stressed during ripening, naturally reducing berry size and increasing skin to juice ratio for greater colour and flavour extraction.

A local weather station gives guidance regarding the micro-climatic conditions. The vineyards are cultivated with a planting density of 4, 000 vines per hectare to limit the yields to about eight tons per hectare (45 – 48 hectolitres) for improved concentration of fruit flavours. The main varieties cultivated are Cabernet Sauvignon (32%), Cabernet Franc (12%), Merlot (11%), Chardonnay (9%), Chenin Blanc (20%) and Shiraz (12%).

The cellar (built in 1993) was refurbished and automated in 2005, with the addition of a new tasting room and conference facility. The cellar capacity is a maximum of 260 tons. Napier produces between 40, 000 and 60, 000 bottles. About half of the fermentation capacity is open fermenters (all stainless steel). The grapes are harvested and sorted by hand. Unbroken berries are placed in tanks for fermentation with regularly punched down throughout the fermentation process in order to ensure gentle extraction. A traditional basket press is used to separate the skins and wine. Napier's flagship, Red Medallion, matures for two years in French oak and rests for two years in bottle before being released. The three varieties are blended halfway through this maturation process. The blend is then returned to barrel to ensure integration of the fruit and wood components.

145

Saint Catherine Chardonnay is a single vineyard wine and the grapes are grown on a south-facing slope. The Chardonnay grapes are whole bunch pressed and the juice is barrel fermented and matured for seven to 10 months. Napier also produces a dry, unwooded Chenin Blanc, a Cabernet Sauvignon for earlier enjoyment and a 5-year pot-still brandy.

A no-nonsense approach to bold wines (Top)
Dedicated picking bins (Centre)
Cool mountain air can change weather conditions within an hour (Left)

ℹ️ Red Medallion (Cab S / F / Merlot), St Catherine Chardonnay 🍷 Cab S / F, Merlot, Malbec, Shz, Chard, Chenin Bl, Colom
🕐 Mon – Fri 9 – 5, Sat 10 – 3, Sun & publ hols by appt ☎ +27 (0)21 873 7829 📠 +27 (0)21 864 2728 ✉ sales@napierwinery.co.za
www.napierwinery.info 📧 5 – 8 y 🛏 00, 01 ℹ️ cellar tours by appt, cottage, venue: conference

Swartland Pocket

View of the Swartland Pocket

Traditionally know for its wheat fields, the Swartland Pocket has developed many vineyards which produce fine quality wine, particularly in the last decade.

Vineyards are cultivated around the towns of Malmesbury, Riebeek-Kasteel and Riebeek West, stretching north towards Piketberg and Porterville. The main vineyard areas are centred the on the lower foothills of the Riebeek-Kasteelberg and Paardeberg mountains.

Long warm summers and water scarcity dictate vine cultivation in this Pocket and play an important role in the variety selection and siting for optimum wine quality. The moderate annual rainfall (400 – 550 mm) and average summer daytime temperature (23.8°C) indicate warm growing conditions, making bush vine cultivation very popular. However, certain vineyard sites on the higher slopes of the Riebeek-Kasteelberg are sheltered from the

afternoon sun by the mountain's prominent peaks at 950 metres above sea level.

Riebeek-Kasteelberg is a sandstone remnant, resting on shale and soils are generally stony, with medium potential. In a northerly direction, towards Piketberg, soils are mainly shale based. Weathered granite intrusions provide reddish-brown soils in certain sites, with excellent water retention properties. The soils on the north-west-facing foothills of Paardeberg Mountain are light coloured and often sandy in nature, which necessitates irrigation. They have a medium potential, the vineyards benefiting from higher altitude and less sun-exposed eastern and southern aspects.

Impressively for this warm producing area, Chenin Blanc has proved itself in bush vines, showing complexity with ripe honeysuckle and tropical fruit characters balanced with good acidity. These wines benefit greatly from gentle oak maturation, enhancing the seriously styled wines, for example Spice Route. Based on the success of single varietal Chenin Blanc, producers have taken this variety to new heights in blended wines. Viognier, Chardonnay and Grenache Blanc add aromatics and mouth-watering fruit flavours to the already dense wine, for a rich palate and developing complexity. The wine from Sadie Family is a good example.

Flagship red variety, Shiraz, produces a wide array of styles from ripe, New World wines (Meerhof, Pulpit Rock) to the more restrained classical style (Kloovenburg, Allesverloren). Even though styles differ, the definite Swartland character, recognisable in all the wines, gives a natural wild scrub character. Rich, spicy Shiraz blends, with blending partners Grenache, Mourvèdre, Carignan and Viognier, show savoury, supple tannins, dense fruit and balanced structure, with Sadie Family Wines and Lammershoek as leading examples. Allesverloren produces a fine port from the traditional Portuguese varieties, with rich prune and plum flavours with a sweet finish.

DRIVING ROUTE: SWARTLAND

Jan van Riebeeck called this softly undulating land between mighty mountain ranges "Het Zwarte Land" (the Black Land) because of the endemic Renoster shrubs which turn black after the rains. The wide, fertile plain is the bread basket of Cape Town with its golden wheat fields reaching the foot of the mountains.

The Swartland Pocket starts some 60 kilometres north of Cape Town. Follow the N1 freeway out of the city and take Exit 10 to the N7. Take the right fork as the road runs parallel to the N1, past the local shopping

centre before turning northwards to join the N7 (at Exit 13), which follows the West Coast.

Reaching the town of Malmesbury, about 63 kilometres from Cape Town, take Exit 65 to the R315 (Malmesbury/Darling). Follow the road as it turns a full 180° and ends in a T-junction. Signage indicates Darling to the right (West) and Riebeek-Kasteel to the left (East). Turn left and follow the signs towards the R45 (Paarl).

At the second traffic light, turn left and then the first right turn-off to Piet Retief Road. This leads past the Old Dutch Reformed church with its magnificent spire. Follow Piet Retief Road out of the town to the rolling hills of the Swartland Pocket. This area is famous for producing powerful white and red wines, particularly Shiraz, which shows strong expression of ripe varietal fruit flavours, spiciness and alcoholic strength.

The warm basin of the Swartland

Soil:	red and brown granite, shale and sandstone from mountain
Climate:	warm, moderate rainfall
White varieties:	Chenin Blanc, Sauvignon Blanc, Chardonnay, Sémillon
Red varieties:	Cabernet Sauvignon, Merlot, Shiraz, Pinotage
Wine styles:	red, white, sparkling, dessert, fortified

147

Along the R45, the R46 turns off north-west towards Ceres/Riebeek-Kasteel. You will return to this point later. About 4.5 kilometres further, turn right at the Aprilskloof Road turn-off. Take the first left and continue along the gravel road. The road makes a long S-bend. About one kilometre further is the Sadie Family Wines cellar on the left. Eben Sadie creates some of the most prestigious wines in the Swartland area. A frequent visitor to Spain, where he makes wine in his bodega in Priorat, Sadie is brimming with passion and mastering the elements to bring concentration and structure to his local wines.

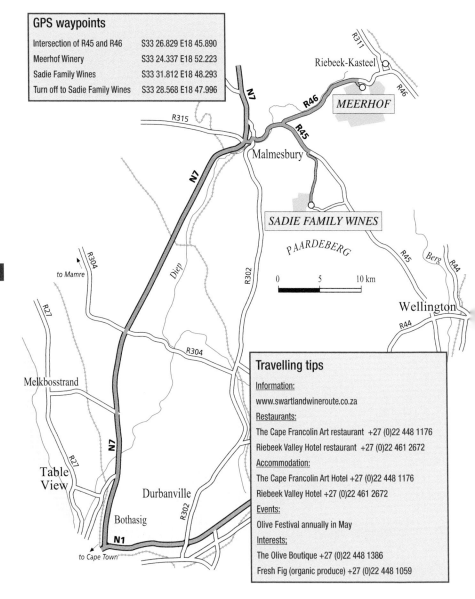

GPS waypoints

Intersection of R45 and R46	S33 26.829 E18 45.890
Meerhof Winery	S33 24.337 E18 52.223
Sadie Family Wines	S33 31.812 E18 48.293
Turn off to Sadie Family Wines	S33 28.568 E18 47.996

Travelling tips

Information:
www.swartlandwineroute.co.za

Restaurants:
The Cape Francolin Art restaurant +27 (0)22 448 1176
Riebeek Valley Hotel restaurant +27 (0)22 461 2672

Accommodation:
The Cape Francolin Art Hotel +27 (0)22 448 1176
Riebeek Valley Hotel +27 (0)22 461 2672

Events:
Olive Festival annually in May

Interests:
The Olive Boutique +27 (0)22 448 1386
Fresh Fig (organic produce) +27 (0)22 448 1059

148

Follow the R46 to Riebeek-Kasteel and the tranquil Riebeek Valley, to the next winery. Meerhof is just short of the top of the Botmanskloof Pass over the Riebeek Mountains. The cellar and garden offer great views. On clear days Table Mountain and the city of Cape Town below, are faintly visible in the distance.

Artists and arts and crafts people have settled and are bringing creative flair to the timeless country lifestyle in the beautiful twin hamlets of Riebeek West and Riebeek-Kasteel, at the foot of the Kasteelberg. The Pocket includes many olive growers, who produce a wide variety of olives and olive-based products. The Olive Boutique in the town is a firm favourite with visitors. Riebeek Valley Hotel offers a variety of health and wellness treatments including t'ai chi, reiki and massage.

Meerhof Winery *Swartland Pocket*

The boutique cellar of Meerhof lies on the crest of the Botmanskloof Pass between Malmesbury and the Riebeek Valley. In the past Meerhof sold its grapes to other producers, but since 2000, Meerhof has been crushing its grapes for its own label. Forty-five hectares of mostly red varieties (95%) are established on the northern side of the Riebeek Mountain. Steep west-facing slopes provide slightly cooler ripening conditions and a low planting density (2, 800 vines/Ha) is used. The shale and clay soils provide good drainage with sufficient water retention and all the vines are trellised with the exception of bush vine Pinotage. The grapes are fermented in open-top fermenters, with regular pump overs to mix skin and juice for colour extraction. Completing malolactic fermentation in tanks, the red wines are transferred to French oak barrels. The wines show teeth-coating tannins, particularly the Shiraz, and ripe fruit flavours.

Shiraz Shz, Cab S, Pinotage, Chard Mon-Fri 9 – 4:30, Sat 10 – 2. Closed Easter Fri – Sun, Dec 25, Jan 1 +27 (0)22 487 2524 +27 (0)22 487 2521 meerhof@wcaccess.co.za www.meerhof.co.za B y 00, 02 conservation area of Renosterveld, meals by appt, BYO picnic, tours by appt

Sadie Family Wines *Swartland Pocket*

"The most excellent wine is one that gives pleasure through its own qualities; nothing which might obscure its natural taste must be mixed with it." Columella's *De Re Rustica*, the most comprehensive account of Roman viticulture, made this timeless judgement over two millennia ago. His successor, Palladius, continued to write on this subject and this philosophy has inspired the names for Eben Sadie's two renaissance wines.

Vineyards are cultivated as trellised and bush vines to maximise water efficiency. Vines receive no irrigation and yields are manually reduced in the extremely dry conditions. The three main soil types add distinctive aspects to the wines: in slate soils grapes retain a higher natural acid; in granite they show more "farmyard", berries and spice and in the sandstone/clay mixture the grapes achieve intense toffee and cassis flavours. White varieties are planted on decomposed granite and alluvial soils with higher draining capacity. Only late ripening Viognier (8 years) is trellised and its canopy protects the sensitive grapes from the sun. All the other white varieties are cultivated as bush vines (35 – 55 years) and produce intensely aromatic fruit.

Hand-picked grapes are cooled, sorted and crushed with about 50 per cent of berries remaining whole. Red varieties are cold macerated and naturally fermented at low temperatures (26°C) with punch downs to ensure slow extraction. The Columella is oak matured for 24 months and bottled without fining or filtration. The wine shows dense berry fruits and spicy herbal undertones. Free-run juice from white varieties is naturally fermented in barrels, with lees maturation adding a creamy mouthfeel to the aromatic and spicy wine.

A small cellar inconspicuously guarding some big wines

Columella (Shz, Mouv), Palladius (Rhône blend: Chenin, Viog, Grenache Bl, Chard) Shz, Mouv, Chenin Bl, Viog, Chard, Grenache Blanc, by appt +27 (0)21 869 8349 +27 (0)21 869 8101 sadiefamily@mail.com Columella 15 – 20 y, Palladius 8 y+ 01, 03 Producer also makes own wine in Spain

Darling Pocket

Heartland – view of Darling town

The Darling Pocket is located around the popular tourist town of Darling, about 65 kilometres north of Cape Town.

The Groenekloof range of granitic hills runs parallel to the coastline, a mere 10 kilometres away. Vineyards are mainly developed on the eastern flanks of these hills, which provide protection from the strong synoptic winds. The artic Benguela current, flows north along this coastline, ensuring cooler growing and ripening conditions than the macro-climate would indicate, giving the area an average summer daytime temperature of 22.4°C and annual rainfall of 538 mm.

The reddish-brown soils are derived from weathered granite and, mainly found on higher landscape positions towards the west, favour the cultivation of various delicate wine varieties. Darling grapes are highly sought after and other areas source grapes from here to blend with their own, producing much

fruitier, naturally acidic wines. None of the wines lack alcohol and their natural acids give a fresh, elegant finish. Consequently, more producers are establishing their own wineries. Even though the summer daytime temperatures are warm with long sunlight hours, the close proximity to the ocean creates cooler than expected growing conditions on exposed slopes and varieties such as Sauvignon Blanc and Merlot do particularly well.

Protected slopes are warmer and more suitable to red varieties such as Shiraz and Pinotage. The low annual rainfall necessitates water conservation and drought-resistant rootstocks. Many vineyards are still cultivated as bush vines as these require less water during the growing season. Where vertical trellising is used, it seldom exceeds a height of 1.5 metres to create a denser canopy and reduce water loss through evaporation from the leaves. The denser canopy also serves to protect the grapes from direct sunlight and possible burn damage.

The pronounced and very distinctive character of Darling's wines, especially Sauvignon Blanc from the Groenekloof area, clearly distinguishes it from the wines of, for example, Durbanville and Constantia. Sauvignon Blanc wines are full of ripe tropical fruit and racy acidity leading to a long finish, such as the wine from Ormonde and Darling Cellars. Other wine producers, such as Groote Post, are doing very well with rich and fruity Chardonnay wines. Just as in the neighbouring Swartland Pocket, the Chenin Blanc from this area shows ripe fruit concentration with citrus notes and a good, dry finish. Tukulu is a good example.

Cabernet Sauvignon is one of the favourite red varieties, showing restraint and firm tannins, both in single varietal and blended wines, with good examples from both Ormonde and Cloof. Tukulu and Darling Cellars produce Pinotage wines with opulent berry fruit, subtle tannins and a hint of smoked beef. The variety's inherent astringency is well managed.

DRIVING ROUTE: DARLING

The Darling Pocket is some 60 kilometres north of Cape Town and directly west of the Swartland Pocket. Follow the N1 freeway

Soil:	granite
Climate:	warm with ocean influence
White varieties:	Chenin Blanc, Sauvignon Blanc, Chardonnay
Red varieties:	Cabernet Sauvignon, Merlot, Shiraz, Pinotage, Cinsaut
Wine styles	red, white, dessert

north out of Cape Town and take Exit 10 to the N7. Take the right fork as it runs parallel to the N1 past a local shopping centre before turning northwards and joining the N7 (at Exit 13), which follows the West Coast. At Malmesbury, about 63 kilometres from Cape Town, take Exit 65 to the R315 (Malmesbury/Darling). Follow the road as it turns a full 180° and ends in a T-junction. The sign indicates Darling to the right (West) and Riebeek-Kasteel to the left (East). Turn right at the intersection and follow the R315 towards Darling, approximately 30 kilometres away.

Approaching the town of Darling, the R315 intersects with the R307. The signage may be a little confusing. As you turn right towards Darling, you are still driving on the R315. The road winds down to the town. Continue through the centre of town to the far side. Signs to the right indicate the turn-off to Ormonde winery.

In the enchanting town of Darling, visit Evita se Perron, a lively place to meet, eat, drink and talk. Humour and enjoyment are the primary aims. It is from this venue that Mrs Evita Bezuidenhout (satirist Pieter-Dirk Uys) keeps an eye on the progress of democracy and entertains guests in her own inimitable style. The word "perron" is a play on the Afrikaans word for a platform at a train station. Evita se Perron has two cabaret venues, a restaurant, bar, arts and crafts market and conference facility – a wonderful venue for functions or wedding receptions.

Eccentric dining – a Darling restaurant

151

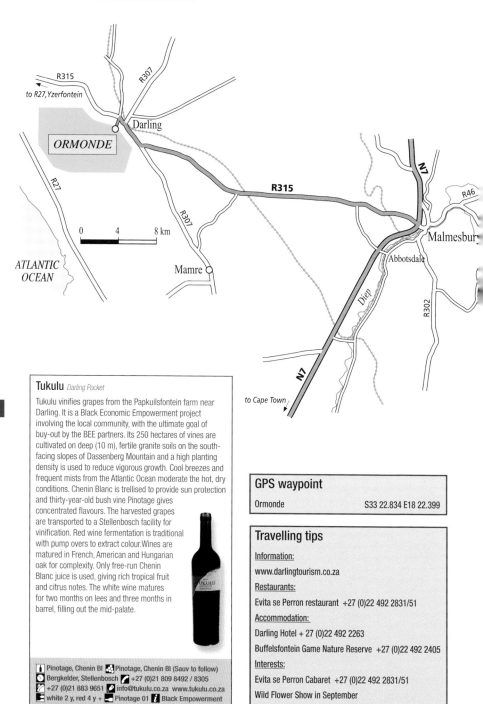

ORMONDE

to R27, Yzerfontein

Darling

R315

R307

ATLANTIC OCEAN

Mamre

0   4   8 km

R315

R307

R27

N7

R46

Malmesbury

Abbotsdale

Diep

R302

N7

to Cape Town

Tukulu *Darling Pocket*

Tukulu vinifies grapes from the Papkuilsfontein farm near Darling. It is a Black Economic Empowerment project involving the local community, with the ultimate goal of buy-out by the BEE partners. Its 250 hectares of vines are cultivated on deep (10 m), fertile granite soils on the south-facing slopes of Dassenberg Mountain and a high planting density is used to reduce vigorous growth. Cool breezes and frequent mists from the Atlantic Ocean moderate the hot, dry conditions. Chenin Blanc is trellised to provide sun protection and thirty-year-old bush vine Pinotage gives concentrated flavours. The harvested grapes are transported to a Stellenbosch facility for vinification. Red wine fermentation is traditional with pump overs to extract colour. Wines are matured in French, American and Hungarian oak for complexity. Only free-run Chenin Blanc juice is used, giving rich tropical fruit and citrus notes. The white wine matures for two months on lees and three months in barrel, filling out the mid-palate.

Pinotage, Chenin Bl   Pinotage, Chenin Bl (Sauv to follow)
Bergkelder, Stellenbosch   +27 (0)21 809 8492 / 8305
+27 (0)21 883 9651   info@tukulu.co.za www.tukulu.co.za
white 2 y, red 4 y +   Pinotage 01   Black Empowerment project

GPS waypoint

Ormonde   S33 22.834 E18 22.399

Travelling tips

Information:
www.darlingtourism.co.za
Restaurants:
Evita se Perron restaurant +27 (0)22 492 2831/51
Accommodation:
Darling Hotel + 27 (0)22 492 2263
Buffelsfontein Game Nature Reserve +27 (0)22 492 2405
Interests:
Evita se Perron Cabaret +27 (0)22 492 2831/51
Wild Flower Show in September
Darling Golf Club +27 (0)22 492 3013

Ormonde *Darling Pocket*

The dynamic winery of Ormonde has grown rapidly over the past five years. The town of Darling was originally laid out on the farm and the winery's gates are literally in Darling with vineyards fanning out on the hills behind the village. Four hundred hectares of vines have been developed on the 4, 500 hectare property and, where vines do not grow, olives have been planted. The Ormonde Reserve wine range uses grapes from older vines to reflect the *terroir*, while the Alexanderfontein lifestyle range is made from younger, developing vines.

The soil consists of decomposed granite with a high percentage of clay (40%) and excessive growth on this fertile soil is a potential problem. The clay provides good water retention as the annual rainfall is only about 500 mm. The vineyards are located on the slopes of the surrounding hills, further increasing water drainage, and the vines are planted to a low planting density of 2, 500 to 3, 000 vines per hectare. The low density encourages deep vine root development. Cover crops are planted between the rows to prevent both further water loss through evaporation and soil surfaces from becoming compacted. These factors allow dry-land cultivation of the vines in a fairly dry climate. With less vegetative growth and a higher concentration of varietal flavours, these Darling wines have a distinctive character. Close proximity to the Atlantic Ocean, only five kilometres away, with frequent mists and sea breezes, ensures much cooler than expected ripening conditions. Temperatures are further moderated by an elevation of 150 – 350 metres.

The vines are trellised to protect them against the prevailing winds and the rows are directed along an east-west axis so that the canopies can protect bunches from direct sun. Due to the relatively cool ripening period, vines are not stressed during summer and give a good acid balance with lower alcohol wines. The vineyards are suckered (removal of excessive young shoots) and leaves are removed to open the canopies to airflow with the exception of the Sauvignon Blanc canopy which is kept slightly denser to protect these heat-sensitive grapes from direct sun. At *veraison* (colour change of grapes) the canopy of the Cabernet Sauvignon (which has a later *veraison*) is opened to allow sufficient sun penetration for colour development. Green harvesting is also done at this stage to reduce the crop of Merlot and Chardonnay in particular.

Grapes are hand picked into small lug boxes to prevent damage. The white varieties are picked only in the cool morning hours to retain their crisp varietal flavours. White grapes are cold macerated for seven days at 6°C to aid glycerol formation and to achieve a fuller mouthfeel. A small percentage is barrel fermented. The flagship Sauvignon Blanc is made in a typical New Zealand style, showing grass notes and rose leaves and although similar to other wines from this area, its wood component makes it distinctly different in structure. The red wines are fermented warm in open-top vessels, using regular punch downs to mix the skins and juice and to achieve maximum colour extraction. The Cabernet Sauvignon/Merlot blend is matured in 100 per cent new wood for 18 months and undergoes a light filtration to remove excess precipitants (proteins and tannins) before bottling.

The gracious homestead (Top)
Well equipped tasting room facilities (Centre)
New plantings in the sought-after red Tukulu soil (Left)

📷 Ormonde Sauvignon Blanc 🏷️ Sauv Bl, Chard, Chenin Bl, Sémillon , Viog, R Riesling, Cab S / F, Merlot, Shz, Mouv, PV, Malbec
🕐 Mon – Fri 9 – 4, Sat, publ hols 9 – 2. Closed Easter Fri, Dec 25, 26, Jan 1 📠 +27 (0)22 492 3540 📠 +27 (0)22 492 3470
✉️ ormondevineyards@iafrica.com www.ormonde.info.co.za 🍷 white 3 y, red 10 y+, 2nd label 5 y 🍇 Merlot 03, Sauv Bl 01
ℹ️ vineyard / day tour with barrel tastings by appt, picnic baskets and BYO picnics, children's facilities, farm produce, walks

Tulbagh Pocket

The Tulbagh basin – home to sculpture, artchitecture and wines

The Tulbagh Pocket lies at the northern end of a north-south running valley, bordered on the west by the Sarons and Obiekwa Mountains, the north by the Groot Winterhoek and the east by the Witsenberg. In this area the vines grow alongside wheat fields, fruit orchards and olive groves. Most of the vineyards are situated on deep boulder beds of the upper tributaries of the Klein Berg River on the foothills of the amphitheatre. This amphitheatre is formed by the southern, south-western and western-facing flanks of the Witsenberg Mountain.

The relatively warm, dry climate is essentially continental due to the isolation of the area. Vineyards are established from the warmer valley floor, up the foothills where the warm meso-climate is tempered by the general southern aspects, high elevation (over 250 m above sea level) and afternoon mountain shadows. Another unique feature of the Tulbagh Pocket is the encapsulating

mountains, shaped like a horseshoe, which trap the cool air from the previous night, reducing daytime temperatures. A south-easterly wind further moderates the daytime temperatures. The annual rainfall of about 550 mm necessitates supplementary irrigation, particularly for newly established vineyards. The average summer daytime temperature of 24.3°C signifies warm conditions during ripening. Vineyards management practices such as row direction and cordon height are used to moderate ripening conditions.

Tulbagh's boulder bed soils closely resemble those of the Rhône Valley in France, whereas the soils on the higher foothills are derived from shale, sandstone colluvium (deposits of soil at the foot of slopes, which accumulate due to gravity) and scree. These are usually stony, with a medium growth potential and good water retention properties. Poor sandy soils typify the valley floor and are rarely used for vine cultivation.

The historical exclusively white production is steadily moving towards noble red varieties, which currently occupy approximately one-third of vineyards. Strong flavours of cut grass and fresh hay with a lemony dimension give the Sauvignon Blanc wines individuality, such as the wines from Saronsberg and Rijks. Chenin Blanc, on the other hand, tends to be more honeyed with rich, nutty flavours and a cool minerality threading the fruit structure. Examples of these are Tulbagh Mountain Vineyards, Rijks and Blue Crane Wines.

In terms of red varieties, Shiraz is the firm favourite, with many single as well as blended wines from many producers, including Manley Private Cellar, Rijks and Bianco. Pervasive black berry fruit spiced with smoked and black pepper notes, the Shiraz wines have good complexity and approachability. Saronsberg

and Tulbagh Mountain Vineyards produce Shiraz blends, using Cinsaut, Mourvèdre, Viognier and Malbec as blending partners. Other red wines include Pinotage (Manley) and Cabernet Sauvignon (Alter Ego).

DRIVING ROUTE: TULBAGH

Tulbagh lies 120 kilometres from Cape Town (90 km from Stellenbosch). From the N1 freeway, take Exit 47 to the left. At the junction turn left onto the R44. Continue on the R44 past Wellington. Turn right onto the R46 (63 km from the N1 turn-off). Seven kilometres further turn left to reach the town.

Pass through the town to the periphery on the northern side. Just before a small bridge, follow the road to the left to Saronsberg. The new winery is tastefully decorated with glass work and an art studio.

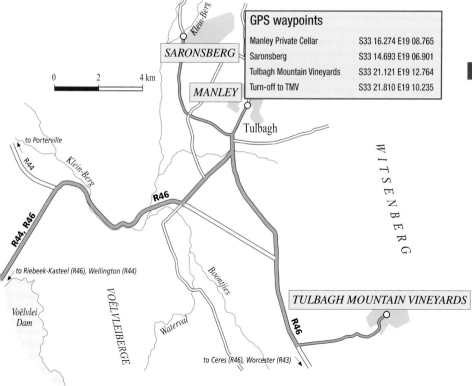

GPS waypoints

Manley Private Cellar	S33 16.274 E19 08.765
Saronsberg	S33 14.693 E19 06.901
Tulbagh Mountain Vineyards	S33 21.121 E19 12.764
Turn-off to TMV	S33 21.810 E19 10.235

155

Return to the small bridge. A few metres further is the entrance to Manley Private Cellar. This family-owned winery also hosts the Hunters Retreat Guest Farm and a small chapel as an intimate country wedding venue. Further along the R46 is Tulbagh Mountain Vineyards. About 10 kilometres from the centre of town, the road crests and a gravel road turns off to the left. Follow this road up to the cellar. Tulbagh Mountain Vineyards produce organically certified wines. There are great views from the tasting room.

Tulbagh has a rich history of Dutch architecture. Church Street, in the centre of town, is home to the largest concentration of national monuments (32 in total) in a single street in South Africa. Wonderful examples of 18th and 19th century architecture exist, many faithfully restored after the devastating earthquake in 1969.

Soil:	boulder beds with large stones
Climate:	warm and dry
White varieties:	Chenin Blanc, Colombar, Muscat d'Alexandrie, Chardonnay
Red varieties:	Cinsaut, Shiraz, Cabernet Sauvignon, Merlot, Pinotage
Wine styles:	red, white, sparkling, dessert

Travelling tips

Information:
www.tulbaghwineroute.com

Restaurants:
Readers Restaurant +27 (0)23 230 0087

Accommodation:
Hunters Retreat Guest Farm (Manley winery)
+27 (0)23 230 0582

Events:
Dutch Festival annually in April

Snow: In the winter months, Matroosberg Reserve offers one of the best spots to experience snow. The reserve also offers various outdoor activities.
Matroosberg +27 (0)22 312 3759

Manley Private Cellar *Tulbagh Pocket*

The boutique winery of the Manley Private Cellar lies in the heart of Tulbagh. Eight hectares of exclusively red varieties were established on gentle north and west-facing slopes on shale and clay soils. In the warm, dry climate water efficiency is vital: irrigation is applied and cover crops improve water infiltration. Canopy density is increased and the rows are directed east to west, offering grapes protection against the blistering sun. By slowly opening the canopy during the ripening season (leaf removal) to allow filtered sunlight and air movement, even Merlot is ripened without sun damage in these extreme conditions. The historic cellar (150 years old) houses the small boutique winery where fermentation yields massive wines (Alc. 15 – 16% by Vol.) from high sugar grapes due to the warm climate. Gentle gravity feed and basket pressing sees young wines to the barrel, and 18 months maturation with some American oak adds a touch of vanilla and spice to the robust berry and mineral characters.

[i] Shiraz (sgl vineyard) [ ] Shz, Pinotage, Cab S, Mourvèdre
[ ] Mon – Sun 9 – 5 (preferably by appt). Closed Dec 25
[ ] +27 (0)23 230 0582 [ ] +27 (0)23 230 0057
[ ] info@manleywines.co.za www.manleywines.co.za [ ] 8 y+
[ ] 02, 03 [ ] cellar tours 10 & 3, light picnic baskets or BYO, luxury B&B, conference venue, weddings, gifts, farm produce, walks

Tulbagh Mountain Vineyards *Tulbagh Pocket*

Tulbagh Mountain Vineyards was created from virgin land high on the Witsenberg Mountain range. Sixteen hectares of organically certified vineyards are now cultivated on the large property. Vines are planted on warm north and north-west-facing slopes and the elevation (400 – 500m) and morning mountain shadows reduce the average daytime temperature by as much as 2°C. Planting density is decreased in the shallow, marginal shale soils to encourage extensive root development. Cover crops further reduce water loss and prevent compaction of top soil layers. The canopies of trellised vines are opened by leaf removal to reduce fungal diseases and to allow in filtered sunlight, which aids colour development in the red grapes. Mourvèdre, cultivated as bush vines, gives a dense, dark fruit. The grapes are sorted before fermenting naturally in small open-top vessels. The wines are pressed and malolactic fermentation is done in barrel. The wine is matured in French oak for 24 months to encourage firm, ripe tannins in these elegant and balanced red wines.

[i] Theta Shiraz, Syrah-Mouv [ ] Cab S, Shz, Mouv [ ] by appt
[ ] +27 (0)23 231 1118 [ ] +27 (0)23 231 1002
[ ] info@tmv.co.za www.tmv.co.za [ ] 6 y+ [ ] 03
[i] organically certified

Saronsberg *Tulbagh Pocket*

Saronsberg is a true phoenix. The state-of-the-art-winery was reborn after a devastating fire in 2002. Today 39 hectares of vines are cultivated at the foot of the Saronsberg Mountain (hence the name). The marginal shale soils are well drained and have a moderate east to south-east aspect, yielding a naturally low crop.

The warm and dry climate, together with medium growth potential soils, allow for early ripening of most varietals, smaller berries with increased skin to juice ratios, a concentrated fruit structure and naturally high acidity levels. Individual blocks are no more than one hectare in extent, offering components for a Rhône and a Bordeaux-style blend, as well as a single varietal Shiraz wine.

Vineyard management is focused on maximising cooling of vines and water efficiency. The low annual rainfall (450 mm) is supplemented by irrigation with run-off water from the mountain. Prevailing south-easterly winds dry the grapes and reduce disease, while simultaneously providing a cooling effect. The planting density varies according to the soil characteristics and vines are trellised, with vertically extending and thinning canopies to allow more air movement and subsequent cooling. Leaf and shoot removal further maximise this cooling effect.

Rows are directed east to west with canopies protecting the grapes from the afternoon sun. Heat-sensitive white and red varietals are planted on the mountain foothills where cooler conditions prevail. Stronger red varietals are planted on the valley floor. Extensive green harvesting reduces yields to ensure proper ripening. Sauvignon Blanc vineyards are harvested several times early in the season, giving a spectrum of green, minty to ripe fruit flavours.

Grapes are hand harvested during the early morning into small lug boxes and cooled to 4°C. Berries are then destemmed, hand sorted and cold macerated for 72 hours to aid colour extraction. A CO_2 gas blanket is used to prevent oxidation and browning during this phase. The must is then slowly heated to 20°C to begin fermentation. In the initial stages of fermentation, the juice is racked and returned to ensure sufficient mixing of skins and juice, with punch downs employed later in the process to prevent extraction of harsh tannins. Skins are pressed and the young wines are transferred to barrel for malolactic fermentation, which allows the integration of wood and wine flavours. The flagship Shiraz is matured for 16 months in 100 per cent new oak, resulting in a spicy, black wine. Components for the Shiraz blend are matured separately for 10 months, blended and matured for a further six months, with Viognier and Mourvèdre adding a softening touch to the powerful Shiraz. Only after 12 months of bottle maturation are the wines released onto the market.

The Chardonnay and Sauvignon Blanc are cold fermented and matured on the lees for three to six months in order to fill out the mid-palate. The racy acidity and wet pebble minerality givers well-rounded classic white wines.

New plantings at Saronsberg (Top)
A garden of sculptures (Centre)
The imposing structure that constitutes the cellar complex (Left)

ℹ️ Full Circle (Shz / Mouv / Viog), Shiraz 🍷 Shz, Mouv, Viog, Cab S, Malbec, Gren, Merlot, PV, Chard, Sauv Bl 🕐 Mon – Fri 8 – 5, Sat 9 – 1. Closed Easter, Dec 25, 26, Jan 1 ☎ +27 (0)23 230 0707 📠 +27 (0)23 230 0709 ✉ info@saronsberg.com www.saronsberg.com
🍴 8y + 🛏 04 ℹ️ artistic tasting room, private art gallery

Robertson Pocket

Vast expanses – the Robertson Pocket

Bordered by the Riversonderend Mountains in the south and the Langeberg range in the north, Robertson is located about 150 kilometres to the north-east of Cape Town. The Breede River is the lifeblood of this low rainfall area (400 mm) and with an average summer daytime temperature of 23°C, the area is relatively warm. However, frequent south-easterly winds often channel moisture-laden air into the valley, cooling the vineyards significantly.

Viticulture is mainly practised along the course of the Breede River and on the mountain foothills. The geology and topography, consequently also the soils, are diverse and quite different to the soils of the coastal belt. Three main soil types are found: sandy soils with boulder beds in the low ravine, dark-coloured lightly textured alluvial soils (promoting high growth vigour) on lower terraces and heavy textured reddish-brown soils on higher foothills.

Some outcrops of limestone (calcium-rich) soils occur from place to place, which explains the area's dominance as a horse stud centre, the pastures being considered ideal for strong bone structure development. These soils dictate rootstock selection and induce moderate growth vigour. Supplementary irrigation is applied in warm summer months. Mainly utilised for Chardonnay cultivation, the limestone soils induce typical mineral characters in the single varietal and sparkling wines from this area.

Planting densities vary from 2, 500 to about 3, 200 vines per hectare depending on the soil potential. Most vineyards are trellised with systems ranging from a 1.2 metre vertical trellis to a double-slanting trellis, which gives a greater leaf surface to protect the grapes from direct sunlight.

Chardonnay is the dominant white variety, with many wineries producing great wines from this variety. The wines show ripe yellow fruit and citrus aromas with an elegant textured structure, enriched by oak maturation. Chalky and mineral characteristics clearly indicate the limestone soil cultivation. (Bon Courage, Graham Beck, De Wetshof and Weltevrede.) The more delicate Sauvignon Blanc is also cultivated in the valley, with the wines depicting passion fruit-dominated flavours with asparagus undertones (Springfield, Quando).

Shiraz is the most prolific red variety and the wine styles range from fragrant all-spice aromas to dark berry fruit. The wines generally have elegant tannin structures and long finishes. (Bon Cap, Bon Courage, Graham Beck, Zandvliet, Viljoensdrift.) A unique Pocket feature is the distinctive fortified dessert wines produced here. These include red muscadel (Graham Beck) as well as white muscadel (Rietvlei, Van Loveren).

Soil:	sandy, alluvial, limestone
Climate:	warm, low rainfall, drastic differences in day/night temperatures
White varieties:	Chenin Blanc, Colombar, Muscat d'Alexandrie, Chardonnay, Sauvignon Blanc
Red varieties:	Cabernet Sauvignon, Shiraz, Merlot, Pinotage, Cinsaut
Wine styles:	red, white, sparkling, dessert, fortified

Organic Wines

Political isolation pre-1994 left South African wine growers unaware of organic viticulture, but recently many have turned to organic, and even biodynamic, practices. The hot, dry summers are beneficial for the non-pesticide approach. Only a few hundred hectares are farmed this way and few producers have embraced it completely. More producers make use of natural vineyard pest control, plant indigenous flora to deter insects from breeding and reduce the amount of chemicals used. Key producers are Bon Cap, Tulbagh Mountain Vineyards, Topaz Wines.

DRIVING ROUTE: ROBERTSON

The Robertson Pocket lies about 150 kilometres or 2 hours drive from Cape Town in a north-easterly direction.

Take the N1 freeway northbound. Pass the town of Paarl to the Huguenot Tunnel through the Drakenstein Mountain range. Have cash available for the toll road as credit cards are not accepted. The drive through the Breede River Valley is a visual feast with hectares of vines spreading out over the river plain.

About 37 kilometres further on, you reach the town of Worcester. At the first traffic light, turn right onto Rabie Avenue. This road crosses over a small bridge for a rail track. At the T-junction, turn left into Durban Street. Drive through the centre of the town. At the next T-junction (traffic light), turn right onto Robertson Road. At the next traffic light, Klein Plasie, a living, open-air museum on the left, is well worth a visit.

About 30 kilometres from Worcester, a sign indicates the turn-off to Eilandia. Turn right to visit Bon Cap Organic Wines. The 6.5 kilometres gravel road is easily accessible. Bon Cap has been a driving force in the production of and education on organic wines.

Return to the R60, turn right and continue for another 6.5 kilometres to the impressive gates of Graham Beck Wines Robertson. This cellar, along with its sister cellar in Franschhoek, produces a wonderful range of wines including whites, reds, blends and sparkling wines. From Graham Beck, continue east on the R60 to the town of Robertson. Pass through the town. On the outskirts, at the circle, take the second exit to Bonnievale on the R317. About seven kilometres further on, Bon Courage is on the right. Bon Courage also produces a wide range of wines. Its Chardonnay, Syrah and sparkling wines are very popular. The restaurant offers lunch and children's facilities. Be sure to visit the "cultivar experience" where you can experience first hand the different grape varieties.

In Worcester, visit the Karoo National Botanical Garden. This jewel of a garden with 144 hectares of natural semi-desert vegetation and 10 hectares of landscaped gardens, features the unique plants of the drier parts of the country. Its greenhouse boasts a world-famous collections of stone plants. Set in the heart of the unspoilt village of McGregor, the Tememos Retreat Centre offers a private world of tranquil beauty. Temenos (Greek Sacred space) is the ideal refuge, a haven of peace and beauty.

Travelling tips

Information:
www.robertsonwinevalley.co.za

Restaurants:
Bon Cap restaurant +27 (0)23 626 1628
Bon Courage restaurant +27 (0)23 626 4178
Jan Harmsgat restaurant +27 (0)23 616 3407

Accommodation:
Bon Cap guest cottages +27 (0)23 626 1628
Jan Harmsgat country house +27 (0)23 616 3407
Dassieshoek Nature Reserve +27 (0)23 626 3866

Events:
Wacky Wine Weekend annually in June
Food and Wine Festival annually in October

Interest:
Temenos Retreat Centre +27 (0)23 625 1871
Kleinplasie & reptile world +27 (0)23 342 2225

160

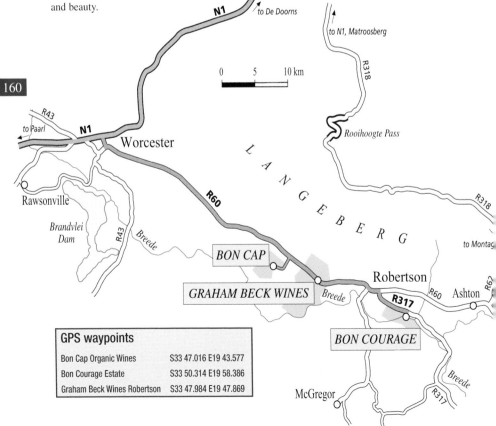

GPS waypoints

Bon Cap Organic Wines	S33 47.016 E19 43.577
Bon Courage Estate	S33 50.314 E19 58.386
Graham Beck Wines Robertson	S33 47.984 E19 47.869

Graham Beck Wines Robertson *Robertson Pocket*

Graham Beck has received international acclaim for its MCC sparkling wine, even though Robertson's extreme daytime and night-time temperature differences are quite dissimilar to that of Champagne. This is also applicable to its soils. Where Champagne is blessed with poor top soil on a limestone bedrock, Graham Beck has duplex soils on a predominantly clay sub-base with limestone. Pinot Noir and Chardonnay, planted on these soils, produce wines of high natural acidity with a distinct mineral character. Receiving sufficient daylight hours coupled with supplementary water management allows Graham Beck to ripen the grapes in mid-January in a stress-free environment.

Vineyards total 190 hectares. Vines have vertically trellised canopies protecting bunches from the direct sun. Prevailing south-easterly summer winds significantly cool the vineyards. Grapes for Blanc de Blanc MCC are harvested slightly riper than normal as greater fruit concentration with alcohol allows the wine to be wood matured. The MCC is bottled for the second fermentation and matured on the lees for 48 months, producing a creamy, flavourful wine with a very fine mousse.

The Ridge Syrah is a single vineyard (4 Ha) planted in 1994. Deficit irrigation practices are implemented during the ripening stages until *veraison* causing the vines to reduce berry sizes, increasing skin to juice ratio. Concentration of colour and flavour in the grapes are easily extracted during cold maceration and fermentation. Malolactic fermentation takes place in barrels and further maturation for up to 17 months gives a powerful, fruity wine with soft, silky tannins.

Overlooking the vineyards from the modern cellar's balcony

[i] The Ridge Syrah, Blanc de Blanc MCC [⚄] Chard, Shz, PN, Cab S, Merlot, Viog, Sang, Mouv
[◑] Mon – Fri 9 – 5, Sat 10 – 3, every 1st Sun of the month 10 – 3 [✆] +27 (0)23 626 1214
[🌡] +27 (0)23 626 5164 [✉] market@grahambeckwines.co.za www.grahambeckwines.com
[▣] Ridge 10 y+, MCC 10 y+ [▬] 92, 93, 98, 00, 03 [i] tours by appt, architectural design award, full disabled access

---

Bon Cap Organic Winery *Robertson Pocket*

Seven generations of the Du Preez family have farmed this property. Bon Cap Organic Winery was created in 2002. The farm is 60 hectares in extent, and vines are cultivated largely in a river valley on poor sandy soils with a shallow clay layer. Here wider plantings compensate for the relatively low soil depth. On the more elevated sites, the soil is composed of fertile red lime, pebbly soils, which have good water retention and drainage. They are planted to the more heat-sensitive varieties like Viognier and Sauvignon Blanc. Due to the relatively warmer climate, canopies are spread (on a vertical trellis) and opened with aggressive leaf removal and suckering to maximise air movement through the vines. Cover crops reduce water loss and vines are irrigated in very warm conditions. Red wines are cold macerated to extract colour and flavour and fermented at low temperatures to prevent harsh tannins. Larger 300 litre and older barrels are used for maturation to ensure a restrained wood character. White wines are aged for six months on the lees after fermentation to add mid-palate weight.

[i] Organic range of varietals [⚄] Cab S, Pinotage, Shiraz, Petit V, Viognier, Chardonnay [◑] Mon – Fri 8 – 5, Sat, Sun, publ hols @ Bistro 10 – 4. Closed Dec 25, 26 [✆] +27 (0)23 626 1628 [🌡] +27 (0)23 626 1895 [✉] info@boncap.co.za www. boncaporganic.co.za [▣] 3 – 5 y [▬] 03, 04 [i] organically certified wines, cottages, wedding & conference venue, bistro, BYO picnics

---

Bon Courage Estate *Robertson Pocket*

Three generations of the Bruwer family have produced wines on the Bon Courage Estate. The estate lies at the confluence of three rivers and is blessed not only with alluvial soils, but also with soil from the surrounding mountain foothills. These diverse soil types provide a range of vine cultivation sites. Red varieties are planted on calcareous red soils, where the fruit flavours are concentrated by difficult growing conditions. Heat-sensitive white varieties are planted in gravelly and alluvial soils with more soil moisture. Canopies are opened to maximise airflow from cooling south-easterly winds. In extreme heat, the vineyards are irrigated. The Syrah, fermented with whole berries to restrain harsh grape tannins, shows complex berry fruit and spice, while the Cabernet Sauvignon has herbal and cassis notes. The red wines mature in a combination of French and American oak, which adds spicy and sweet oak flavours. The MCC matures for 36 months in bottle on its lees, yielding creamy notes, fresh citrus and a lively mousse.

[i] Syrah Inkará (sgl vineyard), Cab S Inkará (sgl vineyard), Jacques Bruére MCC Brut Reserve, Jacques Bruére MCC Brut Reserve Blanc de Blancs [⚄] Cab S, Shz, PN, Chard, Riesl, Sauv Bl, Sém [◑] Mon – Fri 8 – 5, Sat 9 – 3. Closed Easter Fri, Sun, Dec 25, Jan 1 [✆] +27 (0)23 626 4178 [🌡] +27 (0)23 626 3581 [✉] boncourage@mindsmail.com www.boncourage.co.za [▣] MCC 5 y white 3 y, reds 8 y [▬] MCC 00, Shz & Cab 03 [i] tasting room in Cape Dutch homestead (circa 1818), children's facilities

Klein Karoo Pocket

Typical Karoo architecture at The Port Wine House, Calitzdorp

The Klein Karoo is a long, narrow semi-arid area stretching from the rural town of Montagu in the west, through the higher-lying, cooler Barrydale, towards Ladismith, Calitzdorp, Oudtshoorn and De Rust in the east. It consequently supports a diverse *terroir*.

Traditionally, vine plantings were done in the valley's low-lying alluvial soils derived from sandstone or shale. However, with improving viticulture and wine styles, higher-lying cooler sites, in particular soils with clay over gravel, are sought for cultivation in the finger-like valleys and ravines of this beautiful mountainous landscape.

With relative extremes in both climate and soil composition, the larger part of the area is warm with an average summer daytime temperature of 23.6°C. The Klein Karoo is marked by a general shortage of water due to low, unreliable rainfall which only averages about 200 mm per year.

The Tradouw and Barrydale areas are situated at elevations of 400 to 700 metres in the lee of the Langeberg Mountain. Wind-driven clouds from a south-easterly direction often spill over the mountain crest to cool down the daytime temperatures during the growing and ripening season. Weather data interestingly shows an average February temperature of 21°C. By extending harvesting dates, red varieties can be even and fully ripened. Due to the high elevations, extreme winter frost can occur. The soils, mainly consisting of shale, are stony and well-drained. Due to low annual rainfall, these medium potential soils require supplementary irrigation to satisfy the vine's needs during the growing season. Joubert-Tradauw produces Chardonnay and Shiraz wines with rich fruit flavours supported by a good acid balance.

Calitzdorp has long been associated with fortified wines and its reputation is centred on Port. The hot, dry climate is similar to that of the Duoro region in Portugal. The area's soils are drained by the upper tributaries of the Gamka River and vineyards are planted mainly on poor clay soils, avoiding the dark fertile soils on the river banks. These clay soils are well suited to the production of fortified wines made from Muscat and Port varieties (Tinta Barocca, Tinta Roritz, Touriga Naçional, and Souzão), excellent sweet wines as well as full-bodied red wines. Port producers from Calitzdorp have over many years proved to be some of the best this country has to offer in port production.

Planting density of vines varies from as little as 1, 800 vines to 4, 000 vines per hectare, mainly due to varying soil potential. Row directions and trellis systems are adapted from small, untrained bush vines to large

A walk-your-own vineyard tour

Soil:	alluvial, shale, sandstone
Climate:	warm, low rainfall, dry
White varieties:	Colombar, Chenin Blanc, Muscat d'Alexandrie, Chardonnay
Red varieties:	Ruby Cabernet, Shiraz, Pinotage, Merlot, Red Muscadel
Wines:	red, white, sparkling, dessert

Cape Port Wines

South Africa's "Port"-styled wines were historically sweet and made from Tinta Barocca, Cinsaut and even Cabernet Sauvignon and Shiraz. Greater sensitivity to the market introduced drier styles, higher alcohol levels and a mix of the best Port varieties, including the international favourite, Touriga Naçional. The word "Port" has been recognised as the single term to describe a specific product (in this case, the fortified wine from the

O'Porto region in Portugal). European legislation requires that the word be phased out of all South African versions, creating distinctly Cape names, such as Cape Vintage, Cape Late Bottled and Cape Vintage Reserve. The quaint town of Calitzdorp in the Klein Karoo is the unofficial capital of "Port" and hosts an annual festival to celebrate this wine style. Cape "Port" is comparable to its Portuguese cousin in sugar and alcohol levels. However, the former tends to be fruiter. Key producers are Axe Hill, De Krans, JP Bredell.

163

The Klein Karoo – self proclaimed home of South African port

vertically trellised vines according to the topography and prevailing wind direction, maximising the available airflow to assist in cooling the vines. As water is scarce, drought-resistant rootstocks are used and irrigation is applied to regulate growth vigour, mainly using drip systems to prevent water loss through evaporation.

Fortified and red wines are the focus here, with De Krans, Boplaas and Axe Hill being some of South Africa's most well-known Port producers.

GPS waypoints

De Krans	S33 32.105 E21 41.151

Travelling tips

Restaurants:
Port Wine Restaurant +27 (0)44 213 3131

Accommodation:
Port Wine Guest House +27 (0)44 213 3131
Warmwaterberg Spa +27 (0)28 572 1382

Events:
Port Festival annually in July

Interests:
Historic walking route in Calitzdorp

Scenic drives: Seweweekspoort Pass, Rooiberg Pass, Swartberg Pass, Outeniqua Pass

DRIVING ROUTE: KLEIN KAROO

The Klein Karoo Pocket lies about 400 kilometres or three hours drive from Cape Town (about 360 km from Stellenbosch) in a north-easterly direction. Take the N1 freeway from Cape Town. Have cash available for the toll road (Huguenot Tunnel) as credit cards are not accepted. Reaching Worcester, turn right at the first traffic light onto Rabie Avenue. Cross a small bridge and a rail track to the T-junction with Durban Street. Turn left and drive through the centre of the town. At the next T-junction (at the traffic light), turn right onto Robertson Road (R60), and continue through Robertson.

At the T-junction in Ashton, turn left to join the renowned Route 62 (R62) to Montagu, Barrydale and Ladismith before finally reaching Calitzdorp – the unofficial capital of Port in South Africa.

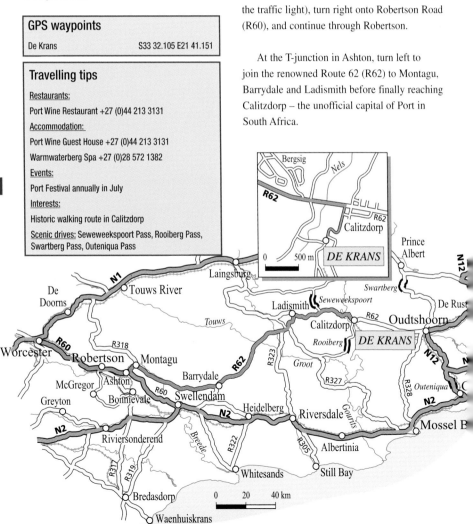

In Calitzdorp, take the second street to the left and pass the stone church building. Turn right at the stop street. On the left you will pass the Port Wine Guest House. The guest house offers classically styled rooms and a restaurant. Follow the road to De Krans, one of South Africa's premier Port producers. De Krans also offers a large range of wines. Do not miss the vineyard walk.

De Krans *Klein Karoo Pocket*

De Krans optimises warm climate cultivation using site selection. Vines are mainly cultivated on hills surrounding the Gamka River. The clay and gravel soils have a low vigour potential and good drainage. Vines are slightly water stressed under these conditions, the effect intensified by increased planting density to optimise the soil depth and water reserves. As a result, the vines naturally reduce canopy growth and produce a smaller berry, translating into concentrated flavours. The Red Stone Reserve is a unique blend (70/30 Touriga Naçional and Cabernet Sauvignon) that truly depicts Calitzdorp *terroir* with soft tannins and an unexpected average alcohol. The Vintage Reserve Port is slightly lower in sugar than others in the area, but high alcohol and tannin extracts give maturing potential. The port is aged in old wooden barrels (least 500 l capacity) which contribute to the slow, controlled oxygenation and subsequent colour and tannin stabilisation rather than wood flavour extraction.

ⓘ Red Stone Reserve (Touriga N, Cab S) 🔖 Touriga N, Tinta B, Temp, Souzão, Cab S, Pinotage, Merlot, Chenin Bl, Chard, Hanepoot ⊙ Mon – Fri 8 – 5, Sat 9 – 3. Closed Sun, Easter Fri, Dec 25 🥂 +27 (0)44 213 3314/64 📠 +27 (0)44 213 3562 ✉ diekrans@mweb.co.za www.dekrans.co.za 🍷 Vintage Port 20 y; red wine 5 – 10 y ⚑ 97, 01, 02, 03 🍇 pick your own grapes (Feb, Mar), BYO picnics, vineyard walks

Diverse agriculture – sun-dried apricots

Infamous and adverturous – view of the Swartberg Pass

165

Other Areas

Mission station – Elim town

ELIM

Promising new vine developments along the southern coast are taking place at Klein River (near Stanford) and Elim, boasting the southernmost vineyards in South Africa. Situated within 10 kilometres of the ocean, these areas have a strong maritime influence. High humidity and subsequent rot as well as strong ocean winds are problematic. Sauvignon Blanc currently accounts for 50 per cent of the vine plantings, with some Cabernet Sauvignon, Petit Verdot and Merlot vineyards in the planning stage.

WORCESTER

The Worcester area boasts the largest surface area of vineyards (nearly 20, 000 hectares) in the country. Brandy production used to be the main production focus of this area with many wines still custom-designed for local *négociants*.

Today, there is a large varietal mix with hillsides producing lower yields of more concentrated fruit. Dessert and fortified wines from the Muscat grape have always produced highly aromatic and luxurious wines. The climate is hot with very low annual rainfall and the area lying in the mountain rain-shadow requires irrigation.

The Worcester area is cultivated along the Breede River, with distinct variations between soils and micro-climates in the different river valleys and tributaries. Low to high potential soils occur and virtually all vineyards are irrigated, using mostly drip irrigation to prevent water loss. Soils are mainly derived from sandstone and fertile red shale. Near Goudini and Slanghoek, the soils and boulder beds are mainly alluvial, consisting of bleached sand reaching dark organic richness. In Rawsonville, vineyards flourish on a flat landscape of alluvial valley soils resting on a bed of river stones providing drainage.

Many vines are untrained bush vines, but where trellising is used, the cordons reach only 80 centimetres. Chenin Blanc and Colombar still dominate vine plantings, while Chardonnay, Sauvignon Blanc as well as Cabernet Sauvignon and Shiraz have become popular.

WEST COAST

Along the west coast of South Africa, large vineyard areas (10, 000 hectares) span the flat land on either side of the Olifants River. This large area stretches from Piekenierskloof, through the Citrusdal valley, the Cederberg on to Vredendal, Lutzville and Koekenaap in the north, following the Olifants River to the Atlantic Ocean near Bamboes Bay. Three main soil types occur: dark and alluvial, calcareous and red sandy soils. Vineyards are limited to deep moisture-retaining soils and available irrigation.

The Cederberg has a high elevation reaching almost 1, 000 metres above sea level. This elevation, combined with sandstone soils, is favourable for wine grape production. Annual rainfall is low at 220 to 370 mm and as the soils have low water retention, this necessitates supplementary irrigation. Generally vines grow vigorously and canopy management is strict to keep a balance between growth and grape production. Planting density is low (2, 200 – 2, 800 vines/Ha) and large vertical and slanting trellises are used.

The area is associated with large volume production of bulk wine, especially for distilling and table wine. Chenin Blanc and Colombar are the dominant varieties, but Muscat d'Alexandrie, Chardonnay and Sauvignon Blanc are also cultivated. Planting of red vines is on the increase with Shiraz and Pinotage as favourites.

NORTHERN AREAS

The most northerly wine-growing area in South Africa includes the Lower Orange River Pocket stretching from Upington to the Augrabies Valley in the west. The annual rainfall is a mere 120 to 160 mm, restricted to summer months in this semi-desert area. Irrigation plays a major part in crop production. The alluvial soils are dark, deep and well-drained, from a medium to heavier texture. Several trellising systems are employed to create micro-climates within the vines to protect grapes from the extreme heat. Douglas and Vaalharts, well known for their signature fortified wines, also make easy drinking table wines. A wide selection of varieties are cultivated, including Chenin Blanc, Colombar, Chardonnay, Pinotage, Shiraz, Cabernet Sauvignon, Ruby Cabernet, Merlot and white Muscadel.

167

Grain and grapes – West coast vineyards

Brandy Route

B randy is truly unique. It is the only alcoholic beverage made from another, namely wine.

Brandy production is made possible by a natural process known as distillation, where the liquid vaporises and then condenses. The Chinese discovered the secret of distillation in 3000 B.C. while scientists such as Hypocrites applied alcohol for medicinal purposes. Fascination with this elixir gave rise to the name "aqua vitae", water of life, as it was widely believed that alcohol could prolong life. It was only in the 15th century that a truly pure alcohol, known as the "soul of the wine" was distilled from wine.

Towards the end of the 16th century, this alcohol was given a German name "Branntwein", (Dutch "brandewijn"), literally meaning "burnt wine". During a 17th century war, French ports were closed for trade and Dutch ships were prevented from loading cargo of newly-distilled brandy. These barrels waited patiently on the quayside of La Rochelle in France for the war to end. When the barrels were finally opened, traders were surprised at the miracle – a once colourless liquid, the brandy was now amber with a rewardingly rich and mellow taste. This discovery led to the development of Cognac. Today good brandy is matured in wood.

South Africa's brandy industry was born a mere twenty years after pioneer Jan van Riebeek set foot on Cape soil. Historical records show that the first brandy from Cape wine was distilled in 1672 on board a Dutch ship lying at anchor in Table Bay. Today the

brandy industry is an important part of the South African wine industry with more than 50 trademarks in the local market. South African brandy consumption is around 40 million litres per year, contributing over R2 billion to the national economy. One of the main reasons for its popularity is the diverse styles in which South African brandy is made. These styles range from firm, upfront brandies that are suited to enjoying with a mixer, to mellow, aged products for neat sipping. South African brandy producers follow strict regulations to ensure that local brandies conform to the highest standards. These regulations ensure that the local brandy industry maintains a reputation of excellence.

BRANDY REGIONS AND PRODUCERS

South Africa has two major brandy-producing regions. The heartland for vines cultivated for brandy distillation is found in the Breede River Valley, between the towns of Rawsonville and Robertson. The second region is the Klein Karoo, a beautiful scrubland between Worcester and Oudtshoorn. These hot, irrigated areas are ideal for cultivating Chenin Blanc, Colombar and Cinsaut, the primary grape varietals used in the production of wine intended for brandy distillation. Yields from these vineyards are higher than those for wine grapes and soils are conducive to producing fruit with the required acid content. Two brandy routes take the enthusiast through these important regions. One route includes the cellars of the Western Cape, the other runs along the R62 route through the Klein Karoo. Distell and the KWV are South Africa's larger brandy producers (by volume), while a number of wineries distil their own brandies, reflecting their unique *terroir*.

ENJOYING BRANDY

Some find the idea of tasting brandy daunting. It need not be. While it is not the same as tasting wine, using the techniques below, you will soon be able to enjoy all the nuances of fine brandies. The South African Brandy Foundation aims to inform and educate the consumer on all aspects of brandy and it welcomes consumers.

When tasting brandy, there are certain techniques and practices that differ from those employed in the tasting of wine. A good starting point is to taste several brandies in a line-up. This gives you the opportunity to compare different brandies. The larger producers provide such opportunities with trained tasters to help you.

APPEARANCE

Line up the brandies, each in a separate glass. You do not have to use a snifter (a special shaped brandy tasting glass). An international wine-tasting glass, such as those handed out at wine shows will do. Fill the glasses about one-quarter, as this allows enough space for the aromas to develop. First examine its colour. The brandy should be clear, with no sediment. The colour ranges from a pale straw yellow to a golden honey.

SMELL

Smell each brandy separately before tasting. Unlike a wine tasting, do not give the glass a vigorous swirl before smelling. The air directly above the brandy develops a complex layer of flavours and aromas. Swirling upsets

the balance and will enhance the alcohol evaporation and drown other subtle aromas. Hold the glass to your face and smell. The first impression is that of wood characters, sweetness and smokiness. Then bring the glass to your nose for a closer sniff to notice subtle differences. One brandy may smell of wild flowers, dried fruit and coffee, while the next may contain scents of tropical fruit, tobacco and leather. At first you might only detect one or two aspects of the brandy, but with practice you will discover the subtle aromas and find the layers in the brandy.

Do not be intimidated by others' comments. Continue to practise more detailed descriptions in your tasting. Also remember that your perception will change and develop over time. Some days you are able to taste more precisely than on other days. Your tasting abilities may even be affected by your eating habits and moods!

Facts about Brandy

- Brandy is distilled from wine, which is made specifically for this purpose. This is referred to as base wine. The grapes are grown for this purpose and are harvested slightly earlier than grapes for table wine to ensure a higher acid content.

- Only healthy, ripe grapes are used for the production of brandy. Poor or rotten grapes are never used, as the unwanted flavours in the grapes will carry through to the final product.

- The base wine is light (lower alcohol, around 11% by Vol.) with a high acidic content to ensure fruit flavours are maintained during distillation.

- Brandy must be distilled twice to ensure the highest purity.

- At least one-third of the final bottled product must be brandy that has been distilled in copper pot stills. The copper pot-still brandy is considered of highest quality and produces the best flavour concentration.

- South African brandy must be matured for a minimum of three years in French oak casks.

- The alcohol content of the final bottled product is between 38% and 43% by volume.

DEVELOPMENT

Brandy also develops in the glass over time. Smell the first brandy and then the rest. Then go back to the first to see how the initial aromas are developing.

TASTING

Some prefer to add a little water to the tasting glass. Although a slight dilution, the water makes it easier to taste on the palate. Adding water is not the rule – many purists prefer to taste brandy neat. The sip is small as brandy is not spat out. There are many flavours which must be allowed to develop on the whole palate. Swallowing allows a different array of flavours to those on the mid-palate to be appreciated. After swallowing, the warmth of the alcohol component becomes apparent. Between sips, rinse your mouth with water or nibble on a biscuit.

Never heat the glass! There is a fine balance between water-soluble and alcohol-soluble components, which become detectable by evaporation of their respective carriers (water or alcohol). Each aroma develops at its own pace, the combination giving you an overall experience. Heating the glass promotes rapid alcohol evaporation. The resultant increased alcohol content will merely burn your nose and distort the balance of aromas.

BRANDY USES

Brandy is a versatile drink. It can be used in many food dishes and cocktails. Brandy can be enjoyed neat as an aperitif, a digestive with meals or with mixers. Brandy with ice and your favourite mixer (cola, ginger ale, soda water or tonic, even fruit juices) makes for a refreshing drink, ideal for South Africa's warm climate. Notice how the characteristic brandy

170

Western Cape Brandy Route	
Avontuur	+27 (0)21 855 3450
Backsberg	+27 (0)21 875 5141
De Compagnie	+27 (0)21 864 1241
Laborie	+27 (0)21 807 3196
Louiesenhof	+27 (0)21 882 2632
Oude Wellington	+27 (0)21 873 4639
Uitkyk	+27 (0)21 884 4416
Upland	+27 (0)82 731 4774
Van Ryn Brandy Cellar	+27 (0)21 881 3875

SA Brandy Foundation	+ 27 (0)21 887 3157
	Fax + 27 (0)21 886 6381
info@sabrandy.co.za	www.sabrandy.co.za

flavour will remain prominent. Premium and estate brandies are usually enjoyed neat, perhaps with ice and a little water. They are characterised by their smooth, full flavour. Traditionally used as a preservative, brandy also adds a special flavour when used in food preparation. As the alcohol evaporates during cooking, the flavour remains and should not overpower the food.

Route 62 Brandy Route	
Barrydale Cellar	+27 (0)28 572 1012
Boplaas	+27 (0)44 213 3326
Grundheim	+27 (0)44 272 6927
Kango Cellar	+27 (0)44 272 6065
KWV House of Brandy	+27 (0)23 342 0255
Mons Ruber	+27 (0)44 251 6550

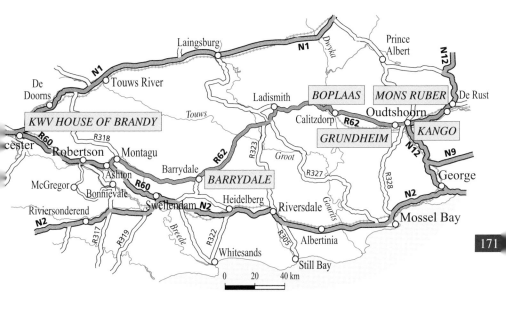

171

Brandy – South Africa's most popular spirit

Garagiste Wine

Ladybird – symbol of organic winemaking

Garagiste (translated as garage owner) is the French term used for a growing number of winemakers who, for want of a farm or cellar, have found an outlet for their passion in their backyards.

In garages, sheds and similar structures dotted around the Western Cape, these self-styled devotees lavish hours of love and attention on one, two or perhaps 12 barrels of wine-in-the-making. With the utmost care and real courage, these garagistes are producing many fine wines. Garagistes traditionally do not own vineyards or wine cellars, and few have any formal training in winemaking. Many make their wines after hours, as they are employed full-time elsewhere. Grapes are bought from independent growers and the wine is usually made in the cellar space rented from an existing wine producer. By outsourcing, they can select the best grapes (within a budget) and have access to all the required processing equipment and analytical facilities without the vast initial cash investment of developing and equipping a full production and maturation cellar.

IN DEFIANCE OF TRADITION

It all began in France in 1992 when Jean-Luc Tunevin started Chateau de Valandraud with grapes bought from the Saint-Emilion area. With meticulous care, he hand-crafted what was to become one of the finest red wines ever made. The Merlot-Cabernet Franc blend was rated a perfect 100 by Robert Parker (US wine critic), securing its place alongside Chateaux Lafite Rothschild, Latour and Margaux. Garagiste operations sprang up around France with winemakers working in defiance of centuries' old tradition. It ignited enormous interest in selective production of boutique quantities. Some garagiste wines command prices reserved for first growth. In recent years, American wine enthusiasts have awarded cult-like status to some of their own garage wines. Richard Niell commented on garagiste in *Decanter* magazine: "The garage phenomenon has given Bordeaux a kick up the collective bum and there is no doubt that we are drinking better wines in a number of appellations because of the ripples that have spread out from the garagistes' activities." Clive Torr, co-founder of South Africa's garagiste movement, comments: "We haven't quite got there, but we are making some superb wines which are slowly being recognised locally and internationally."

Clive Torr pressing Pinot Noir grapes

SOUTH AFRICAN GARAGISTES

In South Africa, Cathy Marshall pioneered the garagiste phenomenon. She crushed her first grapes on Muizenberg beach in Cape Town with friends and family and started the Barefoot Wine Company in 1995. Since its first harvest, Barefoot has grown significantly and is now an honorary member of the Garagiste Movement. Barefoot produces a Syrah, Pinot Noir, Sauvignon Blanc and a fortified red named Myriad while Cathy continues to consult at various wineries. In 1997, Clive Torr vinified the first grapes for Topaz Wines. "I began with a winemaking qualification but no farm or cellar," he says simply. "For me, the greatest honour is to make a wine for my friends and myself. To be creative and receive recognition for your work is very rewarding. In the garage of my house in Paarl, eleven of us got together and made the best Pinot Noir anyone has ever seen. I thought, 'If we can do this with Pinot Noir, a fickle and delicate grape, imagine what else we can do.' And the synergy of all those people spending hours together hand sorting grapes and lavishing attention on the wine was a huge inspiration."

With the inspiration and motivation of Cathy Marshall, Clive Torr and Tanja Beutler, many garagistes are now producing their own wines. "Often these are professionals with a passion for wine. I believe to make it as a garagistes, it takes passion the first year and guts to do it a second year! Every wine created is unique, special and individual. These wines are made with the outmost care and attention to detail," says Beutler. As the number of operations grew, a desperate need for technical guidance and a structured marketing and sales plan emerged. Torr and Beutler spearheaded the convergence and a Garagiste Movement was formed in July 2002. Beutler explains: "We got together at an informal tasting and were simply stunned by the awesome standard of products."

173

Individual attention – grapes ready for hand sorting

The movement provides technical and moral support to aspirant garagiste winemakers. "Logistics are a nightmare and the pooling of resources, equipment and dry goods would streamline operations for members. The movement also supports members in their accreditation applications and compliance with customs and excise regulations," says Beutler.

Ultimately, the coming together of like-minded producers is about marketing. Members and their products are promoted to the local and international wine trade by gaining access to wine events as a group. While never failing to appreciate the importance of commercial considerations, Beutler adamantly maintains; "We have to carry the passion forward, extend the love and dedication that defines garage winemaking." The garagistes pride themselves on the *terroir* of their wines and origin authenticity is a most important aspect.

The Topaz Shiraz 2001 received an outstanding review in *The Wine Advocate*: "A Shiraz that was striking for its sensuality and balance came from a producer whom I had never heard of, South African Wine Master Clive Torr … Garagiste wines [are] less about power and weight than a sensual and almost delicate nuance. Easy to enjoy in a sensual level, they are subtly sophisticated on their expressiveness. The Topaz Shiraz is certainly one of these."

The garagistes' greatest achievement to date has been the five-star rating awarded to The Foundry's 2002 Shiraz in the local *Platter Guide*. Its creator, Chris Williams, is the successor to Giorgio Dalla Cia as chief winemaker at the esteemed South African wine icon, Meerlust.

Small scale – open top fermentation

Dr Philip Mostert, a rural country general practitioner, became a garagiste when he joined Clive Torr on a trip to Beaune, wine capital of Burgundy. Mostert spent the time learning everything from cleaning a cellar to picking, sorting and crushing grapes. "It was one of the best experiences of my life. I returned home determined to make 2002 my first vintage." He did and the success of his wine caught everyone off guard. His Dispore Kamma Syrah 2002 received a Grand Gold Medal and Best Garagiste Producer award at the Michelangelo International Wine Awards in 2003.

Many new garagistes are making wines. For most, the single point of entry into the market is through the Garagiste Movement. Contact the Garagiste Movement at tanja@topazwine.co.za for purchases and more information.

Facts on garagiste winemaking

- Total maximum production 9, 000 litres
- Certification and registration by SAWIS (South African Wine Information Systems) and the Wine and Spirit Board
- Project must be totally funded by garagiste
- The wine must be made by garagiste in South Africa

Notes

Chapter 3

Tasting and Understanding Wines and Styles

Tasting and Understanding Wines and Styles

Old and new – a fine collection ready for tasting

Wine tasting, as opposed to wine drinking, is an art form that teaches us to focus on quality and not quantity. And because wine stimulates all our senses – sound, sight, taste, smell and touch – it is an invitation to hedonism.

WINE TASTING IS NOT SIMPLY WINE DRINKING

Wine gives pleasure associated with the natural desire to eat and drink. Wine used to be like any other drink, consumed at all times of the day, but when it became a strong symbol in the celebration of Catholic Mass, its status rose significantly to that of a "special" or exclusive beverage. Today wine is consumed as the first choice lifestyle product of moderation. It has become synonymous with culture and style, playing a major role in the economies of many nations. Wine is also deemed essential to man's survival and is linked to a range of health benefits, as is seen in the French paradox.

Wine may reduce the risk of heart disease, stress and related diseases. Excessive drinking, however, has detrimental effects, ruining the health, dulling the senses and corroding the social structure.

Were it not for our memory and cultural education, tasting wine (and any other food) would remain a strictly sensory pleasure. But one of the attractions of tasting is the identification of an aroma, recognising a certain style of wine or particular vintage. Wine becomes a magical journey in time and space. It does not have to include jargon, pretences or snobbery.

The French paradox

It seems paradoxical that the French, enjoying a diet based on cheese, bread and meat, are generally very healthy and have a low risk of heart disease and obesity – diseases associated with protein and fat-based eating habits. Their secret is the moderate consumption of wine on a regular basis.

178

Quality stemware for quality wines

Novices often wonder whether wine tasting itself is not a sufficient pleasure or whether the efforts to describe a wine are wasted. In fact, tasting wine is similar to criticising a painting. Pleasure is always said to be heightened by knowledge. To describe a glass of wine is to prolong enjoyment as each glass of wine tells a unique story, representing a particular technique, recalling a specific time of harvest and reminding us of a specific place of origin. Wine is uniquely individual, telling us a story if we know how to listen.

WHAT IS A GREAT WINE?

Wine as an agricultural product is influenced, not only by the winemaker, but also by weather conditions and agricultural pests and diseases. Wine must be produced from healthy, good quality grapes and not have any obvious faults. It should not contain excessive additions or harmful substances. Wine can either be made from one specific grape variety or from a blend of different varieties. These varietal characteristics must be well preserved in the wine, leading to the intensity of flavours and aromas and an overall balance in the wine. On the highest level, wine represents the specific vintage or year of harvest, the ability to age successfully and is an expression of *terroir* or geographical

Wine ingredients

Water – 80 – 90 per cent water, quantity varying with alcohol content.

Alcohol – ethyl alcohol produced by yeast from sugar, accounts for 8 – 20 per cent of volume.

Acids – from grape origin (tartaric, malic) or produced by fermentation (lactic, acetic). Total acidity ranges between 2 – 9 grams per litre. Main source of acid flavour in wine and stimulates saliva production.

Phenolic compounds
Pigments: yellow and red pigments give wine its colour (200 – 500 mg/l)
Tannins: contained in grape skins and pips or extracted from wood barrels. Provide astringency that puckers the mouth. Thickens the saliva and makes wine seem dry. Excessive tannins may cause bitterness.

Sugars – all finished wine has a portion of unfermented sugar, called residual sugar. Contributes to the basic flavour of sweetness, creates a balance with acid and gives viscosity. Sugar and alcohol together create richness.

Salts – wine's major salts are potassium and sodium; however, their tastes are disguised by alcohol and sugar.

Carbon dioxide (CO$_2$) – wine contains various amounts of CO$_2$. It becomes detectable at 500 mg/l and creates bubbles at 1, 000 mg/l; adds freshness by accentuating the acidity and also diffuses the aroma.

Aromatic substances – these substances give wine its aroma and taste and account for the complexity and richness. Based on their volatility, they contribute to odours ranging from floral and fruity to herbaceous and even spicy. The intensity of odour is influenced by the alcohol and water content.

identity – a specific site from which the grapes were harvested. Competition wines are not necessarily the best drinking wines. They tend to hold the greatest concentration, fruitiest bouquet, highest alcohol and most pronounced tannins. They are made to impress. One sip may be enough as they could be overpowering and require food to be best enjoyed. A wine of understated elegance, in the words of Jan "Boland" Coetzee, will "drink like water".

SERVING WINE

Wine should always be served at room temperature and, as a general rule for South African conditions, all wines should be served slightly chilled. A wine served too cold (from the fridge or cooling system, normally 5°C), can be slightly warmed by cupping the glass in your hands. Even a small rise in temperature can make an acidic, watery white wine seem more interesting, as more flavours and aromas are released at a slightly higher temperature. When tasting, first look at the wine, smell it and then taste it. These steps will give clues about the grape variety or varieties in case of a blend, where it was harvested, how the wine was made and the quality.

A good decanter will properly air wine

Serving wine in the correct order will allow you to enjoy each style at its best. It is not a crime to mix wines, but as your senses become duller through the course of a tasting or meal, the progress should be in order of alcoholic strength. Older wines containing sediment may benefit from decanting. Drinking a murky glass of wine because you were trying to save the last few millilitres hardly seems worthwhile. Glass decanters are available from all good wine shops. About six standard wine glasses can be filled to a reasonable level from one 750 ml bottle of wine.

Glasses and bottles – A "waiter's friend" is by far the most efficient way to remove a cork. Avoid silly cork-pulling gadgets. When opening MCC or sparkling wine, do not allow the cork to shoot out as you will lose some pressure (bubbles) and wine. Let the cork

---

Serving wine

White before red, Light before tannic, Simple before complex, Young before old, Dry before sweet

---

Serving temperatures for wine

RED WINES	VARIETIES	TEMPERATURE
Very tannic	Cabernet Sauvignon, Shiraz, Pinotage	16° – 18°C
Medium body	Pinot Noir, Merlot, Cape Blends, Bordeaux blends	14° – 16°C
Light body	Other red varieties, blended reds	10° – 12°C

WHITE WINE	VARIETIES	TEMPERATURE
Wooded	Chardonnay, Chenin , Sémillon Blanc	12°C
Non-wooded	Sauvignon Blanc, Chenin Blanc, Sémillon	10°C
Sparkling wines		8° – 10°C
Sweet wines	Late and Noble Late Harvest, Semi-sweet	8° – 10°C

ROSÉ WINES	VARIETIES	TEMPERATURE
Light	Light body Rosé, Blanc de Noir	8° – 10°C
Medium body	Rosé	12° – 14°C

slip out slowly with a gentle sigh. Choose the right shaped glass, clean, transparent and tulip-shaped with an opening narrow enough to concentrate the aromas. Glasses must be tall enough to allow for swirling. Hand-blown crystal is not necessary, but will enhance the experience. Wash glasses in warm soapy water, rinse thoroughly and dry standing or hung upside down on a glass rack.

APPEARANCES: LOOKING AT WINE

The first step to enjoying wine is to look at it in the glass; this will reveal something about how the wine was made, how it was stored, its age and alcohol content. Tilt the glass sideways, holding it over a white surface or up to the light. The important elements to notice are clarity, colour, intensity and viscosity.

Clarity – Observe the brightness and clarity from the top of the glass on a white background. A clean and clear appearance is the first step to ensuring a healthy wine. If the wine seems dull and has little variance from the centre of the glass to the rim, it is probably a very ordinary specimen. Most good wines look interesting, shining brightly with a colour hue changing towards the rim. A great wine with great depth of colour, though not transparent, should be clear. However, deposits or dullness do not necessarily indicate a spoilt wine.

Colour – Colour intensity depends on the amount of pigment in the wine and can be observed by looking through the top of a glass at the light-permeability. The colour shade can be determined by studying the distinguishable colours visible in the meniscus of a tilted glass. South African red wines age faster than European examples and using colour shade, a relatively accurate estimate can be made as to its age. If two colours appear in the meniscus, the wine is less than three years of

age. Three distinctive colours indicate the wine is aged between four and seven years and if any browning is visible, the wine is older than seven years.

Most white wines start out having a greenish tinge and bottle maturation transforms the colour to pale yellow. If however a green tinge remains, it may indicate excessive use of sulphur dioxide (an anti-oxidant). Rosé wines, when produced from red grapes with minimum skin contact, produce lightly coloured wines. Good quality red wines have a similar maturation path to whites: starting out with an almost blue or purple colour, with maturation they will change to cherry red, orange and eventually brown. Differing from white wine, the colour of youthful red wine is influenced by variety, but most age to the same hues.

Blind tasting *(pictured above)*

Tasting wine "blind" does not mean you cannot see the wine; it refers to the identity of the wine being hidden. The purpose is to identify the origins and winemaking style from its characteristics.

Shade

Pour equal amounts of white wine into several glasses and add 1, 2, 5, 10 and 20 drops of red wine. Arrange the glasses in ascending order. Notice how the colour of the white wine changes with increased amount of red wine added. This change indicates the shade of colour.

Table of colours

WHITE WINES

Colourless	Very young, protected from oxidation, possibly tank vinification (less than 1 year)
Pale yellow / green	Grapes from cooler areas, harvested less ripe (less than 2 years)
Yellow / straw	Ultimate colour achievement for most SA white wines, point of consumption (1 – 3 years)
Yellow / gold	Sweeter table wines in youth. Wood matured wines. (3 – 4 years)
Copper / gold	Sweet dessert wines. Greatest table wines (5 – 6 years)
Brown / amber	Very old, possibly oxidised, poor storage and excessive light

ROSÉ

Stained white wines, pink highlights	Good rosé wines
Onion	Inferior shade, spoiled by oxygen
Pink / orange	Common for wines from warmer production areas

RED WINES

Blue / purple	Very young red wines. Good shade for Pinotage or Pinotage blend. Lesser quality wines never leave this infantile stage (less than 1 year)
Ruby / cherry red	Optimum development for most blended red wines (2 years)
Red / garnet	Point of consumption for most as further aging will do little good (2 – 4 years)
Red with orange border	A sign of maturity. Age shows in aromas and flavours (3 – 5 years)
Mahogany	Truly exquisite wines take on this shade without loss of crispness (5 – 7 years)
Amber / brown	Advanced age. Brown tinge is first noticed at the glass edge. Browning may also result from too much exposure to air (5 – 10 years)

Intensity – The intensity or colour density refers to the amount of pigment in the solution. Two wines may have the same colour but one is darker and more difficult to see through when placed on a white background. What do these changing colour densities indicate? Good colour intensity denotes good tannin content from fully matured grapes; the wine should age well and benefit from its years in bottle. It also indicates that the wine has been allowed a reasonable length of time in contact with the skins, which provides greater density of fruit, bouquet and palate. A pale colour, although occasionally a characteristic of a grape variety, could indicate a fast, poor vinification process, overcropping of vines or simply an inferior vintage with fewer sun hours during the ripening stage. A low density does not necessarily indicate a poor or spoilt wine. Great colour intensity most often relates to concentrated fruit flavours, complexity and structure, characterising a superior wine.

Viscosity – The threadlike "tears" or "legs" formed on the inside surface of a wine glass when swirled are due to a liquid's viscosity. Alcohol and sugar content provide viscosity to a wine, modifying the surface tension. This in turn causes liquid running down the glass surface to form tears. The amount or shape of tears is *not* an indication of wine quality.

Intensity

Pour a deeply coloured wine into several glasses and add 20, 40 and 80 per cent water respectively. Arrange the glasses in ascending order. Notice that the colour hue stays the same, but the intensity varies.

From light to dark

Too pale – Causes: poor extraction, wet harvest, unrestricted yields, young vines, unripe grapes, rotten grapes, fermentation at too low temperatures. Deduce: wine of poor vintage, poor aging ability

Deeply coloured – Causes: good extraction, limited yields, older vines, sufficient vinification. Deduce: good or great wine. Wine with a future.

Differences in smell

Aroma	odours from the grape itself
Bouquet	odours arising from the processing of the grapes – vinification, wooding and maturation
Aroma	defines the perception of smell, via our nose or retronasal passages
Flavour	associated with the liquid in our mouth. Chemically based and supported by smell
Cleanliness	the wine should have a very distinctive smell of grapes. Any dusty, musty or animal-related smell is an indication of a faulty wine

AROMA: SMELLING THE WINE

Assessing the wine's bouquet is based on what is known as the "nose" of wine. We tend to think that "smell" is detected by our nose and "taste" is sensed in our mouth. In fact, the lines between these distinctions are very blurred. Elements to notice are cleanliness, aromatics and intensity.

When pouring, ensure the glass is filled no more than a third to allow enough space for the aroma to collect. Smelling while holding the glass still, will yield very subtle and fleeting aromas. Swirl the glass and smell again. Agitating the glass to disturb the surface of the wine will bring out the least volatile aromas. Allow the wine to settle in the glass and smell it again. As the wine moves from a reductive state in the bottle to an oxygenated state in the glass, many aromatic components develop at varying speeds due to aeration and oxidation, which encourages volatile compounds to collect on the liquid surface. For example, meat and smoky notes disappear as soon as the wine is aired, whereas fruit and wood aromas are brought out by aeration.

The aromatics of wine can be divided into six main families: vegetal, floral, fruit, wood, spice and empyreuma (cocoa, toast, gingerbread, etc.), while other, less common, aromatics such as mineral, chemical and animal odours also occur. Wine aromas originate from three major sources: the grape berries themselves (primary); the vinification or winemaking process (secondary) and the maturation process (tertiary).

Grape aromas – All grapes possess their own unique identity and pass this on, in varying degrees, to the wine. In white wines, for instance, aromas of roses and spice are associated with Gewürztraminer and white fruits with Sauvignon Blanc. In red wines a note of red berries indicates Cabernet Sauvignon, while black-skinned fruits and black pepper suggest Shiraz.

183

Berry aromas in your wine

Maturing wine – oak barrels at Whalehaven, Walker Bay

Aromatics also differ from one region to another. Compare a green, mineral-styled Sauvignon Blanc from Cape Point with a ripe, fruit-driven Sauvignon from Robertson. Riesling grapes represent a striking example of the exchange between grape variety and *terroir*. Depending on the soil, Riesling wines may express delicate floral aromas or heavier scents of truffles. The level of ripeness when grapes are harvested also influences aroma – unripe Sauvignon Blanc tends to show vegetal aromas such as sage leaves and grass; even an unattractive cat's urine smell. However, when fully ripe, Sauvignon Blanc can give a complex bouquet of white-fleshed fruit, florals and musk.

Fermentation bouquet – Grape juice is not very aromatic, apart from the obvious smell of grapes. Some aromas are present in a latent state as precursors in berry skins and they are brought forward by alcoholic fermentation. Yeast, responsible for this conversion, produces alcohol and carbon dioxide along with various secondary products influencing aroma. Fermentation with natural-occurring yeasts, although risky, brings a different spectrum of aromas. During malolactic fermentation, natural or selected bacteria soften the acidity of wine by converting malic acid to lactic acid,

and produces flavours such as fresh butter, butterscotch and hazelnut.

Maturation bouquet – Following processing, wine (mostly reds and heavier whites) matures for varying lengths of time, depending on the style. During maturation the primary and secondary aromas diminish as the wine loses its youthful character and elegance and integration develops. Maturation in tank protects wine from oxidation and small quantities of sulphur are added as an anti-oxidant. Oxidation is avoided in most instances as it spoils wine; however, with barrel maturation controlled oxidation is the objective.

Oak barrels impart various aromas and flavours such as vanilla, toast, cigar box, spicy, coconut and smoky characters due to extraction of wood compounds. In this case, controlled oxidation stabilises the newly introduced compounds. Once bottled, wine enters a reductive state and develops the aromas that come with age: leather, meat, game, mushrooms and smoke. Wine is a living entity with a life cycle: birth, development and maturity, followed by decline and death. A wine that retains some of its fruit after maturation and aging has every chance of becoming a great, matured wine.

FLAVOUR: TASTING WINE

Tasting a wine on your palate is above all a question of appreciating the synthesis of flavours. You must appraise the balance of the wine's structure; distinguish the entry, mid-palate and finish and discern the elementary flavours, tannins and alcoholic warmth. This is the essence of wine tasting.

The traditional approach to tasting is aimed at determining the four elementary flavours: sweet, acid, salty and bitter, on specific areas on the tongue. It has been discovered that all sensations are registered on all areas of the tongue. Also, there are many more "taste" sensations than the basic four.

• **Olfactory sensations** are perceived by the retronasal passage. When aromas reach the temperature of the mouth, they are perceived as more intense than in a colder wine. The rise in temperature brings out the less volatile elements. These "flavours of the palate" are important; they are the fundamental signature of the wine.

• **Taste sensations** are chemically based and perceived on the tongue. A compound dissolves in the saliva and is detected by the mouth's receptors. Taste includes the four basic perceptions of sweet, acid, salt and bitter, as well as various other flavours (fruit, wood, meat, etc.) and is supported by the retronasal passage (foodstuffs taste bland when one's nose is blocked).

• **Tactile or feeling sensation** is illustrated best when tasting a red wine (or a white wine fermented in wood), when tannins create a perception of astringency or chewiness that gives the wine texture. Tannins are directly linked to the fluidity and viscosity of saliva. Excessive tannins make your mouth dry. The sensation is thus physically based as opposed to chemically.

• **Thermal or temperature sensations** depend on the actual temperature of a wine which influences the perception of flavours and aromas. Alcohol content is also important; when excessive, it makes a wine seem warm.

STAGES OF TASTING

Wine is taken into the mouth and aerated by breathing air over it. The first few seconds is known as the "entrance" or "attack" of a wine. First impressions are of sweetness and subtle aromas. Roll the wine around in your mouth for a few seconds, noticing how aromas and flavours develop and temperature, viscosity and astringency become apparent. These developing characteristics are called the "mid-palate" and indicate a wine's complexity. You may spit the wine out; however, there are dimensions that can only be savoured when wine is swallowed. Take some time to appreciate the different flavours when you spit out wine and when it is swallowed. The intensity of a wine's "finish" will reveal its ultimate quality in persistence, balance and structure.

ELEMENTARY FLAVOURS

The main elements which can be noted in wine include: sweetness, acidity, bitterness, aromatic character, body, persistence, balance and typicity.

Sweetness – Sweetness in wine results from a portion of unfermented sugar, about 1 – 4 g/l in dry wines. This subtle sweetness helps to create a balance by softening harsher characteristics such as acidity, bitterness and astringency. Certain wine styles, for instance late harvest wine, have much higher levels of sugar (50 – 150 g/l) resulting in an authentic sweet taste and a more viscous liquid. South African law forbids sugar additions.

Tasting test for sugar

A bowl of sugar has no distinctive smell, but place granules of sugar in your mouth and you have a distinctive taste. Whenever you drink a liquid, wine, fizzy drink or juice, try to access its sweetness. There are various flavours associated with sugar – ripe fruit flavours, vanilla and glycerine. Even excessive amounts of alcohol can contribute to a wine tasting slightly sweeter.

Acidity – This is the vital spark. It forms the backbone of a wine, giving crispness, liveliness and an appealing "zip". Excess acid makes a wine tart while too little makes it bland and lifeless. Tartaric acid is the most common and important acid present in grapes and has a crisp taste resembling that of a fresh Granny Smith apple.

Tasting test for acid

Smell some vinegar and notice how your tongue curls up in anticipation. Acid has such a strong effect on the tongue that it is the easiest of all tastes to imagine without any liquid or solid stimulus.

Most drinks have a refreshing acidity to them – fizzy drinks, milk and fruit juice like grapefruit and orange juice. To give you an idea of what various acids taste like, taste the following: cream of tartar (tartaric acid), apple juice (malic acid), lemon or grapefruit juice (citric acid), milk or yoghurt (lactic acid), vinegar (acetic acid) and fizzy drinks (carbonic acid).

Bitterness – Less prominent than sweetness and acidity, bitterness is important in a balanced wine. Caused by tannins, it is often confused with astringency. Bitterness is a taste perceived in the back of the mouth, while astringency is a physical sensation of puckering that is sensed in the entire mouth.

Body – This describes the intensity of wine flavours and the weight of a wine in which alcohol plays a major role; a higher alcohol level results in a weightier wine.

Persistence / Finish – An intense aromatic refers to the continuation of an aromatic sensation on the palate, a lasting impression after the wine has been swallowed. A richer and denser wine will coat the palate more substantially and prolong stimulation of the senses. The ideal is a comfortable, lengthy reminder of a wine's character; the opposite is a wine with a short finish, with flavours disappearing quickly.

Balance – This depends on the relationship between the various chemical components. There is a balance of flavours where tastes (sweet substances, acids, tannins, salts) come together in the mouth, each either adding to the qualities of another or neutralising another. A wine's harmony is essentially derived from the balance between sweetness, acidity and bitterness. Sugar counteracts acidity as well as bitterness. Wines containing excessive acid are called "green", while wines with insufficient acid are called "flabby", "flat" and "bland". A wine with noticeable but not unpleasant acid is often called "crisp".

Flavour and aroma – The balance between flavour and aroma indicates quality as aromas "carry on" from the nose to the palate, and the expectation created by a wine's aroma is matched by the experience of taste. The development of aromatics during the life of a wine competes with the primary fruit aromas. Great wines are remarkable for the ability of their fruit content to last and evolve, moving from white-fleshed or red fruits to cooked or soft fruit and prunes.

Typicity – Typicity relates to two factors: *terroir* or place of production and the specific grape variety (or varieties). *Terroir* incorporates location effects such as climate, soil and vineyard management of a particular site, to form a unique origin. The variety refers to how strongly specific characters associated with a particular variety have been preserved in the resulting wine.

FAULTS IN WINE

A faultless wine is not necessarily a quality wine; it may be dull even if technically sound. Being informed about wine faults will save you drinking a spoilt wine or, even worse, discarding future purchases of good wine from a good producer based on one faulty bottle.

Most particles found in wine are quite harmless, merely a nuisance and can be done away with without discarding the precious liquid. The following guidelines may help you decide on a course of action. Remember, life's too short to drink bad wine!

Harmless

These faults are harmless even when ingested. However, in spoiling the appearance of wine, some enjoyment may be lost.

Dull surface	At best it is simply an ordinary wine. At worst, there is a serious fault.
Pieces of cork (or deposits from the lip of the bottle)	A bottle with a disintegrating cork was opened and served carelessly. Decant the wine into clean glasses, maybe use a sieve.
Crystals	White crystals in white wines and fragments of dark deposits in red wines are in fact the same substance – Harmless solids created through the maturation of wine, usually crystals of tartaric acid. These tartrates are dyed dark red by colour pigments in red wines, but in white wines they may look like sugar or glass fragments. To avoid confusion, deposits are removed by cold stabilisation (inducing crystal formation under very low temperatures and filtering wine clean). A wine with deposits shows it has not been over treated.
Excess acid	Due to an under-ripe crop or over acidification in overripe years. Look for another vintage from the producer.
Excess tannin	Under-ripened grapes, over-extraction or over-wooding.
Excess carbon dioxide	Recently bottled (with use of carbon dioxide gas), should subside after a minute or two.

187

Problematic

These faults are more serious and the wine should not be consumed.

Oxidation	Wine smells of honey, wax or a grain bag. In limited quantities, oxygen may contribute to the aroma profile (barrel aging), but in excess it spoils wine. Incorrect or prolonged storing and extreme temperature changes dry the cork and allow oxygen into the bottle.
Vinegar	Advanced oxidation or bacterial spoilage creates acetic acid or vinegar.
Mouldy	Smells of old, wet shoes, due to poor storage.
Corked	Smells of wet cardboard and intensely mouldy. Problems arise when the cork is spoiled by bacterial infection or by sulphur in a wine combining with chlorine in the immediate vicinity.
Mousiness	Smells of rodent urine. Caused by *Brettanomyces* bacteria, a problem mainly in reds when wine is stored in barrels without proper sanitation.
Haziness (cloudiness)	A protein instability found in white wines. Protein is a natural product of grapes and at high concentrations forms a cloud. It is tasteless and harmless but visually unacceptable.
Iridescence or film on surface	Serious micro-organism or enzymatic problems. Wine could be oxidised or vinegary.
Stringiness	Strings are clearly visible holding wine up to a light source, cause by bacterial spoilage.
Rotten eggs or rubber	Smell caused by sulphur-related compounds.

STYLES OF WINE
IN SOUTH AFRICA

South African wines have certain distinctive characteristics of New World wines in that they show good extract (from the grape skins) and new oak barrels are used extensively. Another hint to South Africa as origin is the acid structure, which is slightly different from that of Old World wines. Because of the warmer climate, addition of acid is permitted and generally gives a distinctive, recognisable flavour profile.

QUALITY LEVELS

South African wines in general can be categorised into the following four quality categories:

Lower end wines – These wines are generally based on Cinsaut as a red variety and certain Chenin Blanc wines.

Everyday drinking wines – These wines typically have very limited use of new oak or have been vinified using old barrels, wood staves and chips. The Nederburg range excluding private bins and auction wines typify this class.

Cult wines		Vintage
Klein Constantia	Vin de Constance	2000
Ernie Els Wines	Ernie Els Signature	2004
De Toren	Fusion V	2003
Boekenhoutskloof	Syrah	2001
Sadie Family Wines	Columella	2002
De Trafford	Cabernet Sauvignon	2003

Icon wines		Vintage
Kanonkop	Paul Sauer	2002
Rust en Vrede	Estate Wine	2002
Vergelegen	Cabernet Sauvignon	2003
Meerlust	Rubicon	2001
Thelema	Shiraz	2003

Upper echelon wines – Upper echelon wines are typified by the selection of only exceptional components: outstanding blocks within a vineyard or the best tanks or barrels. Examples are Pinotage from Camberley or Bellevue, Chardonnay from Mulderbosch, Sauvignon Blanc from Neil Ellis and Cabernet Sauvignon from Buitenverwachting.

Show wines – In the past, South Africa had very few cult or icon wines, but with better *terroir*, site selection, complementary variety placements and the use of "new" varieties, the list is growing.

Meerlust's only white wine – an aromatic barrel fermented Chardonnay

188

The art of blending – In the last five years, South African winemakers have turned to blending white wine varietals. The two main varietals are Chardonnay and Chenin Blanc, although more complex tri-varietal blends use Viognier as well as Sauvignon Blanc. No one specific area stands out as the optimum, although cooler climate regions do produce the highest quality. The top blends are Vergelegen white (Sémillon / Sauvignon Blanc) and Palladius (Sadie Family Wines) based on Chenin Blanc, Viognier and Chardonnay.

Single vineyard wines – Currently there is no legislation allowing recognition of a single vineyard on a South African wine label. There are, however, many examples of single vineyard wines as the focus on *terroir* wines increases. The future will see this explored as a particular feature of wines.

Red wines

STYLE	CHARACTERISTICS
Fresh, fruity	Light in colour. Raspberries, red apple and cherries; absence of dense tannin. Juicy, plummy wines, unoaked. Merlot, Grenache, Pinotage, Gamay. For early consumption.
Medium body	Firm structure and density. Red berry fruit, spice, chocolate. Gently oaking. Classic wines for meat dishes.
Powerful, spicy	Intensely mouth filling, inky black and complex. Higher alcohol (riper picking), powerful tannins (new oak barrels) and ripe fruits. Cabernet Sauvignon, Shiraz, Zinfandel and Mouvèrdre. Improves with proper cellaring.

White wines

STYLE	CHARACTERISTICS
Crisp, light bodied	Pale colour. Fresh cut grass and wet stones. Low alcohol, crisp acidity, unwooded.
Aromatic	Bone dry to medium sweet. Honey, diesel, straw (Riesling); citrus and peach (Viognier) and florals (rose on Gewürztraminer).
Steely or mineral	Grippy mouthfeel, flinty and firm fruit on palate. Produced in cooler climates. Flint and gun powder (Sauvignon Blanc); limes (Riesling); hazelnut (Chardonnay) and wax or wet stones (Chenin Blanc, Sémillon). Good food partner.
Full bodied, rich	Honeyed with tropical fruit, creamy, mouth filling. From warmer climates, increased alcohol levels and wooded. Vanilla (wooded Chardonnay), nectarines and pineapple (Chenin Blanc, Sémillon).

Other

STYLE	CHARACTERISTICS
Sparkling	Toast, cookie dough, sweetness. Aggressive mousse, disappearing quickly.
MCC (Sparkling)	Toast, nut, biscuit, buttery. Fine and persistent mousse. Crisp acidity, lingering finish.
Rosé wines	Made from red grapes with minimum skin contact. Lighter alcohol, delicate fruit flavours, rarely tannic or structured. Zinfandel, Pinotage, Cabernet Sauvignon blends.
Sweet wines	Apricots, peaches, spice. High sugar and viscous.
	Late and Special Late Harvest produced from grapes left on vine, resulting in high sugar content.
	Noble Late Harvest wines (NLH) produced from grapes attacked by *Botrytis cinerea*. Benevolent form removes water from berries, concentrating sugar, acid and flavour compounds (noble rot). Wines are rich, sweet and perfumed without being sugary while concentrated acid provides structure and balance. Aggressive form of *Botrytis* results in loss of crop. Chenin Blanc, Sémillon, Sauvignon Blanc, Weisser Riesling, Gewürztraminer.
Fortified wines	Berry, tar, chocolate flavours. Port style wines use Portuguese varieties (Tinta Barocca, Tinta Roriz, Touriga Nacional) or French varieties.

WHITE VARIETALS WINES

CHARDONNAY
Melon, grapefruit and pineapple
Buttery and nutty

Chardonnay is found in all South Africa's grape cultivation areas, from the cool coastal climate to the extremely warm Orange River region. Chardonnay wines can be classified into cool and warm region styles, although the soil in which they grow plays a predominant role in the flavour profile. Chardonnays can be wooded or unwooded. Traditionally wines were heavily oaked, but evolved over the past decade to a lighter, more elegantly oaked style as a result of international consumer market demands. The wines will be exposed to wood either by fermentation or aging in barrels, but are seldom applied to the entire crush. The unwooded component brings a crisp acidity and fresh fruit flavours to the finished product. In higher price brackets, wines are aged in barrels with frequent stirring of the lees (Fr. *bâttonage*). *Bâttonage* increases the mellowing effect of lees and wines show more buttery, popcorn and creamy nuances. Acidity levels vary in Chardonnays, although in higher quality wines, the trend is to halt malolactic fermentation at an early stage and thus increase the malic acid proportion. This gives a good balance.

Warm Pockets – The Olifants River and Orange River areas are both extremely warm and not favourable for this fairly heat-sensitive variety. To avoid typical baked, jammy characters, grapes are often picked earlier during the ripening period. The resultant wines are lower in alcohol (typically around Alc. 12.5% by Vol.) and show a tropical fruit palate with a lack of citrus character. Often thin, the wines tend to have a short finish and little elegance, a style more for quaffing.

Robertson Pocket – Although this area has a warm climate, predominantly limestone soils impart a distinct lime character. Wine styles are often rich in character with strong tropical fruit characters balanced with a lime citrus character.

Coastal Pockets – These Pockets produce elegant Chardonnay styles with good finesse. The fruit flavours vary from strong citrus (lemon, orange, tangerine) in the coolest areas to more tropical fruits (melon, peach,

---

Sparkling Wine

Champagne's ruling body (CIVC) ruled out the name champagne for Cape sparkling wine long before the European Union trade agreement in 2002. South African producers came up the term *Méthode Cap Classique* (MCC) to describe their style of bubbly production. While *Méthode* and *Classique* refer to the classic Champagne method of bottle fermentation, *Cap* points to the South African geographical origin.

Most MCCs are made with Chardonnay and Pinot Noir, and little Pinot Meunier is used. Some incorporate a touch of Chenin or Pinotage. Blends are evenly distributed between Blanc de Blanc or only white grapes (Chardonnay) and the traditional Chardonnay/Pinot Noir blend. South Africa's quality sparkling wines (Chardonnay/Pinot Noir blends) are some of the best value for money in the world. Best Pockets for MCCs are Franschhoek, Robertson, Paarl and Stellenbosch with producers like Graham Beck, Villiera and Steenberg leading the way.

Manual remuage at Steenberg Vineyards

pineapple) in warmer areas. The citrus component ranges from lime notes to more distinct grapefruit notes. The touch more alcohol is noticeable in increased palate weight and wooded examples show vanilla, butter and oily characters. The best Pockets for Chardonnay are Stellenbosch, Durbanville, Cape Point and Walker Bay.

CHENIN BLANC
Quince, apple and pear drops
Sweet barley and honey

Chenin Blanc is the most prolific in South Africa but the percentage of plantings has been reduced based on historically poor quality performance. This variety dominates in warmer Pockets such as the Klein Karoo, Olifants River, Swartland, Paarl, Worcester and Robertson. A good blending partner for other white varieties such as Chardonnay and Colombar, the bulk of Chenin Blanc fruit is still used for brandy spirits production. Warmer regions yield light-textured tropical wines with good acidity for a refreshing summer drink. These wines are unwooded and appeal to the broad consumer market.

However, in the last five years, some notable, outstanding quality Chenin Blancs have been produced in a variety of styles, mainly from the Stellenbosch area and in particular Pockets along the Helderberg and Schaapenberg Mountains. When cool fermented, Chenin Blanc shows pear drops, quince and apple flavours, becoming more peachy and melon-like in fuller dry wines. Wood fermentation and aging produces structured wines in a heavier style. With *Botrytis* development in the grapes, wines become rich in barley, sugar and honey characters. Notably the sweeter and wooded styles have excelled in the international Chenin Blanc competitions, particularly in France.

SAUVIGNON BLANC
Flinty, mineral, zesty
Cut grass, nettles, asparagus, green pepper
Gooseberry, passion fruit, mango

South Africa's Sauvignon Blanc style is midway between that of Europe and New Zealand. This variety is fast becoming a signature white grape of South Africa. Styles vary from a grassy, herbaceous style to the riper, tropical, gooseberry style. Sauvignon Blanc's style depends heavily on berry ripeness. To add complexity, grapes are picked in three stages. Slightly under-ripe grapes give the green grass, green pepper and tinned pea flavours. Medium ripeness yields green fig and white asparagus flavours, while fully ripe grapes show fruity nuances such as gooseberries and yellow fruit.

Sauvignon Blanc is very *terroir* sensitive and generally cooler regions are preferred as these give the green pepper or methoxypyrazine notes, as do chalky limestone soils. The best Sauvignon Blancs come from the Cape Point, Stellenbosch (various Pockets), Robertson (due to soil type) and Durbanville area. The aromas and flavours range from freshly cut grass and tropical fruit (Durbanville) to green pepper, flint and fig (Darling), floral, gooseberry and peach (Simonsberg). Only the cooler climate Sauvignon Blancs of South Africa can age well; others should be drunk young.

OTHER WHITE VARIETIES
Varieties that account for less than one per cent of plantings are categorised here.

Riesling (Rhine Riesling) – Flavours of apple and lime, honey and petrol. These have mostly been uprooted in South Africa, but colder coastal Pockets (Constantia and Elgin, Stellenbosch) make wonderful dry Rieslings which can age successfully. However, the variety-typical terpene character becomes evident earlier than in the Old World wines.

Viognier – Typically peach, apricot as well as jasmine. This up-and-coming variety has gained popularity over the past five years. South African Viognier wines show intense peach blossom aromas while young. However, this floral nose dies rapidly with age. Cultivated mostly in the Stellenbosch area, there are also a number of vineyards in the Swartland and Paarl. Some wines are slightly wooded to add complexity and palate weight to balance the intensely powerful nose. Viognier is also blended at times with Shiraz to give a Côte Rôtie style.

Sémillon – Flavours of lime and citrus, also marmalade and some sweetness. Sémillon was planted extensively in South Africa in the previous century. However, due to lack of demand, Sémillon was mostly uprooted. The Franschhoek Pocket currently has the largest plantings of Sémillon. In cooler areas wines taste grassy with an oily, lanolin mouthfeel. Often a small amount (5 per cent) of Sauvignon Blanc is blended with Sémillon to enhance its grassy flavours. In warmer regions wines tend to be wooded, giving a fuller mouthfeel and yellow fruit flavours.

RED VARIETAL WINES

South African red wines can be very alcoholic, up to 16 per cent alcohol, although the average percentage is 14 – 14.5 per cent by volume. In the last five years, grapes have been picked riper (later in the season) and more detailed attention has been given to sorting of fruit. Gentler processing reduces extraction of excessive tannins, making wines softer and more accessible at a younger age while maintaining a good maturation potential. South African winemakers generally use new oak barrels; however, with a gentler winemaking

approach, percentages of new wood have been reduced. This philosophy yields fruity, austere wines balanced with good extraction which expresses a New World fruit character, but maintains some of the Old World undertones.

CAPE BLENDS

The new Cape Blend style is gaining popularity. The first distinct characteristic relates to the origin and indicates a blend made within a particular Cape area. The second indicates use of the truly South African variety, Pinotage, as a blending partner. At present there are no specific regulations in terms of varieties and percentages required. Kaapzicht's stunning victory in claiming the title Best Blended Red Wine in the World at the 2004 International Wine and Spirit competition is very encouraging. This blend contains approximately 40 per cent Pinotage. Warwick's Three Cape Ladies was selected for the Top 100 in *Wine Spectator's* 2004 line-up and contains approximately 30 per cent Pinotage.

CABERNET SAUVIGNON
Capsicum (green pepper)
Blackcurrant and plums
Cedar, eucalyptus, vanilla and coffee

Cabernet Sauvignon wine from newer clones are black fruit driven (blackberry and blackcurrant), while older clones show more herbaceousness with green pepper aromas. Cabernet Sauvignon maintains a characteristic flavour profile irrespective of the *terroir*. Since this variety requires some warmth to ripen, the flavour profile tends to evolve from herbaceous to richer dark fruits as you travel inland from the coast. The award-winning Cabernet Sauvignons are concentrated around the Stellenbosch area. Bordeaux blends are also very popular, blending Cabernet Sauvignon with Merlot and small amounts of Cabernet

Franc. Occasionally Cabernet Sauvignon may be blended with Shiraz, but this is an exception rather than the rule.

PINOTAGE

Plums and raspberries, hints of banana
Smoky, spicy

Pinotage wines fall mainly into two styles, one being very individual and robust, the other leaning towards the elegance of its Pinot Noir parent. A youthful wine has a distinctive jammy, red fruit taste (raspberry and mulberry) mixed with spicy notes. Harvested very ripe, Pinotage may show hints of banana and undesired burnt rubber, nail varnish or acetone characters which are eliminated with improved cultivation and high fermentation temperatures. During aging, the aromas evolve towards strawberry, wet pine needles and mushrooms (a Pinot Noir character). Pinotage is generally made in one of three styles: unwooded; a lighter fruity style; or a wooded style. We also find Pinotage in some Cape Blends. The belt from Stellenbosch, through Franschhoek towards Paarl and the Swartland is the main cultivation area.

SHIRAZ

Black pepper, spice, smoke
Leather, savoury, chocolate

Shiraz produces inky, aromatic red wines with smoky, floral, minty, peppery and spicy aromas. The occasional medicinal character is undesired and may flow over into a eucalyptus character. In cool climates Shiraz shows mint, pepperiness and spice. Warm climate cultivation gives raspberry and blackberry fruits, evolving to chocolate, tarry and gamey notes with age. Shiraz is popular in South Africa and cool climate areas are relatively unexplored in favour of warmer climates. No regional suitability has really been established but Shiraz excels in Paarl, Wellington and various Stellenbosch

Pockets. Vineyards are still fairly young, due to historical disease problems and a search for optimum clones. Although not as bold as Australian examples, South African Shiraz wines are typically New World with the style moving from earthy-oxidative to more upfront fruitiness. A period of excessive oaking with America oak in particular has also come to an end resulting in more elegant wines.

MERLOT

Capsicum, bell pepper, blackcurrant
Chocolate, spice, soft mint

Merlot plantings have steadily increased at the expense of other red varieties. Merlot has an easy mouthfeel, berry fruit flavour coupled with chocolate and mint. Grown mostly in coastal regions, Stellenbosch, Franschhoek and Paarl are the predominant Pockets. South Africa struggles to make world-class single variety Merlots, but certain examples are very promising. The softer mid-palate and smooth tannins make Merlot an excellent blending partner and it is often combined with Cabernet Sauvignon. Cooler regions with soils that have slightly higher clay content produce minty Merlots while flavours in warmer regions are dominated by violets.

PINOT NOIR

Raspberry, strawberry, cherry
Incense, game, perfumed

This Burgundian grape commands a small percentage of total plantings in South Africa. Initial plantings yielded a very organic wine due to the character of the Swiss BK5 clone. In the past 10 years, newer clones have yielded robust and fruit-driven wines. The best Pinot Noirs hail from Walker Bay due to cool growing conditions. Elgin is also an up-and-coming area for Pinot Noir due to increased plantings in the last four years.

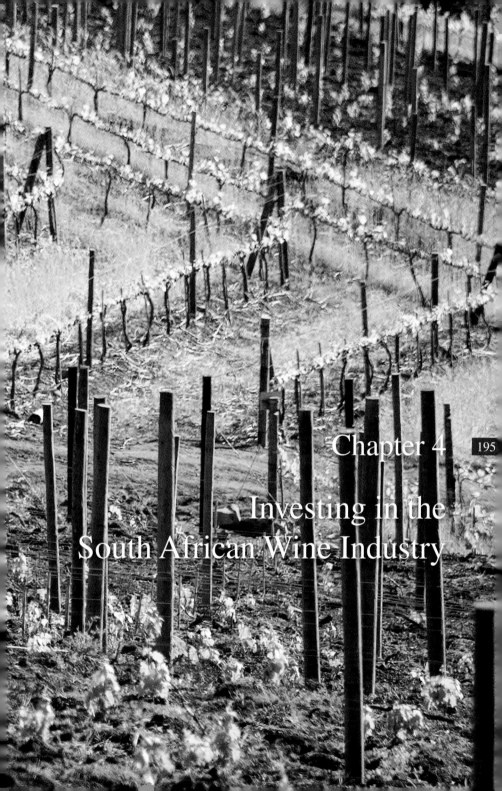

Chapter 4

Investing in the
South African Wine Industry

Investing in the
South African Wine Industry

Hidden Valley's new winery designed around gentle grape handling

Southh Africa remains an investor's land of opportunity. From starting a small South African wine collection to owning a beautiful wine estate, there is value to be found in every sector of the market.

Over the past decade, the local wine industry has maintained a steady growth. As the country's fiscal strategies started to produce the desired results – driving down inflation, steadying the currency and increasing the country's growth – winemakers and estate owners have prospered. However, entrepreneurs who banked on a weak currency, winemakers who ignored quality and exporters who sought mass volume all fell outside the parameters of good investors. As the media seek out sensation, the headlines far too often highlight such examples, lamenting the woes of short-term opportunists. As in any investing community, the principles of a blue-chip investment can easily be related to a good wine: enduring quality, relentless attention to

detail and controlled growth. These form the cornerstone of the investments discussed in the section below.

INVESTING IN A
VINEYARD OR WINERY

At present, both virgin land and established vineyards are attracting great interest from both local and international investors. The goal of owning a winery is to ensure that the venture is profitable. Cultivating grapes can certainly be profitable, but one must realise that, due to the forces of nature, farming always remains uncertain.

Just as other investments are phased to reach a desired production level, returns from a vineyard should be evaluated over a long-term period. This does, to a large extent, counter rapid changes in the weather and pests, which could drastically change quality and quantity in the short term. Consulting experts will assist you in achieving good returns from your vineyards. Focusing on selected cultivars, matching the area's *terroir* and producing quality wine for the local and international market should bring investment success. How the production is constituted remains of ultimate importance.

Although supply and demand are vitally important economical factors, it is also true that good quality wine will always find a market, provided price levels are on target. Establishing a wine production facility while outsourcing the grape supply is more cost effective initially, but risks remain as you relinquish some control over the cultivation process and therefore your ultimate investment success.

In compiling cost estimates for a wine producing property, the first consideration is the cost of land. This varies between areas and is directly related to the size of the property. In prime areas, virgin land can reach €60, 000 per hectare (10, 000 m²). Developed estates could well cost double that amount. Undeveloped land requires substantial funds to establish vineyards. This alone could cost about €15, 000 per hectare. Irrigation equipment and water aside, annual maintenance costs including sprays, fertilisers, pest control and pruning come to around €1, 400 per hectare. The cost of water and irrigation depends on the location of the property, available water sources and the needs of the grape variety.

THE VINES

Wine grapes are an annual crop. Harvesting in South Africa takes place between January and March, in contrast to the European or US production seasons, where harvesting occurs from August to November. Harvesting is done mostly by hand – machine harvesting is rare –

and grapes may be used for own production or sold to another party for vinification. Many producers buy in grapes to supplement their own production or to diversify the style and flavour of their wines. A new trend among grape farmers is to keep back a few tons of their crop in order to produce their own boutique wines on the estate.

The planting and cultivation of vines varies greatly across different production areas and the quality and style of wine depends on planted vine cultivars in each particular area, their cultivation and the actual winemaking. Planting density ranges from 500 to 2, 000 vines per hectare. Hectares are the most common unit of measure for vines in South Africa. One hectare constitutes 100 metres by 100 metres or 10, 000 m², roughly two football fields side-by-side. Vines are cultivated as bush vines or on trellising with various designs of wire support systems. Cultivation strives for an optimum balance between vine growth and grape quality: too many grape bunches per plant can do long-term damage to a vine and result in a diluted wine; when too little fruit is produced, the financial returns may be insufficient.

197

Vines can grow almost anywhere, but this does not necessarily ensure grapes of high quality. Quality crop production is often a function of site and grape variety choice, given the specific *terroir* and rootstock requirements. Too often these basic rules are not considered with costly consequences. Topography of the land as well as the soil conditions directly affect vineyard layout and cost. The first crop from a vineyard can be harvested at the end of the second year after planting, but young vines produce only 40 per cent of their potential at this early stage. During the third year, production reaches approximately 60 per cent of total capacity.

Aeration – pump-over of red wine

During these initial stages, buying in grapes from other well-established producers in the area could be a consideration, in order to establish a presence for these wines in the market in a short space of time. Most modern planting densities produce between five to seven tons per hectare. Certain cultivars tend to produce consistently higher or lower yields and production also varies over vintages. As a rough guideline for producing quality wine, a normal year's harvest should not exceed 50 tons of grapes from a mature 10 hectare vineyard. Vines are hardy plants and have a long lifespan, although acute infection with pests or disease and even wrong rootstock choices may demand that vineyards are replanted sooner than expected.

WHERE TO START?

Success requires consulting experts during the planning phase, ranging from field experts, the financial sector, local producers and industry entrepreneurs. Seeking expert advice enables you to evaluate winemaking possibilities on a particular property. Creating a future profile scenario including specified goals and a cost analysis should provide a clear road map and ensure that all factors have been addressed before the transaction is finalised.

DEFINE THE WINE STYLE

To achieve a unique and personal style of wine, you should define the characteristics and goals in advance and communicate these clearly to all involved.

Start by carefully investigating site conditions and possible location advantages (inter and intraregional). *Terroir* characteristics such as climatic features, temperature and sun exposure, as well as aspects and their applied use are essential considerations in order to achieve the vineyards' highest potential. For example, the root drying technique naturally limits the amount of bunches per vine but, though very effective, the practice is still relatively unexplored in South Africa. Creating a distinguished wine is achieved by either working with a single cultivar or blending complimentary cultivars. The wine's style definition is important and you should ensure that the style includes origin-distinctive characteristics that are both regional and site-specific. A knowledgeable and experienced winemaker will prove to be a great asset in this process.

ESTABLISHMENT AND RUNNING COSTS

At present, establishing one hectare of vineyard on a standard plot, excluding cost factors such as steep slopes, shallow soils or major soil chemical requirements, will cost approximately €15, 000. Sites located on very steep slopes with compacted soil that requires chemical adjustments or additional drainage, will naturally result in a significant increase in establishment costs.

The production of one bottle of wine has a minimum cost of €3.75. The market price for quality wines can range from €5 to €15 per bottle, with some wines reaching as much as €25 per bottle. The establishment cost of a standard 200 ton wine cellar is around €600, 000 with a 50 / 50 split between the structure and equipment required. A cellar focusing on red wine production and thus requiring barrel maturation facilities for 200 tons, requires further investment in barrels and space. The first harvest will require 580 barrels (Bordeaux 225 l) and, should the maturation period exceed twelve months, this will result in the following harvest requiring another 580 barrels. Not all of these barrels will be new and, once the two-year harvest cycle has been reached, new barrels become second-fill barrels and the replenishment costs become significantly less.

New French oak barrels will set you back approximately €650 each, resulting in a theoretical cost of €377, 000 for your first set. The maturation facilities require floor space, preferably well insulated. Most winemakers prefer a basement or even an underground facility. However, the most important factor is reliable temperature and humidity control mechanisms. The associated costs for the maturation cellar will depend on your architectural tastes and the required engineering. Keep in mind that you will need

Boutique winery – Bein Wines produces only 1,000 cases annually

enough floor space for at least two consecutive harvests, anticipated growth, plus ample room to manoeuvre the unwieldy barrels.

ESTABLISHING A BRAND

Be informed about brand-building principles. Once you define a wine style, create a marketing strategy. It may be a while before your wine shows the character you ultimately want, especially when working with very young vines or buying in grapes. In the interim, a second label may be a worthwhile option. A second label allows you to make and sell wine, use the property name as visual brand recognition and establish a client base, while creating an expectation for the premium label. A second label may require lower production costs as grapes from young vines are less expensive than premium blocks. At the same time you can maintain lower maturation costs, as you could mature the wine in second or third-fill barrels instead of only new barrels, while generating cash flow.

SPECIALIST VITICULTURISTS AND BALANCED VINEYARDS

Quality wine starts with quality vineyards when creating a solid foundation on which to build your success. High quality grapes can only be cultivated with meticulous attention during the establishment and cultivation of the vineyards by trained and experienced viticulturists. Although minor chemical adjustments are allowed, the winemaking process depends essentially on the quality of the raw material and a great wine can never be made from poor or diseased grapes. On the other hand, high quality grapes are merely refined into great wine by yeasts, wood, oxygen and the gentle hand of time. Without a solid chemical and physical base, a wine has no future.

199

Establishment costs are high and replanting a vineyard delays full production by another four years. By matching the grape variety to soils and aspects of a specific site, costly mistakes are avoided, while the best possible grape quality can be achieved earlier in the life of the vine.

A MATURATION CELLAR AND PHASED DEVELOPMENT

To simplify initial stages, you can buy in grapes and initially outsource the crushing, pressing and fermentation. This means that you will only be working with fermented wine and barrels in your maturation cellar. A fully operational wine cellar that handles the entire vinification process – from harvested grapes to bottled wine – has a breakeven point (costs vs. revenue) which is usually attained from the production of 80 tons or more, producing between 600 and 750 litres of wine per ton. Potential above-average returns can be realised once production exceeds 130 tons.

A growing number of investors enter the market as boutique wine producers. A phased development in the form of a boutique cellar, starting with as little as 20 tons, is an option that allows the investment to grow on both capital as well as a growing stream of revenue. An initial layout of around €50, 000 is required to equip such a cellar with new equipment, but would not include the barrels. An alternative is to source previously used equipment from a reputable dealer, and invest the balance in good quality barrels.

Scaling up to a production of 165 tons or more will result in the doubling of operational costs, and may well include the appointment of an assistant winemaker. For example, the production of 230 tons will result in approximately 18, 000 cases

(12 bottles to a case), depending on the grape varietal and pressing intensity. Such a production run requires a reasonable staff compliment, expertise and experience. The required experience can be hired. Many "flying winemakers" or consulting winemakers provide unbiased services to start-up wineries. Crosscheck references and taste their product before committing to the relationship.

MARKETING THE WINE

Defining the style of wine goes hand-in-hand with identifying a target market where the wine will be sold. Various marketing opportunities are available: cellar door, local sales, international sales, trade shows and internet sales. Expertise from an experienced marketing team should provide a good platform from which to build marketing efforts. Getting to know your market is vital in order to communicate successfully and sell to your clients. Trade shows, wine tastings and international travel should be priorities, as well as a good understanding of regulations on sales and exports.

Enjoy the journey! There is no greater satisfaction than to see the fruits of your efforts. The journey is part of the experience and should be as joyful as the end result.

REVENUE EXPECTATIONS

Income considerations from wine grape production and winemaking are based on:
- grape yield (a function of weather and viticulture practices such as yield per hectare),
- grape pricing (a function of specific cultivar and *terroir*-based supply and demand),
- winemaking (a function of wine type and style),
- and the market position of the wine.

Grapes are sold by the ton and prices vary according to area, grape variety and chemical analysis. Average tonnage prices for white noble varieties in 2005 were roughly €500, whereas noble red varieties averaged around €530 per ton. For example, a 10 hectare vineyard, yielding 50 tons of red grapes priced at €500 per ton, would have a gross income of €25, 000. Running expenses would be around €15, 000. A gross profit for the year in this scenario, excluding debt service, could be about €10, 000.

South Africa's diverse climate and topography allows growers to produce grapes for a wide range of wine styles (dry, sweet, sparkling) from the same grape variety. Each Pocket has a unique climate, soil and landscape which produce wines unique to that Pocket. Buying or cultivating grapes within a respected *terroir* could mean better quality and higher prices.

Currently an official subsidy programme by government compensates new winery developments. In terms of this programme up to 30 per cent of the establishment cost of a winery can be recouped in non-taxable cash over three years. Also, depreciation allowances are favourable for investors. It is vital to obtain expert advice early in the process in order to ensure that correct legal structures and qualifying parameters are put into place to support the property's future profile.

Useful facts and figures

One glass of wine contains:
- 125 ml of wine
- 0.5 kg of grapes

One bottle of wine contains
- 750 ml of liquid (25.6 ozs)
- 6 standard glasses of wine
- 1.1 kg of grapes (39 ozs)

One case of wine contains:
- 12 bottles of wine
- 72 glasses of wine
- 13 kg of grapes

One barrel of wine contains:
- 225 l of wine (most popular size barrel)
- 1, 800 glasses
- 300 standard bottles
- 25 cases of wine
- 330 kg of grapes
- (300 l, 500 l and other size barrels also exist)

One hectare (100 m x 100 m) of land averages:
- 5 tons of grapes
- 3, 750 l of grape juice
- 16.5 barrels (225 l)
- 4, 950 bottles (750 ml)
- 29, 700 glasses

Typical production figures:
- 10 Ha (at 5 tons / hectare)
- 37, 500 l
- 49, 500 bottles (750 ml)
- 4, 125 x 12 bottle cases

The cost of a bottle of wine includes:
- Bottle: glass
- Closures: cork / plastic / glass top / screw caps
- Covers: wax / foils / shrink-wrap plastics
- Labels: front / neck / back / other
- Other: muselet / champagne corks / foil covers
- Wine
- Marketing and distribution
- Losses: wine tasting, faults, marketing samples
  The cost of a bottle of wine can run up to €3.50 or more

STARTING A SOUTH AFRICAN WINE COLLECTION

For anyone with more than a passing interest in wine, stocking even a modest wine cellar is as rewarding as building up a collection of fine books or music. In this age, very few are fortunate enough to live in a house with a functional basement, therefore the term "cellar" is used very loosely. A cellar can be any space dedicated to the storage of wine, beneath the staircase, an unused fireplace, a cupboard, a Eurocave® (a commercially available, temperature and humidity-controlled cabinet) or a converted fridge.

A cellar should enjoy a constant cool temperature, 11°C is optimal, but consistency is more important than the actual temperature. Fresh air should circulate reasonably freely through the cellar. Sufficient humidity will prevent natural corks from drying out: aim for 75 – 80 per cent humidity. Drier cellars should be humidified. Those that are too humid can be improved with a bit of gravel on the floor. Gravel also greatly reduces the risk of breakage should bottles be dropped. Use a sturdy, stable packing system such as racks, shelves or bins in which to pack wine bottles. Choose a system that makes for easy adding or removing of bottles, as this can become a cause of frustration if not properly managed. The cellar must be secured against thieves and uninformed persons and it may be wise to insure the contents of your cellar.

ORGANISING WINE

In an extensive cellar, it is worth setting up a spreadsheet using letters and numbers to identify each row and column. This allows you to put your hand on any bottle of wine, provided you keep the system up to date every time a bottle moves. To start a cellar, dedicate specific areas to the most important sets of wine. Use the following sets as examples: current drinking wine, everyday drinking, special occasion wines, aging wines, or arrange the wines by country of origin or style.

THE COLLECTION

The word "collection" suggests selecting wines that will develop further complexity and character after a few years' bottle age, not simply stocking up on wines to be enjoyed

Elegant design – wine storage facility in a controlled environment

immediately. There are many examples of the latter on supermarket and specialist wine shop shelves and it seems a waste to devote cellar space to them. The wine suggestions provided are for special occasions and maturation, but not necessarily for financial investment.

Unlike many of their European counterparts, South African winegrowers are not prohibited by legislation when it comes to matching *terroir* to variety. Consequently, individual farms historically planted a wide range of different grape varieties. This approach is, laudably, changing as winemakers learn which areas best suit which varieties. While there are – and always will be – exceptions, the list of suggested wines below is based largely on this first tentative research. Obviously, personal taste is paramount; those who prefer red wine to white wine will bias

Home cellar – functional, using expandable wine racks

their cellar accordingly. This Pocket-based selection of South African wines is offered as a possible starting point for a 150 bottle cellar. Should you have spatial constraints, you may want to halve the quantities and start with a total of 75 bottles.

Number of bottles	Wine	Geographical Region (Pocket if available)
6	MCC – sparkling wine	Stellenbosch, Robertson
6	Chardonnay – cooler climate, mineral examples	Walker Bay
6	Chardonnay – fruitier, warmer styles	Stellenbosch-Simonsberg, Robertson
12	Chenin Blanc	Stellenbosch-Simonsberg, Devon Valley, Helderberg
12	Riesling	Constantia
6	Sauvignon Blanc	Elgin, Constantia
6	Sémillon	Constantia
6	White blends	Constantia, Elgin, Helderberg
12	Cabernet Sauvignon – more restrained styles	Stellenbosch, Helderberg, Blaauwklippen, Annandale
6	Cabernet Sauvignon – bolder styles	Paarl, Wellington
3	Cabernet Franc	Stellenbosch-Simonsberg, Helderberg
12	Red blends (Bordeaux style)	Stellenbosch-Simonsberg, Helderberg Blaauwklippen, Annandale
6	Merlot	Stellenbosch, Paarl
6	Pinotage	Bottelary, Paarl
12	Shiraz	Paarl, Swartland
6	Pinot Noir	Walker Bay, Elgin
12	Red blends (Cape blends)	Stellenbosch, Paarl
6	Mediterranean blends	Paarl, Swartland
9	Cape port style	Helderberg, Klein Karoo

Chapter 5

205

Local Knowledge

Local Knowledge

Unusual road sign that tell a story

Local knowledge is one of the most valuable possessions when you are travelling, yet it is not for sale. Experience can only be experienced. The local knowledge and practical tips provided in this section serve as a guide to assist you to get the most out of your stay.

VISITING SOUTH AFRICA

Make sure all medical insurance policies, prescriptions and important travel documents are up to date and that you have copies in a safe place. Although South Africa does not have many of the tropical diseases (yellow fever, etc.), malaria is more prevalent in some northern areas of the country. The Winelands are fortunately a safe area in terms of diseases. Insect repellent comes in handy on warm summer evenings and sun block is a requirement in the hot African sun. The following guidelines are provided to help you plan your outings.

Global Positioning System (GPS) is probably the single most useful equipment modern travellers can add to their vehicle. Most of the major South African cities and their surrounds are digitally mapped for use with a GPS unit.

We have recorded GPS waypoints for the wineries detailed in the text. These waypoints can be used to find your way accurately around a driving route. The waypoints have an accuracy of roughly 10 metres, which will be more than sufficient to guide you to your destination.

We have used Garmin™ equipment exclusively for the purposes of mapping our way around the Cape Winelands. Every driving route described has been digitally mapped and can be downloaded from the Cheviot Publishing website, http://www.cheviot-publishing.com. Once downloaded onto your computer, the maps can be uploaded onto your

Garmin™ GPS unit, providing you with turn-by-turn instructions for the selected driving route. Follow the route from one winery to the next, and arrive at your destination relaxed.

Should you not have access to the internet, please contact the publishers for a copy of the waypoints and driving routes on CD (contact details on page 4). The digital GPS maps will provide you with additional information that might not be included in this Guide.

TOURING THE WINELANDS

South African wineries are surprisingly approachable and many, including the most famous, welcome visitors to their cellars and tasting facilities to sample their products. At larger wineries, visitors are welcomed at the tasting room where wines can be tasted and purchased and where most winery tours start.

When visiting smaller wineries, however, you are most often hosted by the winemaker or owner. Should you want to meet the winemaker in person, enquire in advance of the planned visit, as these skilled cellar masters are a little shy of attention, particularly in harvest time from January to March.

Finding your way made easy

Practicalities

The local time is GMT + 2 hours

To check time: dial 1026

Fights: Internal flights from Johannesburg to Cape Town take two hours

Water: tap water is safe for consumption

Electricity: South Africa uses 220V

Average daytime temperatures: Jan 25°C, Apr 22°C, July 14°C, Oct 20°C

Climate: hot, dry summers (Sept – Mar); rainy, cold winter (Apr – Oct)

Emergencies: Police 10111; Ambulance / Fire 10177

Money: major banks are open Mon – Fri 9 – 15:30, Sat 9 – 11. ATMs are located at most major banks

Traveller's cheques: can be exchanged at all major banks (with photo ID / passport)

Phones: 1023 for enquiries, international inquiries 0903. Cape Town and surrounds dialling code 021. International access code starts with 09. Dialling internationally to South Africa starts with +27.

Post Office: open Mon – Fri 8:30 – 16:30, Sat 8 – 12

Public Holidays: 1 Jan, 21 March, 27 April, Good Friday, Easter Monday, 1 May, 9 Aug, 24 Sept, 16, 25, 26 Dec

VAT: value added tax of 14% on most goods, generally included in price stated

Security: South Africa is generally safe for travellers, especially in the Winelands. As in all countries, the most important rule is to be aware of your surroundings. Lock your vehicle when leaving it and keep any valuables out of plain sight

Mobile / Cellular telephones: Available from the phone rental companies at airports, which should provide you with emergency numbers. South Africa has a very good mobile signal in most areas and you can use your mobile phone in emergencies

Tourist information: Usually located in the centre of town, tourist information centres provide information, suggestions and in many cases bookings for trips, restaurants and accommodation

Opening time: Shops, wineries and businesses do not close over lunch

Enjoy wine responsibly! Do not drink and drive

WHEN TO TRAVEL

The timing of a visit to a particular Pocket depends on the requirements and expectations of the visitor. For sightseeing, spring and summer (September to February) are best – the vineyards are lush and the new harvest is maturing, but you will have to share the space and attention with other tourists. Harvest time from January to March is a photographer's dream – no one who has watched the pickers in the vineyards or tasted the ripe grapes will ever forget the experience. Keep in mind that farms are a beehive of activity during harvest – picking, fermenting and pressing grapes – and few wineries allow access to the production cellar or winemaker at this time.

Visiting the Winelands after harvest time (end of March to April), you witness vineyards changing colour in an exquisite autumn display. It is true that, mostly the red and brown colours of leaves are due to a vine disease, but they pose no threat to grapes or wine and are an eye's delight. Not only is this time of the year cooler, but also generally a bit more affordable, particularly in terms of accommodation. It is also advisable to carry a bottle of fresh water in your vehicle.

Autumn colours in the vine

VISITING CELLARS

Regarded as a New World wine producer, South Africa has a wide range of wine cellars – everything from the garagistes, making wine in a shed behind the house, to the ultramodern winery employing hi-tech equipment. Most cellars have a dedicated tasting facility and some incorporate gift shops filled with branded glasses, caps, sweat shirts and corkscrews. Many also offer local produce such as cheese or olives, and may include a restaurant.

Wineries indicate their location along the roads, but legislation restricts the amount of names per indication. Do not be discouraged if the name of your favourite winery is not on display along the road – a good map will lead you there. Some smaller producers prefer to offer tastings by appointment only, restricting visits to hours that do not interfere with work.

Note that most wineries are closed on the following days: Easter weekend, Christmas (25 – 26 Dec) and New Year's Day (1 Jan). Certain wineries are open to visitors on weekends and public holidays. Please consult individual winery profiles or phone the cellar. Tasting facilities stay open over lunchtime.

PLANNING YOUR TRIP

Decide which Pockets and producers you wish to visit and consult relevant maps. Calculate about one hour for each wine farm visited and try to join at least one cellar tour. It gives an interesting glimpse into the inner workings of winemaking. Preferably arrive for lunch between 12:30 and 13:30 as most restaurants do not serve lunch after 15:00. Arrive at the last cellar at least one hour before closing time to ensure sufficient time to taste its wines. Enjoy wine responsibly! Do not drink and drive; appoint a designated driver.

AT THE WINE FARM

A nominal fee is charged for wine tasting to recoup the value of wines used and to keep out unwanted elements. Tasting fees are generally refunded on purchase. If you find nothing of interest, there is no need to feel pressured into buying. At the same time, avoid wasting the producer's time by overstaying your welcome. Usually the tasting glass is included in the fee and can be taken as a souvenir of your visit. Tasting facilities do not allow the use of other wines / liquor on their premises. To prevent misuse of liquor, wineries will limit the amount of wine provided to visitors during a tasting.

Taste dry white wines first, proceed to red wines and sample sweeter wines last. Sparkling wines can be enjoyed in between to clean your palate. The tasting order will allow your palate to progress naturally and allow you to best enjoy each wine style. Do not swallow all wines tasted. Use the spittoons provided! Smoking is not allowed in tasting rooms. Some cellars will serve you at a table; others only serve at the tasting counter. Enquire from the tasting room assistant.

PURCHASING WINE

Most cellars allow the purchase of mixed cases of wine. Wine can be delivered to your door on request and at a reasonable fee. Enquire at the winery about international agents or distributors and their shipping arrangements. Most cellars offer secure packaging for your wines, particularly for air cargo.

Cash and most international credit cards are accepted at wineries. Due to the high incidence of fraud, cheques are generally not accepted. Remember that wine is a unique gift from the region.

Wine shop at Neethlingshof

PACKING AND STORING WINE

ON THE ROAD

Packing wine bottles when travelling can potentially cause problems. Cardboard boxes supplied by most wineries make for easy handling and protect bottles against breakage. However, purpose-made Styrofoam wine cartons are preferable, preventing breakage, damage to the label as well as temperature changes. Most standard-sized bottles will fit snugly inside. These cartons are available from most specialised wine shops. Never allow wine bottles to roll around in your vehicle as breakage is the most probable outcome.

209

Travelling tips

- Wines travel best laid on their side to keep the cork moist.
- Bottles with screw tops can be kept upright.
- Keep in a cool, dark place.
- Never leave wine bottles loose in a vehicle, especially not in the luggage compartment where temperatures can get very high.
- Pack wine bottles in a carton or foam box to protect them from possible damage.
- Avoid sudden temperature changes (day and night) and parking areas with exhaust fumes as higher temperature ages a wine more quickly.

Safe wine travel – temperature and shock control

IN THE AIR

Only small quantities of wine can be accommodated onboard a flight. Countries differ on how much wine and other alcoholic products you may bring across their borders. Generally the limit it is around three litres of wine and one litre of spirits. Styrofoam packing is ideal when flying. Placing wine in a suitcase is always a risk – breakage may occur if it is not packed tightly with towels and it significantly increases luggage weight.

A winery agent in your city / country may save you the trouble. Enquire about international availability when you visit wineries. Alternatively, use a freight company to get your wine home safely. It is worth spending the money to keep your precious wines in a stable environment and the memories of the visit safe.

AT HOME

Open bottles – Bottles half-empty after a meal need not be wasted. Ask the *sommelier* to keep the cork of the bottle opened at your table. If it breaks or crumbles, ask for a clean cork. Stopper the bottle and store upright in a cool, dark place.

The Vac-u-vin® system is a very handy tool – a special rubber stopper is placed in the bottle neck and a hand-held vacuum pump is used to extract the air. It is inexpensive and by far the best way to secure half bottles. The Vac-u-vin® system is readily available from wine and speciality gift shops.

Closed bottles – Safely storing wine is easily achieved in most households. Wines require a cool, dark, quiet place to rest. Specially designed fridges or "wine coolers" are best, but should this be out of your price range, follow these simple guidelines:

- Wines are best stored laid down on their side to keep the cork moist and avoid oxidation and subsequent spoilage.
- Bottles with screw caps may be stored upright.
- Choose a cool, dark place in your house, preferably an underground space but, failing this, an unused cupboard or space under a staircase will do.
- Ideal storage temperature is 14 – 16°C with humidity at 80 per cent.
- Avoid sudden temperature changes. The specific storage temperature is less crucial than keeping it constant. Extreme temperature variations cause wine to age prematurely or even spoil. Rather store at a slightly higher temperature and avoid great variations between daytime and night-time temperatures.
- Do not place wines in an attic, garage where cars are parked or against an outside wall of your house. Placing bottles against an inside wall is a better option as wines experience fewer temperature changes.
- Wooden wine racks are a great way to store and have easy access to your wine collection. Use only untreated wood as the chlorine used in treatments may

damage wines causing a "corked" taste.

- Larger racks are good for your MCCs and sparkling wines, certain red wines in tapered bottles, as well as magnum bottles.
- Keeping a journal of what you buy helps to organise your cellar.
- Use name tags to identify bottles and avoid pulling wines out of racks repeatedly to check what they are.
- Dedicate specific areas within the storage space to sets of wines. For example: everyday drinking, special occasion and maturing wines.
- Wine is a living thing; it does not last forever and it will "die" eventually. Read up on your wines to ensure you enjoy them at their peak.
- Storing wine under favourable conditions will ensure that it matures at the best rate and that it will reach the best possible maturation.
- If you have a special wine that you want to keep for display purposes, why not enjoy it with good friends and display the empty bottle. It is no use displaying vinegar from your favourite winery.

Wine accessories and gift ideas

Decanter

Glass decanters allow you to separate sediment from the wine and are attractive on the table.

Drip catcher

(1) a thin metal disk rolled up and placed in the bottle neck to catch drops of liquid when pouring, or (2) a collar that fits around the bottle neck. It works and is inexpensive.

Bottle mats

Placed under bottles for display on the table and essential to keep table cloths clean.

Pourer baskets

To keep old, fragile wines on their side as in the cellar. Be very careful when uncorking.

Ice bucket

Crucial for keeping both red and white wines at the correct temperature. Keep a few around the table and pop wines into an ice bucket only when needed. Many are works of art but remember their job and choose those that are tall enough to immerse even the bottle neck.

Wine thermometer

A bit ostentatious, but a must for the serious wine lover.

Bottle holders

Can look very handsome next to the table. Could be from wood, wicker or metal, but avoid plastic.

Vac-u-vin®

A rubbery, silicone stopper placed in the bottle neck, with a hand-held vacuum pump to secure it. The best possible way to store opened wines.

211

Small gifts for big enthusiasts

DRIVING IN SOUTH AFRICA

Renting a vehicle – Various agents are available. To rent a car, you will need a valid driver's licence, may not have a criminal record and must make immediate payment, mostly using a credit card and proper insurance. Most rental companies have branches at airports and in cities and may be found on the internet. Smaller companies offer cheaper rates, but terms may not be flexible or fit your needs.

Petrol / Fuel – Fuel or petrol stations are locally referred to as "garages". Most are open 24 hours a day, but in small towns they might close at 20:00. Usually the premises include a small shop stocking soft drinks, candy, takeaway meals, newspapers and cigarettes, but no alcohol. Diesel, Lead Replacement and Unleaded fuel are available.

Payment – Petrol stations do not accept credit cards, including international cards. Payment can be made in cash.

Side of the road – South Africans drive on the left-hand side of the road, similar to the United Kingdom.

Speed – Maximum speed in a residential area is 60 km/h; on the freeway 120 km/h. The speed limit is indicated by a white circular sign with a red outline.

Sidewalk cafés in old-town Stellenbosch

Driver's licence – Local law requires that you have your driver's licence with you at all times when driving. International driver's licenses must be accompanied by the original driver's licence from the country of origin.

Traffic flow – Due to urban growth, a major traffic flow problem has arisen with lack of road signage, compounded by traffic often flowing directly into the fast lane. This can be unnerving if you are not used to driving on this particular side of the road.

Parking – In certain areas official parking attendants with hand-held devices record the registration number of the vehicle and parking time. Payment is accepted in cash only and settled upfront with the attendant. Non-payment is fined. In smaller towns, roadside meters are used. Parking near the centre of town can cost as much as R6.50 per hour. High-density areas limit the duration of parking, indicated on signs.

Parking attendants – Official attendants wear identification. Unemployed people and even children frequent areas where there are no official parking attendants, asking for money for supposedly looking after your car. Giving in to these requests only encourages further begging.

Cellular phones and other electronic devices – The use of a cellular telephone while driving is only permitted when using a car kit or a "hands-free" kit.

EATING IN SOUTH AFRICA

Restaurants, delis, food shops – The Winelands have abundant eating establishments. Some wineries have their own restaurants and their suggested wine and food pairings are always a good idea. Delis and food shops charge for plastic carrier bags. You may supply your own.

Reservations – Booking is advisable at most restaurants and can be made by phone.

Eating in the Winelands – many wineries offer delightful eateries

Service fee – Ten per cent of the value of the meal is usually included for tables of more than six people.

Ordering wine and Bring your own (BYO) – Wine bottles should be brought to the table unopened and the person who ordered the wine should be consulted as to whether it is the correct wine and vintage. In South African culture, it is acceptable for people to take their own wine to a restaurant. They are charged a corkage fee. It is advisable to enquire in advance about the restaurant's policy on BYO, as some may have a very high charge per bottle, limit the amount of bottles you are allowed to bring or simply do not allow it at all. Restaurants will not allow you to bring your own bottle if they have that particular wine on their list.

Faulty wine – Be sure to check the wine for faults when it is opened at your table and reject a suspicious or faulty wine. Faults must be pointed out to the waitron / *sommelier* and if it is indeed a faulty wine, you should not be charged. See the section Faults in wine (Chapter 3, page 187) for common faults and problems.

ACCOMMODATION IN SOUTH AFRICA

Staying in the Western Cape is a pleasurable experience, amidst towering mountains, rivers and vineyards. The Wineland towns offer a wealth of accommodation.

B&B and guest houses – Generally small establishments with only a few rooms. Offer accommodation with breakfast included.

Hotels – Generally larger establishments, accommodating larger groups such as families. Breakfast is provided at an additional cost.

Reservations – Make a reservation ahead of time, by telephone, email of fax. Be sure that you receive confirmation. Most establishments require a deposit.

Service fee – Required at luxury establishments.

Services – The establishments can inform you about the best local services and products. Ask your host for a reference or visit your local tourist information centre. The information centre is a good place to meet and plan excursions.

GLOSSARY

Accessible, approachable: flavours are in harmony, wine is ready to drink.

Acid, acetic: caused by acetic acid bacteria, has a vinegar taste.

Acid, lactic: produced from malic acid by malolactic bacteria during malolactic fermentation. Gentler tasting acid, also found in milk.

Acid, malic: naturally occurring in grapes, acidic taste.

Acid, tartaric: naturally occurring in grapes, very strong acidic taste. Excess may result in harmless crystals forming in bottled wine, aesthetically undesired.

Acid, volatile: caused by bacterial spoilage in wine, imparts a vinegar smell.

Acidity: naturally occurring chemical compound in grapes, forms backbone and gives structure to wine. Wines with good acidity are described as crisp, fresh and alive. Two main acids are malic and tartaric. In South Africa adding certain acids (which occur naturally in grapes) is allowed because of the hot climate.

Aging, barrel: aging wine in barrel causes extraction of flavour compounds from wood – woody, smoky, cigar box, meaty, vanilla, toast. Adds to complexity and quality of wine. Also allows very slow oxidation, resulting in stable colour and flavour.

Aging, bottle: development of flavours / aromas in bottle. Positive: softening of tannins and greenness, wine becomes more integrated. White wines become less acidic and more syrupy. Negative: overaging leads to wine going stale.

Alcohol: produced by yeasts from grape sugar. Gives fullness, richness and sweetness to wine and acts as a preservative. Too much alcohol gives a burning sensation. Measured in volume of total liquid.

Aroma: the fragrance or smell of wine. Aromatics belong to various chemical families classified according to their volatility. Mostly created by a series of closely related chemical substances rather than a single substance being solely responsible for a particular flavour or aroma.

Astringent: a physical characteristic of wine, mouth-puckering sensation caused by tannins. Also closely related to bitterness.

Backbone: a wine with structure, not flabby or insipid. See *Acid, Tannin*.

Baked: hot, earthy character associated with overripe grapes.

Balance: the harmony between the major wine components – acid, alcohol, sugar, tannins, wood and fruit. A definite quality indicator.

Balling / brix: measurements of sugar levels in grapes, expressed as degrees. Used to determine ripeness for harvesting.

Barrel: a wooden wine container made from oak. Various sizes: 225 l, 300 l, 500 l and larger. Most popular is French and American oak. Hungarian oak is gaining popularity because of reduced cost.

Barrel fermentation: fermentation in oak barrel. Gives greater complexity due to integration of extracts from wood. Mostly used for full-bodied white wines – Chardonnay, Chenin Blanc, Sémillon and Viognier.

Bâttonage: stirring of yeast lees in the storage container, usually wooden barrels. Intensifies butter and creamy flavours, softens acidity. Very labour intensive, increases price.

Bead, mousse: the bubbles in sparkling wine. A very fine, long-lasting bead is most desirable.

Bitterness: a taste sensed on the finish (back area of mouth). Slight bitterness may be related to cultivar and is acceptable; too much is unpleasant and regarded as a winemaking fault.

Blend: a wine made from two or more different grape varieties, vintages, vineyards or containers. Used to bring out desirable attributes of all components, as well as erasing possible weaknesses in a particular component.

Bloom: (1) flowering of grape vines, (2) the

natural wax covering found on grape skins, protects against diseases.

Body: sensation of fullness on the palate. Related to alcohol, tannins and concentration.

Botrytis cinerea: a fungus that attacks ripe grapes, depleting water from berries and concentrating sugar and other compounds. Benevolent form results in "noble rot" responsible for great sweet wines; aggressive form results in loss of crop.

Bottle shock: a state of "flavourlessness" noticeable in wine directly after bottling. Most fruit flavours disappear; acid and alcohol stands out. Can last up to a few months. Most wines recover completely with rest.

Butter: flavour and aroma associated with barrel-fermented white wines. A rich creamy smoothness.

Canopy: the leaves and shoots on a vine plant.

Cap: fermenting (red) wine produces carbon dioxide and pushes grape skins to the surface, forming a cap.

Carbon dioxide: odourless, colourless gas resulting from alcoholic fermentation.

Chaptalisation: French term for addition of sugar to grape must in order to raise alcohol levels. Not permitted in South Africa.

Charmat: method of sparkling wine production in sealed tanks under pressure. An easier and cheaper alternative to bottle fermentation.

Clarify: winemaking operation which removes lees (dead yeast cells, fragments of grape skins and pulp, pips, etc.) from juice or wine. May result in slight loss of flavour.

Clone: a sub-group of genetically identical plants within a particular variety, propagated from a single vine to perpetuate its selected or special characteristics.

Complex: a wine with multiple flavour levels from the vineyards, winemaking techniques and bottle development. A quality indicator.

Cork: wine bottle stopper made from bark of cork tree. A natural product. Defects may result in tainted wine.

Corked: A wine smelling mouldy, dusty and of wet cardboard. Caused by chemical compound TCA (trichloranisole) which is formed by sulphur and chlorine. TCA diminishes the fruit character of wine, substituting a damp, mouldy smell. Wine must be smelled, not cork.

Crisp: refers to acidity. Positive: fresh, clean. Negative: too tart, sharp.

Cultivars: grape varieties.

Dense: having intense texture, flavour-packed.

Depth: having many layers, intense.

Dosage: sugar added to *Méthode Champenoise* or *Méthode Cap Classique* wines after second fermentation.

Dry: fermented wine, all sugar is converted to alcohol. See *Residual sugar.*

Dry-land cultivation: cultivation of vines with rain as main water supply. Supplementary irrigation may be used in extremely hot or dry conditions to prevent damage to vines.

Duplex: layered soil, generally sand over clay.

Earthy: wine with soil-derived flavour, mineral, damp, mushroom.

Easy: undemanding wine, ready to drink.

Elegant: stylish and refined.

Entry / attack: sensation as wine enters the mouth. (Sweetness, florals and fruit flavours.)

Esters: natural chemical compound, responsible for floral aromas in wine.

Extract: sum of all solids in wine – tannins, sugar, acids, glycerine, minerals, pigments, etc. Expressed g/l. An indication of substance and quality: 18 g/l is low; above 23 g/l for white wine is significant; a full-bodied red wine would be above 30 g/l.

Fermentation, alcoholic: biochemical conversion of sugar to alcohol and carbon dioxide by yeast. Enhances flavour by (1) releasing flavours from their sugar-linked precursors, and (2) by forming new flavour compounds from chemical building blocks existing in juice.

Fermentation, malolactic: biochemical conversion of malic acid to lactic acid by bacteria. Results in softer / reduced acidity and a more rounded, mellow flavour.

Fermentation, natural / spontaneous: alcoholic fermentation without addition of yeast. Naturally occurring yeast on equipment populates juice when contact occurs. Potentially risky due to high temperatures. Off-flavours may occur.

Fermentation, stuck: unfinished fermentation resulting in higher than normal residual sugar, due to yeast death, possibly on sensitivity to excessive alcohol. High potential for spoilage.

Filtration: method of clearing wine by passing liquid through membranes or cellulose pads to remove suspended solids, yeast or bacteria. Filtration may result in reduction of wine flavour and aroma, therefore the shift to unfiltered wines. Sweet wines must be filtered to remove yeast to prevent refermentation, pressure build-up and possible bottle explosion.

Finesse: description of polished, balanced wine.

Fining: traditional method of clearing wine. Insoluble substances bind with wine components and precipitate out so that wine can be filtered clean. Used to reduce tannins or unstable proteins.

Finish / aftertaste: the lingering flavours of wine on the palate after swallowing – its persistence. Should be pleasant. A long finish is a quality indicator.

Firm: compact, has good backbone.

Flabby: wine lacking structure, backbone, result of too little acid.

Floral: aromas and tastes with floral aspect, as opposed to fruity. Desirable in fine white wines.

Forward: opposite of a shy wine. Pronounced flavours and aromas.

Free-run: juice obtained from crushed gapes before pressure is applied. This juice is purest and most aromatic.

Fresh: refers to acidity. Lively, young. A sweet wine without sufficient acid will cloy; enough acid and taste is fresh and uncloying.

Full: high in alcohol and extract.

Glycerol: product of alcoholic fermentation. Results in oily, mouth-filling character, supports sweetness. Leaves "legs" in an agitated glass.

Green: unripe, tannic and hard. Can refer to wine with excessive acid, unripe characters.

Grip: firm on palate and finish. Acid, tannin and alcohol are contributors.

Herbaceous: grassy, hay-like character. May indicate unripe grapes.

Honey: honey and/or bees wax flavours are typical of sweet-style wines, Noble Late Harvest or straw wines. Also an indicator of bottle age, maturity.

Hot: burning sensation caused by excess alcohol in wine.

Intensity: strong character, good expression of flavours. Not flabby.

Lean: thin, lacking fruit flavours and body.

Lees: sediment that occurs during winemaking or bottle aging. May be used to add flavour and complexity by allowing contact time with wine.

Length: enduring, the wine flavour lingers on palate long after swallowing.

Light: wines with less than 10% Alc. by Vol.

Maceration, carbonic: method of fermentation using whole (uncrushed) berries. Grape bunches are placed in a closed fermenter with carbon dioxide gas. Fermentation occurs within berries, which then burst. Light-styled wines relating to *Beaujolais Nouveau* (low in alcohol and concentration).

Maceration, cold: winemaking method used mainly for red grapes prior to alcoholic fermentation. Crushed grapes (skins and juice) are held at sufficiently cool temperatures to prevent fermentation for a few hours to a few days. Used for extraction of grape varietal flavours.

Meaty: savoury, also aroma of raw meat. Frequent in Shiraz and Merlot.

***Méthode Cap Classique* (MCC):** South African term as alternative to the word Champagne. Sparkling wines produced by bottle fermentation.

Méthode Champenoise: classic method of making sparkling wine by inducing fermentation in bottles.

Mouthfeel: sensations experienced in the mouth when tasting (body, heat and weight).

Must: skins, juice and pulp of crushed berries may contain whole berries or bunches. Red wine is fermented as must including grape skins, white wine as juice only.

Neutral: wine that has no expressive flavour.

New World: accessible, bold wines; expressive fruit, wooding and alcohol. Geographically refers to the Americas, South Africa, Australia and New Zealand.

Oak: main source of wood used to make barrels, on occasion cherry or other woods may be used but in limited quantities. See **Barrel**.

(O)enology: the study of winemaking.

Old World: subtle wine, less oak and alcohol, more varied and vinous. Geographically refers to Europe.

Oxidation: chemical process requiring oxygen. Changes due to exposure to air: uncontrolled results in spoilt wines, vinegar taste; controlled (in barrels) results in stabilisation of flavour and colour, desirable development of wine.

pH: measurement of hydrogen in wine, indicating acidity. Has no unit. Used in determining ripeness of grapes for harvest. Optimum level for juice and wine is between 3.1 and 3.4.

Pump over: mixing of fermenting juice and berries by removal and reintroduction of juice.

Punch down: manual mixing of fermenting juice and berries.

Reductive: without exposure to oxygen.

Residual sugar (RS): unfermented sugar remaining in wine after alcoholic fermentation.

Stabilisation: process in which chemical components achieve a balance, stable or unchanging arrangement.

Stabilisation, cold: wine-clearing method to prevent crystal formation after bottling. Crystal formation induced by chilling wine and filtering

clear liquid off the crystals. See **Acid, Tartaric**.

Sulphur: chemical compound, preservative. Used in vineyards to prevent spread of disease, as additive in wine to prevent oxidation and browning. Direct exposure to sulphur may cause difficultly in breathing.

Tannins: astringent and bitter compounds found in grapes and oak, a natural preservative. Oxidises slowly and promotes aging. Excessive tannins create harsh, aggressive wines. Over time, tannins combine with pigments to stabilise colour. Condensation reduces the astringency.

Terpenes: natural grape compounds giving strong floral aromas, important in Riesling, Gewürztraminer and Muscats.

Terroir: the interplay of natural elements that make up the environment where vines grow: soil, climate, slope, aspect, altitude. Emphasises the importance and uniqueness of a wine from a specific site, the expression of the wine's origin.

Veraison: ripening stage indicated by colour change in grape berries.

Vin (de) Paillé: "strawed wine" made from grapes dried between straw lattices.

Watery: thin, diluted wine resulting from (1) overproducing vines, (2) very young vines, or (3) a winemaking mistake. Not to be confused with a light-bodied wine, which is a particular style that retains elegance and balance.

Yeast: single cell micro-organisms responsible for conversion of sugar to alcohol in winemaking.

Yeast, natural wild: yeast populations present in vineyards, grapes and wineries. Frequently participate in early stages of fermentation due to low levels of alcohol and sulphur. May be responsible for entire fermentation under special circumstances.

Yeast, selected, cultured, dry: yeast produced in mass, sold in freeze-dried format, usually from a singular type.

Yeasty: pleasant wine smell of warm bread or yeast, frequent in barrel-fermented white wines and MCC sparkling wines.

Photography and Illustration Credits

Every effort has been made to trace the copyright holders and we apologise in advance for any unintentional omissions. We would be pleased to insert the appropriate acknowledgements in any subsequent edition of this publication.

Cheviot Publishing would like to thank the following individuals and companies for their kind permission to reproduce their photographs on the pages as indicated:

Boudewijn Scholten: 65

Elmari Swart: 128, 129, 132

Jacques Smit: 151, 166, 167 bottom

Kleine Zalze Wines: 82 top, 82 middle, 82 bottom, 213

Meerlust Administrators: 188

All other images by Jaap Scholten.

For further information contact www.cheviot-publishing.com or jaap@scholten.co.za

Cheviot Publishing would like to thank Dawid Saayman for his kind permission to reproduce his illustration on the page 23.

Cheviot Publishing would like to thank Barry of Birdmen Paragliding for facilitating the aerial photography shoot over Meerendal Wine Estate.   www.birdmen.co.za

Notes

Notes

Notes

Notes

Notes

Notes

Notes

Wine Producing Regions of South Afric[a]

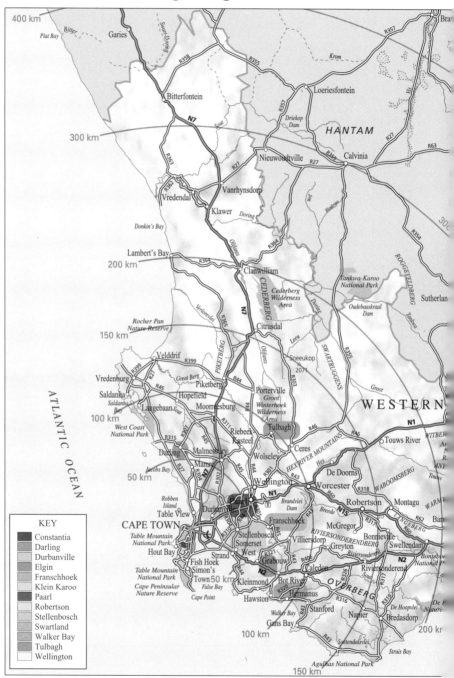